AF835028

Quantum Computing

Quantum computing is a rapidly emerging technology that harnesses the laws of quantum mechanics to solve problems too complex for classical computers. It is a multidisciplinary field comprising aspects of computer science, physics, and mathematics that utilizes quantum mechanics to solve complex problems faster than classical computers. It is a computational technology that uses the principles of quantum mechanics, such as entanglement, superposition, and interference, to process, store, and manipulate large amounts of data and perform complex calculations that conventional computing systems and supercomputers cannot fathom.

Quantum Computing: Research, Applications, and Advances provides a comprehensive overview of the foundational principles of quantum mechanics that underpin quantum computing. It explains such concepts as superposition, entanglement, and quantum gates to demystify the esoteric nature of quantum phenomena. It delves into the current state of quantum computing research, presenting an insightful analysis of the latest breakthroughs and technological advancements. From the race to achieve quantum supremacy to the development of scalable quantum hardware, the book offers a detailed exploration of the key players, their methodologies, and the challenges they face as they push the boundaries of quantum computing capabilities. It explores the practical applications of quantum computing across various domains. From cryptography to optimization problems and drug discovery, the book also illustrates how quantum algorithms have the potential to outperform classical counterparts to open doors to new possibilities where traditional computing falls short. The book integrates theoretical concepts and practical applications. The highlights include the following:

- Quantum computing in machine learning
- Harnessing quantum computing for predictive analysis
- Quantum-powered financial fraud detection
- Enhancing deep learning with quantum computing
- Quantum computing in medical imaging

Innovations in Intelligent Internet of Everything (IoE)
Series Editor: Fadi Al-Turjman

Advances in Technological Innovations in Higher Education: Theory and Practices
Edited by Adarsh Garg, B.V. Babu, and Valentina E Balas

Computational Intelligence in Healthcare: Applications, Challenges, and Management
Edited by Meenu Gupta, Shakeel Ahmed, Rakesh Kumar, Chadi Altrjman

Advances in SIoT (Social Internet of Things)
Edited by Gururaj H L, Pramod H B, Gowtham M

Blockchain, IOT and AI technologies for Supply Chain Management
Edited by Priyanka Chawla, Adarsh Kumar, Anand Nayyar and Mohd Naved

Renewable Energy and AI for Sustainable Development
Edited by Sailesh Iyer, Anand Nayyar, Mohd Naved and Fadi Al-Turjman

AIoT: Artificial Intelligence of Things
Edited by Arun Sekar Rajasekaran, Fadi Al-Turjman, Suganyadevi S

AI and Machine Learning for Mechanical and Electrical Engineering
Edited by T. Rajasanthosh Kumar, Surendra Reddy Vinta, Sagar Dhanraj Pande, and Aditya Khamparia

Artificial Intelligence Learning Facilitators: Creating Smart Education Systems
Edited by Dr. Fadi Al-Turjman

Generative AI 2.0 and Data Analytics
Edited by Adarsh Garg, John Walsh, and Fadi Al-Turjman

Quantum Computing: Research, Applications, and Advances
Edited by Arun Sekar Rajasekaran, Suganyadevi S., and Fadi Al-Turjman

For more information about the series, please visit: https://www.routledge.com/Innovations-in-Intelligent-Internet-of-Everything-IoE/book-series/IOE

Quantum Computing

Research, Applications, and Advances

Edited by
Arun Sekar Rajasekaran,
Suganyadevi S.,
and Fadi Al-Turjman

CRC Press
Taylor & Francis Group
Boca Raton London New York

CRC Press is an imprint of the
Taylor & Francis Group, an **informa** business
AN AUERBACH BOOK

Designed cover image: Shutterstock

First edition published 2026
by CRC Press
2385 NW Executive Center Drive, Suite 320, Boca Raton FL 33431

and by CRC Press
4 Park Square, Milton Park, Abingdon, Oxon, OX14 4RN

CRC Press is an imprint of Taylor & Francis Group, LLC

© 2026 selection and editorial matter, Arun Sekar Rajasekaran, Suganyadevi S., and Fadi Al-Turjman; individual chapters, the contributors

Reasonable efforts have been made to publish reliable data and information, but the author and publisher cannot assume responsibility for the validity of all materials or the consequences of their use. The authors and publishers have attempted to trace the copyright holders of all material reproduced in this publication and apologize to copyright holders if permission to publish in this form has not been obtained. If any copyright material has not been acknowledged please write and let us know so we may rectify in any future reprint.

Except as permitted under U.S. Copyright Law, no part of this book may be reprinted, reproduced, transmitted, or utilized in any form by any electronic, mechanical, or other means, now known or hereafter invented, including photocopying, microfilming, and recording, or in any information storage or retrieval system, without written permission from the publishers.

For permission to photocopy or use material electronically from this work, access www.copyright.com or contact the Copyright Clearance Center, Inc. (CCC), 222 Rosewood Drive, Danvers, MA 01923, 978-750-8400. For works that are not available on CCC please contact mpkbookspermissions@tandf.co.uk

For Product Safety Concerns and Information please contact our EU representative GPSR@taylor andfrancis.com. Taylor & Francis Verlag GmbH, Kaufingerstraße 24, 80331 München, Germany.

Trademark notice: Product or corporate names may be trademarks or registered trademarks and are used only for identification and explanation without intent to infringe.

Library of Congress Cataloging-in-Publication Data
Names: Rajasekaran, Arun Sekar editor | S., Suganyadevi editor |
Al-Turjman, Fadi editor
Title: Quantum computing : research, applications, and advances / edited by
Arun Sekar Rajasekaran, Suganyadevi S., and Fadi Al-Turjman.
Description: First edition. | Boca Raton, FL : CRC Press, 2026. | Series:
Innovations in intelligent Internet of everything (IoE) | Includes
bibliographical references and index. |
Identifiers: LCCN 2025049899 (print) | LCCN 2025049900 (ebook) | ISBN
9781032958286 hardback | ISBN 9781032960739 paperback | ISBN
9781003587835 ebook
Subjects: LCSH: Quantum computing | Quantum computers
Classification: LCC QA76.889 .Q27 2026 (print) | LCC QA76.889 (ebook)
LC record available at https://lccn.loc.gov/2025049899
LC ebook record available at https://lccn.loc.gov/2025049900

ISBN: 978-1-032-95828-6 (hbk)
ISBN: 978-1-032-96073-9 (pbk)
ISBN: 978-1-003-58783-5 (ebk)

DOI: 10.1201/9781003587835

Typeset in Times
by SPi Technologies India Pvt Ltd (Straive)

Contents

Editors

Arun Sekar Rajasekaran received his Bachelor's degree in Electronics and Communication engineering from Sri Ramakrishna Engineering College in 2008, his Master's degree in VLSI Design in 2013, and his PhD in Low-Power Very Large Scale Integration (VLSI) design from Anna University, Chennai in 2019. He is currently working as Professor and associate head in the Department of Electronics and Communication Engineering at SR University, Warangal, Telangana, India. He has nearly 13 years of teaching experience. He had published more than 35 studies in Science Citation Index Expanded (SCIE)-Indexed Journals, namely, *IEEE Transactions on Industrial Informatics, IEEE Transactions on Intelligent Transportation Systems, IEEE Transactions on Vehicular Technology, ACM Transactions*, Springer, Elsevier, IET, and Wiley publications. His areas of interest are Low-Power VLSI design, Network security, Blockchain, Body area networks, and Image processing. He is Senior Member of the Institute of Electrical and Electronics Engineers (SMIEEE), Life Member of the Indian Society for Technical Education (LISTE), Fellow of the Institute of Electronics and Telecommunication Engineers (FIETE), a member of the International Society for Research and Development (ISRD), and a member of the International Engineering Association of Nations Group (IEANG).

Suganyadevi S. is an Assistant Professor in the Department of Electronics and Communication Engineering at KPR Institute of Engineering and Technology, Tamil Nadu, India. She received her BE degree in Electronics and Communication Engineering from Anna University, Chennai, Tamil Nadu, India in 2012 and her ME. degree in VLSI Design from Anna University, Chennai, Tamil Nadu, India in 2014. she has completed her PhD at Anna University, Chennai, Tamil Nadu, India in 2025. She is a University Rank Holder in her undergraduate studies and a Gold Medalist in her postgraduate program. She has published around 30 papers in international journals and conferences, contributed to over 10 book chapters, authored 1 book, and edited 3 books. She holds more than 10 patents and serves as a reviewer for several reputed journals including *IEEE Transactions on Image Processing*, the *ACM Computing Surveys*, *Computers in Biology and Medicine* (SCIE), *Informatics in Medicine Unlocked* (SCIE), *Cognitive Computation*, *Artificial Intelligence Review*, *Molecular Ecology*, *The Imaging Science Journal* (SCIE), *The Journal of Supercomputing* (SCIE), *International Journal of Computing and Digital Systems* (SCIE), *Concurrency and Computation: Practice and Experience* (SCIE), *Bulletin of Electrical Engineering and Informatics*, *Applied Artificial Intelligence*, *Research in Comparative and International Education*, *Journal of Experimental and Theoretical Artificial Intelligence*, *Health Informatics Journal*, *Computer Methods in Biomechanics and Biomedical Engineering*, *Connection Science*, *and Scientific Reports*. She has received a total of ₹7.44 lakhs in funding from the Department of Health Research–Indian Council of Medical Research (DHR–ICMR) and ₹30,000 from DRDO. She is Life Member of the Indian Society for Technical Education (ISTE), and her research interests include Machine Learning and Image Processing.

Professor Dr. Fadi Al-Turjman received his Ph.D. in computer science from Queen's University, Canada, in 2011. He is the "advisor to the chairman of the board of trustees on AI and informatics" at Near East University (NEU), Turkey, and the founding/current dean for AI and Informatics faculty in the same university. Prof. Al-Turjman is the head of Software Engineering Department, and the founding director for the AI and Robotics Institute and the International Research Center for AI and IoT at NEU. He has been awarded the lifetime golden-award of Dr. Suat Gunsel from Near East University for the year 2022, in addition to several other recognitions and best research awards at key international venues. Prof. Al-Turjman is a leading authority in the areas of smart/intelligent IoT systems, wireless, and mobile networks' architectures, protocols, deployments, and performance evaluation in Artificial Intelligence of Things (AIoT). His publication history spans over 700 SCI/E publications, in addition to numerous keynotes and plenary talks at flagship venues. He has authored and edited more than 100 books about AI, cognition, security, and wireless sensor networks' deployments in smart IoT environments, which have been published by well-reputed publishers such as IEEE, Taylor and Francis, Elsevier, IET, and Springer. Prof. Al-Turjman is leading a number of international conferences and workshops in flagship AI and IoT societies. Currently, he serves as a book series editor with distinguished publishers, and the lead guest/associate editor for several top tier journals, including the IEEE Communications Surveys and Tutorials (IF 23.9) and the Elsevier Sustainable Cities and Society (IF 10.8).

Contributors

Fadi Al-Turjman
Software Engineering Department, AI and IoT research center, AI and Informatics
Faculty, Near East University
Mersin, Turkey

R. Abinaya
Department of Computer Science and Engineering
Sri Ramakrishna Institute of Technology
Coimbatore, Tamil Nadu, India

S. A. Amala Nirmal Doss
Department of Computing
Muscat College
Muscat, Sultanate of Oman

S. Amsaveni
Department of Electronics and Communication Engineering
Nandha College of Technology
Vaikaalmedu, Tamil Nadu, India

Sivakumar Annamalai
Department of Safety and Fire Engineering
Excel Engineering College
Komarapalayam, Tamil Nadu, India

Umaamaheshvari Annamalai
Department of Electronics and Communication Engineering
Coimbatore Institute of Engineering and Technology
Coimbatore, Tamil Nadu, India

Mohamed Uvaze Ahamed Ayoobkhan
Department of Computing
De Montfort University
Almaty, Kazakhstan

J. David Rathnaraj
Department of Mechanical Engineering
Sri Ramakrishna Institute of Technology
Coimbatore, Tamil Nadu, India

K. K. Archana
Department of Computer Science and Engineering
Sri Ramakrishna Institute of Technology
Coimbatore, Tamil Nadu, India

K. Balasamy
Department of Artificial Intelligence and Data Science
Bannari Amman Institute of Technology
Sathyamangalam, Erode, Tamil Nadu, India

G. Deebanchakkarawarthi
Department of Computer Science and Engineering
Hindusthan College of Engineering and Technology
Coimbatore, Tamil Nadu, India

D. Ganeshkumar
Department of Electrical and Electronics Engineering
Dr. Mahalingam College of Engineering and Technology
Pollachi, Tamil Nadu, India

R. Immanual
Department of Mechanical Engineering
Sri Ramakrishna Institute of Technology
Coimbatore, Tamil Nadu, India

G. Indhumathi
Department of Electronics and Communication Engineering
Rajalakshmi College of Engineering
Chennai, Tamil Nadu, India

K. Janani
Department of Electronics and Communication Engineering
Kongu Engineering College
Perundurai, Tamil Nadu, India

R. Jayavadivel
School of Computer Science and Engineering
Presidency University
Bengaluru, Karnataka, India

R. Jeevitha
Department of Computer Science and Engineering
KPR Institute of Engineering and Technology
Coimbatore, Tamil Nadu, India

Kafila
School of Business
SR University
Warangal, Telangana, India

Pratibha C. Kaladeep Yalagi
Department of Computer Science and Engineering
Walchand Institute of Technology
Solapur, Maharashtra, India

N. Kavitha
Department of Electronics and Instrumentation Engineering
Hindusthan College of Engineering and Technology
Coimbatore, Tamil Nadu, India

C. M. Lingesh
Department of Electronics and Communication Engineering
Sri Krishna College of Technology
Coimbatore, Tamil Nadu, India

N. Madhan Kishore
Department of Electronics and Communication Engineering
Sri Krishna College of Technology
Coimbatore, Tamil Nadu, India

D. Magdalene Delighta Angeline
Department of Computer Science and Engineering
Joginpally B.R. Engineering College
Hyderabad, Telangana, India

G. Mahesh Gopal
School of Engineering and Technology
Wollega University
Nekemte, Ethiopia

C. Mariyammal
Department of Computer Science and Engineering
Karpagam College of Engineering
Coimbatore, Tamil Nadu, India

G. B. Mohankumar
Department of Electrical and Electronics Engineering
Nandha College of Technology
Vaikaalmedu, Tamil Nadu, India

Kathirvelu Murugan
Department of Electronics and Communication Engineering
KPR Institute of Engineering and Technology
Coimbatore, Tamil Nadu, India

C. Nandagopal
Department of Electronics and Communication Engineering
M. Kumarasamy College of Engineering
Thalavapalayam, Tamil Nadu, India

A. Napolean
Department of Electronics and Communication Engineering
Alva Institute of Technology
Mangalore, Karnataka, India

R. Naveenkumar
Department of Electronics and Communication Engineering
Sri Krishna College of Technology
Coimbatore, Tamil Nadu, India

B. Nithish Gokul
Department of Electronics and Communication Engineering
Sri Krishna College of Technology
Coimbatore, Tamil Nadu, India

Yogeswari Palanisamy
Department of Electronics and Communication Engineering
KPR Institute of Engineering and Technology
Coimbatore, Tamil Nadu, India

Govind Kumar Pandey
Department of Computer Science and Engineering – Artificial Language and Machine Learning
Dayananda Sagar University
Harohalli, Karnataka, India

K. Poornima
Department of Electronics and Communication Engineering
Nandha College of Technology
Vaikaalmedu, Tamil Nadu, India

T. Prabakaran
Department of Computer Science and Engineering
Joginpally B.R. Engineering College
Hyderabad, Telangana, India

Kudali Prasanthi
School of Business
SR University
Warangal, Telangana, India

V. Preetha
Department of Computer Science and Engineering
Sri Ramakrishna Institute of Technology
Coimbatore, Tamil Nadu, India

S. V. K. R. Rajeswari
Department of Computer Science and Engineering – Artificial Language and Machine Learning
Dayananda Sagar University
Harohalli, Karnataka, India

M. Rajyalaxmi
School of Business
SR University
Warangal, Telangana, India

A. S. Renugadevi
Kongu Engineering College
Perundurai, Tamil Nadu, India

Ramiz Salama
Department of Artificial Intelligence and Software Engineering
Near East University
Marin, Turkey

I. Samuel Peter James
Department of Computer Science and Engineering
Shadan Women's College of Engineering
Hyderabad, Telangana, India

N. Sanjana
Department of Computer Science and Engineering
Sri Ramakrishna Institute of Technology
Coimbatore, Tamil Nadu, India

G. Saranya
Department of Electronics and Communication Engineering
Rajalakshmi College of Engineering
Chennai, Tamil Nadu, India

V. Shanmugavalli
School of Computer Engineering
Manipal Academy of Higher Education
Bengaluru, Karnataka, India

Talla Shirisha
School of Business
SR University
Warangal, Telangana, India

N. M. Sivamangai
Department of Electronics and Communication Engineering
Karunya Institute of Technology and Sciences
Coimbatore, Tamil Nadu, India

M. K. Sundaram
Department of Computer Science and Engineering
SIMATS Engineering College
Chennai, Tamil Nadu, India

M. Vallikannu
Department of English
Vel Tech Rangarajan Dr. Sagunthala R&D Institute of Science and Technology
Chennai, Tamil Nadu, India

Koteswara Rao Veginati
School of Business
SR University
Warangal, Telangana, India

K. Vijayalakshmi
Department of Artificial Intelligence and Data Science
JNN Institute of Engineering
Chennai, Tamil Nadu, India

N. Vini Antony Grace
Department of ECE, R.M.D. Engineering College
Kavaraipettai, India

Preface

Quantum computing is a revolutionary paradigm that applies the principles of quantum mechanics—such as superposition, entanglement, and interference—to perform computations far beyond the capabilities of classical systems. Unlike traditional computers that process data using binary digits (bits), quantum computers use quantum bits (qubits), which can represent multiple states simultaneously. This allows quantum systems to tackle complex problems in optimization, cryptography, machine learning, and more—many of which are unsolvable by today's most powerful supercomputers.

This book, *Quantum Computing: Research, Application, and Advances*, provides a comprehensive and multidimensional exploration of quantum computing, guiding readers through its theoretical foundations, system architectures, and transformative real-world applications. It presents quantum computing as a multidisciplinary field where physics, computer science, and mathematics converge, offering readers insights into how this technology is reshaping the future of computation.

The book begins with an accessible introduction to quantum mechanics for computing, demystifying core concepts such as quantum gates, quantum circuits, and qubit behavior. It then delves into practical implementations and architectures of quantum systems, from algorithm development to quantum communication protocols. Readers will find insightful commentary on global initiatives and investments—from the U.S. National Quantum Initiative to China's billion-dollar research laboratories—highlighting the international race to quantum supremacy.

This book is a valuable resource for researchers, academics, industry professionals, and students interested in understanding both the fundamentals and advanced applications of quantum technologies. Whether you are new to the subject or an experienced professional seeking to explore new perspectives, this volume provides a structured and comprehensive journey through the quantum computing landscape.

This book specifically focuses on emerging research and practical applications of quantum computing, including but not limited to the following topics:

1. Quantum Computing in Artificial Intelligence
2. Quantum Computing Transforming Machine Learning: An Overview
3. Quantum Computing in Machine Learning
4. Harnessing Quantum Computing for Predictive Analysis: Understanding the Social Media Impact on Stock Market Investment
5. Quantum-Powered Fraud Detection: Revolutionizing Financial Security
6. Quantum Computing in Healthcare
7. Quantum Computing in Healthcare: Applications and Challenges
8. Enhancing Deep Learning with Quantum Computing: Its Challenges, Opportunities, and Applications

9. Design and Optimization of Quantum Arithmetic Circuits for Next-Generation Quantum Systems
10. Quantum Key Distribution: Visualizing the Foundations of Future-Proof Secure Communication
11. Challenges and Opportunities of Quantum Computing in Medical Imaging
12. Quantum Computing and Industry Transformation
13. Next-Generation Quantum Algorithms: Trends, Techniques, and Applications
14. Applications of Deep Learning Technology for Mobile and Quantum Computing
15. Effective Quantum, Artificial Intelligence (AI), and Cloud Implementation
16. Quantum Supremacy and Its Applications

Acknowledgments

We, the editors, extend our deepest gratitude to the management of SR University, KPR Institute of Engineering and Technology, whose support and encouragement were crucial throughout this book proposal. Special thanks to the Department of Electronics and Communication Engineering for their insights and contributions that greatly enriched the content. We are immensely thankful to all the editors and authors of the chapters, whose expertise and dedication are reflected on every page. Each of you has brought invaluable knowledge and depth to this effort. We also express my heartfelt appreciation to my family for their unwavering support and understanding, which have been my anchor throughout this book proposal.

Thank you all for your contributions to this publication.

1 Quantum Computing in Artificial Intelligence

V. Shanmugavalli, A. S. Renugadevi, R. Jayavadivel, and K. Janani

1.1 INTRODUCTION

In recent years, a discipline with the potential to drastically change the use of machine learning (ML) and data processing environments has emerged from the novel fusion of neural networks and quantum technologies. This combination of artificial intelligence and quantum technology, known as "Quantum Technology," has the potential to unleash currently unheard-of processing power, allowing us to address difficult issues that were previously thought to be intractable. Superposition and entanglement [1], two basic ideas in quantum mechanics, are used in utilizing quantum technology to handle information in methods which are inefficient for traditional computers. These quantum characteristics could speed up a variety of artificial intelligence (AI) systems, increasing the speed and precision of calculations. This introduction addresses the core notions of AI and quantum technology [2].

1.1.1 Quantum State

Science makes use of quantum states, especially entangled ones, and information processing technology disseminates and examines this data [3]. Therefore, even for jobs like increases up [nondeterministic polynomial time (NP-Complete)], qubits could solve complex mathematical problems faster than we initially thought was conceivable. Using quantum, People can now use computers to address challenges like merciless research and massive number breakdown that computational complexity just cannot control. The quantity of quantum in a specific algorithm is an often-used metric to illustrate a person's proficiency with quantum technology [4]. This number has now reached the range of a few orders of magnitude (hundreds of qubits) and triple magnitudes of an order (millions and millions of qubits) with regard to ubiquitous computing power and quantum annealers [5].

1.1.2 Basics of Quantum Technology

Understanding the basics of quantum technology is required to comprehend quantum machine learning (QML). Quantum computers employ qubits, or 0 and 1, to represent information, while classical computers use bits. Qubits can represent many values at once because they might be in a superposition of modes. Their computing capability is significantly increased by these features [6].

DOI: 10.1201/9781003587835-1

1.1.3 The Revolution in AI

Over the last few decades, AI has advanced significantly, allowing machines to carry out tasks such as autonomous decision-making, processing natural language, and identifying images. However, particularly in deep learning and neural network training, the constantly increasing demand for processing power has started to surpass the capacity of traditional computers [7].

1.1.4 Advantage of Quantum

When it comes to solving AI-related challenges, quantum machines might offer a significant advantage. In machine-learning tasks, their proficiency in tackling intricate optimization issues, vast datasets, and mimicking quantum systems is essential. The integration of AI and quantum technology across domains that include financial modeling, drug discovery, and cryptography offers the potential for novel discoveries and solutions.

1.1.5 The Architecture of Quantum AI

The field of computational learning includes a wide range of methods and strategies. It includes both fully quantum algorithms designed for particular purposes and quantum-enhanced conventional ML methods. Both practitioners and researchers can now explore the impact and advantages of quantum ML—thanks to the development of optical software and hardware platforms [3].

1.1.6 Path Ahead

The advancement of quantum technology necessitates the resolution of several challenges, including hardware development, scalability, and error correction. Although the journey is still in its early phases, to properly utilize quantum computing's promise for AI applications, researchers are putting forth endless effort.

It shall go deeper into the key elements of this quantum neural networks course, innovative topics, such as quantum techniques, applications, and the most recent advancements in quantum hardware and software [8]. Our objective is to give readers a comprehensive understanding of how AI and quantum technology are related, as well as their transformative potential in ML, through these investigations.

1.2 THEORETICAL FOUNDATIONS OF QUANTUM TECHNOLOGY

1.2.1 Quantum Bits

Conventional Bits, which stand for 0s and 1s, are the fundamental informational units used in classical computing. Qubits, on the other hand, can represent both 0 and 1 at the same time due to the fact that they are in a superposition state. The capacity of qubits to reside in a linear mixture of states allows quantum systems to examine

TABLE 1.1
Difference between Bits and Qubits

Bits	Qubits
Logic gates (AND, OR, and NOT)	Quantum logic gates (Hadamard gate, Phase gate, and Controlled-NOT gate [C-NOT])
Hold either a one or a zero	Hold a one, a zero, or both
Information takes the discrete values 0 and 1	Information take the value $\|0\}$, $\|1\}$ or $a\|0\} + b\|1\}$ in the superposition state.
Bits are slow	Qubits are faster
With 2 bits, you can store 4 possible values {00, 01, 10, 11} but only one of those at a time.	With two qubits in superposition, you can store the same four values simultaneously $\|00\}$, $\|01\}$, $\|10\}$, $\|11\}$

many possibilities simultaneously. For some applications, this feature serves as the foundation for the acceleration in quantum algorithms. A qubit's superposition coefficients determine whether it has the potential to collapse into either of its base states, which are 0 or 1. This gives quantum algorithms a greater likelihood [2]. Table 1.1 depicts the difference between bits and qubits.

1.3 QUANTUM MECHANICAL PRINCIPLES

1.3.1 Superposition

Superposition denotes the combination of all feasible qubit configurations. Superposition of qubits can build multidimensional computational spaces. These spaces allow for novel representations of complex situations. Figure 1.1 depicts the superposition mechanical principle.

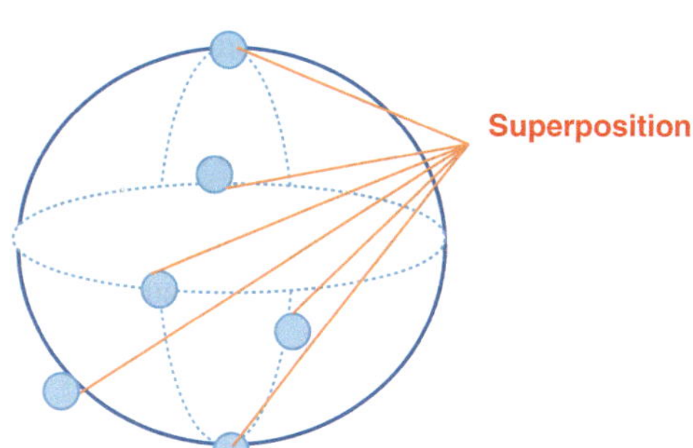

FIGURE 1.1 Superposition.

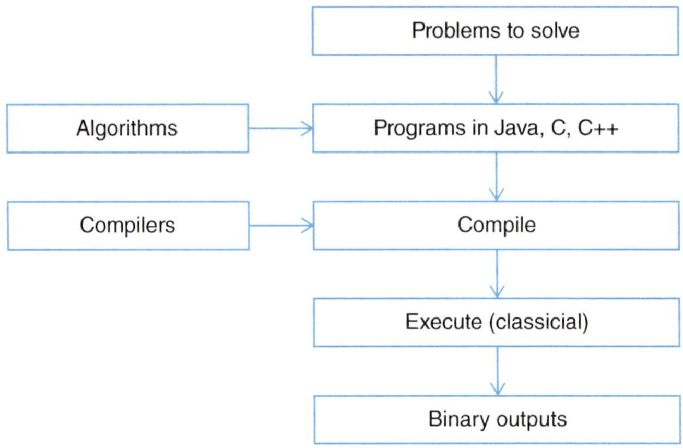

FIGURE 1.3 Steps involved in classical computing.

of data, since incomplete or skewed data might produce unreliable results. Data preparation, or the cleaning, organizing, and modification of data, is also crucial to guarantee that models can effectively learn and generalize from the information provided. Data governance, privacy, and ethical issues are increasingly important as AI advances, ensuring that AI systems are trustworthy and accountable (Figure 1.3).

1.5 CONCEPTUALIZING QUANTUM AI

1.5.1 Quantum AI

Quantum AI, which sits at the nexus of neural networks and quantum technology, uses the special characteristics of quantum physics to improve ML and data processing. Because qubits, the building blocks of quantum computers, can exist in multiple states at once, they can perform complex operations at unprecedented speeds when compared to classical computers. These potential makes it especially intriguing for jobs like financial modeling, drug development, and large-scale data analytics since it enables faster data analysis, better pattern detection, and more efficient optimization. Nevertheless, error correction and the requirement for reliable quantum algorithms are two obstacles in this young sector. As research improves, quantum artificial intelligence (AI) has the potential to alter enterprises by giving solutions to problems that classical systems cannot now address [5].

1.5.1.1 Enhancements to ML via Quantum Technology (Figure 1.4)

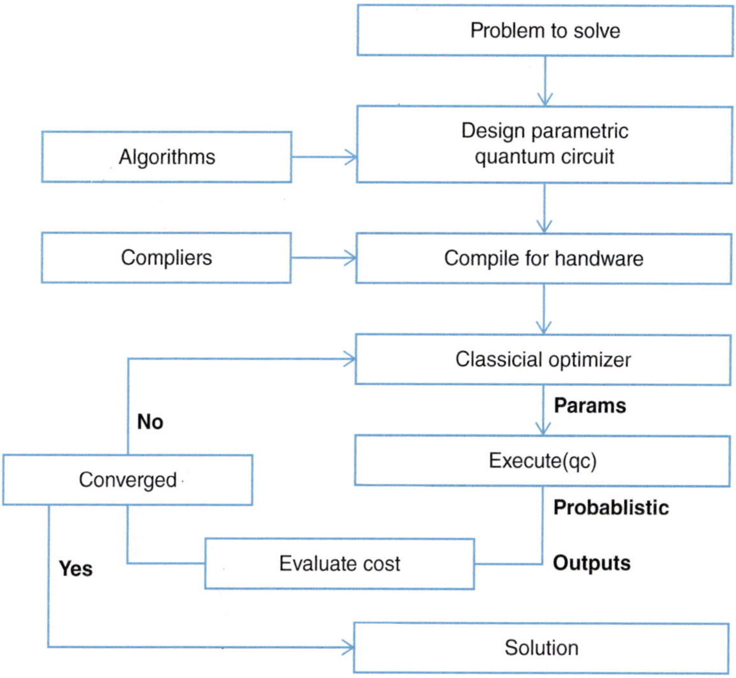

FIGURE 1.4 Steps involved in quantum computing.

1.5.2 Quantum Acceleration in Learning

- **Quantum Advantage**: Quantum algorithms can accelerate tasks related to AI, including recognizing patterns, data analysis, and improvement.
- **Quantum Speedup**: ML is being revolutionized by quantum algorithms, which can execute some calculations tenfold faster than their conventional equivalents. Figure 1.4 depicts the steps involved in quantum computing.

1.5.3 QSVMs

One fundamental ML issue that can be resolved is support vector machine classification with the quantum method QSVM [11]. QSVM boosts the effectiveness of kernel techniques used in support vector algorithms by utilizing quantum characteristics.

1.5.4 Principal Component Analysis (PCA) in Quantum

One popular method for reducing dimensionality in classical ML is principal component analysis. Quantum PCA is appropriate for huge datasets since it uses quantum methods to speed up the dimensionality reduction process [12].

1.5.5 Quantum Clustering Algorithms

Clustering is a crucial task in unsupervised ML that can be effectively performed using quantum techniques like k-means. Cluster assignment optimization and the processing of intricate data structures are two uses for quantum clustering algorithms.

1.5.6 Quantum Encoding for Data

Techniques for encoding quantum data, including image translation and frequency packaging, convert conventional information into quantum information that can be handled (Figure 1.4). Using the methods of quantum technology on quantum data visualizations, these encodings may allow for quantum speedup for traditional ML applications.

1.5.7 Networks of Quantum Neural

The goal of the developing discipline of quantum neural networks is to improve artificial neural networks by utilizing quantum characteristics. Deep learning models may perform better thanks to quantum neural networks' ability to analyze quantum input and carry out quantum operations [13].

1.5.8 Libraries for QML

Qiskit and TensorFlow Quantum are two libraries that provide frameworks and instruments. These sets include tools to help scientists and developers develop code for QML in their exploration of integrating quantum technology into ML algorithms [3].

1.5.9 Quantum Generative Models in Quantum

Realistic data distributions are the objective of quantum Boltzmann machines and other quantum-model-generation tools. These models can be used for data synthesis and generative adversarial networks (GANs).

1.6 HARDWARE LIMITATIONS AND TECHNOLOGICAL CHALLENGES

1.6.1 Quantum Computers

Quantum processors, which employ qubits as their basic processing units, are important to quantum equipment [8].

- **Qubit Technology**: Among the technologies utilized to develop quantum processing devices are Topological qubits, trapped ions, and superconducting qubits.
- **Qubit Connectivity**: A key component of a quantum processor's performance, qubit connectivity affects the kinds of quantum algorithms that can be run.

1.6.2 Correction for Quantum Errors

The phenomenon known as quantum decoherence arises from a qubit's sensitivity to external influences. Techniques for error correction are crucial to lessening the impact of incoherence. Table 1.2 illustrates a comparison between conventional and quantum technologies.

Codes for Quantum Error Correction: Dynamic error-correcting programs, like a surface code, can be used to find and correct mistakes that could happen when quantum matter is being calculated.

1.6.3 Control and Quantum Gates

The fundamental components of quantum computers are quantum gates that allow qubit manipulation. Accurately implementing quantum algorithms requires precise control over quantum gates [5].

Control Based on Pulses: Control in superconducting qubits is often accomplished by means of quantum gates implemented by microwave energy and other techniques.

1.6.4 Suppliers of Quantum Hardware

Among the top businesses and associations in the quantum hardware space are Google, International Business Machines (IBM), Rigetti, Honeywell, IonQ, and

TABLE 1.2
Comparison between Conventional Technology and Quantum Technology

	Conventional Technology	Quantum Technology
Computational units	A transistor is used to calculate, which can stand for either 0 or 1.	Qubits are used for calculations, taking simultaneously levels 0 and 1.
Computing capacity	The number of transistors has a 1:1 relationship with the increase in power.	The power grows exponentially with the number of qubits.
Error rates and environment	Run at room temperature and have low mistake rates.	Requires ultracold temperatures and high mistake rates.
Suitability	Classical computers are best suited to perform the majority of daily processing.	Optimization problems, data analysis, and simulation.

others. With the goal of raising the qubit count, lowering error rates, and improving quantum performance, these suppliers are actively creating quantum processors.

1.6.5 Scalability of Quantum Hardware

The industry's largest obstacle is the scalability of quantum technologies, which means adding more qubits while maintaining or improving their quality. To solve complex ML and AI challenges that demand substantial quantum resources, scaling quantum processors is crucial (Table 1.1).

1.6.6 The Ecosystem of Quantum Hardware

Quantum development kits and quantum cloud platforms enable users can utilize and test quantum technology from a distance. The resources needed to design, simulate, and execute these ecosystems enable quantum algorithms on actual quantum processors [14].

1.6.7 Progress in Quantum Hardware

Quantum Volume: This measure evaluates a quantum processor's overall performance by integrating connection, error rates, and qubit count.

Achieving advantage entails proving that quantum processors are capable of solving specific issues more quickly or effectively than traditional computers. Table 1.3 depicts the advantages and disadvantages of Quantum hardware.

1.6.8 Difficulties with Quantum Hardware

Rates of Error: Reducing error rates and increasing qubit coherence times continue to be major obstacles in the advancement of quantum technology.

Physical Restrictions: The design and operation of quantum processors are complicated by a number of physical restrictions, including the requirement to operate at extremely low temperatures.

TABLE 1.3
Advantages and Disadvantages of Quantum Hardware

Advantages	Disadvantages
Traditional computers can never match the speed of quantum computers.	Building a quantum computer is challenging and requires specialized parts, costly technology, and large cooling systems.
Regardless of how complex the issue is, quantum computing enables.	Errors can be caused by environmental conditions, depending on the nature of qubits and quantum physics.
Complex simulations may be executed by quantum computers due to their high speed and complexity.	Only in certain fields and for particular jobs could quantum computers lead to breakthrough answers.

Scaling Complexity: The more qubits there are in a quantum system, the more difficult it is to manage its complexity.

Quantum Decoherence: Due to their extreme sensitivity to outside noise, quantum systems can lose their coherence and produce computation mistakes.

Cryogenic Cooling: Hardware design is made more difficult by the fact that the majority of quantum systems must function at temperatures that are incredibly low, almost at zero degrees.

Fabrication Challenges: Building uniform, reliable qubits with consistent properties is difficult due to manufacturing variability.

1.7 PRACTICAL APPLICATION OF QUANTUM AI

1.7.1 Drug Discovery and Materials Science

Accurate modeling of chemical reactions and molecular structures is made possible by quantum simulations. Drug development procedures are optimized through using QML to predict the properties and behavior of molecules. Figure 1.5 illustrates Quantum computing's use in AI.

1.7.2 Portfolio Optimization and Financial Modeling

Quantum techniques are employed in economic duties like portfolio optimization, option pricing, and risk assessment. Investment strategy optimization and market trend prediction are aided by QML [12].

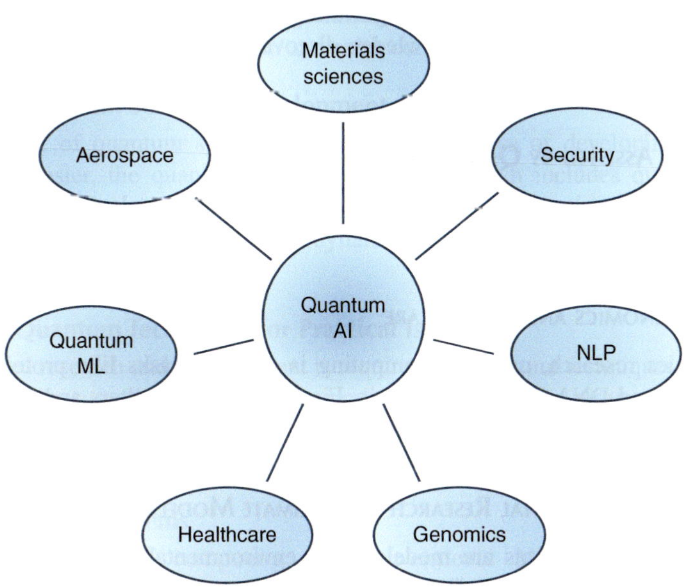

FIGURE 1.5 Quantum computing's use in AI.

1.8.1.6 Quantum Workforce and Education

The development of quantum ML is hampered by a lack of quantum specialists and researchers. To develop a qualified workforce, funding quantum education and training initiatives is crucial [12].

1.8.1.7 Cryptography Secured by Quantum

The creation and implementation of quantum-resistant encryption systems must be given top priority since quantum computers pose a danger to traditional encryption techniques. Quantum-secured cryptography improves the security of cryptographic systems through the application of quantum physics concepts. By employing quantum states such as photons, quantum cryptography, and in particular quantum key distribution (QKD), guarantees that keys are shared securely, in contrast to classical encryption techniques that depend on intricate mathematical problems for security. The no-cloning theorem, which forbids an eavesdropper from secretly copying quantum information, is one of its main characteristics [13]. The communication parties are alerted when the quantum state is changed by any effort to intercept the key. Since quantum cryptography is theoretically immune to both conventional and quantum computer threats, it offers a degree of security that traditional cryptography techniques cannot match. This is particularly relevant given the threat that emerging quantum computers pose to existing encryption methods [6].

1.8.1.8 Security and Ethical Issues

While data processing and analysis could be revolutionized by QML, it also brings up moral questions about data security, privacy, and equity. To resolve these issues and create moral standards for QML, work must be done.

1.8.1.9 Standards

To guarantee reliability and compatibility in contexts involving quantum technology, standards in the industry for ML in quantum systems must be established. Standardization of hardware, software, and security features is necessary. Even though quantum technology has the chance to revolutionize technology, numerous barriers need to be overcome before its full promise can be realized [5]. The vulnerability of qubits, which limits the dependability and computation time due to decoherence and inaccuracy caused by ambient noise, is one of the most urgent problems. Developing effective quantum error correction requires an enormous number of physical qubits to represent a single logical qubit, posing scalability hurdles. Additionally, building large-scale quantum systems involves complex engineering, including cryogenic cooling and minimizing interference between qubits. The development of quantum algorithms also lags behind hardware advancements, with only a few practical algorithms available, and integrating quantum processors with classical systems introduces latency and data transfer issues.

1.8.2 Future Directions

1.8.2.1 Quantum Cloud Services

It is anticipated that quantum cloud platforms will become more widely available, allowing a wider spectrum of users to test out QML and hardware [1].

- **Quantum Internet**: Using quantum repeaters and QKD, quantum communication protocols are being developed for safe data transfer.
- **Distributed Quantum Computing**: Enabling collaborative quantum computations across networks to enhance scalability.

1.8.2.2 Libraries

A multitude of tools and resources for the creation and study of quantum algorithms will be made available by the constant growth of libraries for QML [3].

- **Qiskit ML**, developed by IBM, offers tools for implementing quantum circuits and combining them with classical ML models, allowing users to explore algorithms for classification, regression, and clustering.
- **PennyLane** by Xanadu is another popular framework that supports quantum neural networks and enables smooth transitions between quantum and classical systems and hybrid quantum–classical algorithms, with automatic differentiation for quantum circuits.
- **TensorFlow Quantum** (TFQ), developed by Google, builds on TensorFlow, enabling the creation and training of quantum models alongside classical neural networks for ML tasks.
- **Cirq**, from Google, provides tools for developing and simulating quantum circuits, which can be used in QML workflows when combined with other libraries like TFQ.
- Although it is primarily focused on quantum optimization and simulation tasks, a powerful framework for developing QML algorithms is provided by the **Quantum Development Kit (QDK)**, which includes the Q# coding language.

These libraries are pushing the limits of what is feasible with classical methods and establishing the groundwork for the next generation of quantum-enhanced ML [13].

1.8.2.3 Quantum Advantage in Various Domains

Climate modeling, healthcare, banking, and other industries stand to benefit greatly from QML. Progress in these areas will be driven by ongoing research and collaboration.

QML algorithms offer faster data processing and pattern recognition in the domains of AI, which could transform industries such as financial forecasting and medical diagnostics. Climate modeling and energy optimization also stand to gain, with quantum systems capable of simulating large-scale quantum systems to improve renewable energy solutions and grid management [6].

1.8.2.4 Innovation in Quantum Hardware

Continuous advancements in quantum hardware will result in the creation of ever-more-potent and dependable quantum processors, creating new prospects for applications of QML. Existing platforms, such as trapped ions and superconducting qubits, are being improved, while emerging alternatives, such as photonic, topological, and neutral atom qubits, offer promising paths toward improved coherence and scalability [14]. A key challenge is mitigating decoherence, as qubits are extremely sensitive to environmental noise, necessitating advanced cryogenic systems and error-correction protocols.

1.8.2.5 Research on Quantum ML

New quantum algorithms that will be used in AI and data analysis will continue to be produced by interdisciplinary research at the nexus of quantum technology. Developing quantum versions of conventional algorithms, such as quantum support vector machines and quantum neural networks, is a key area of research aimed at increasing computing efficiency in pattern recognition and data processing. The Quantum Approximate Optimization Algorithm (QAOA) and the Variational Quantum Eigensolver (VQE) are two examples of variational algorithms being used in the study of hybrid quantum-classical MSL models. By using quantum data encoding techniques to efficiently represent conventional data in states of quantum information, researchers are investigating ways to benefit from quantum speedups. With the development of quantum hardware, QML research could have an impact on fields like AI, financial modeling, and drug discovery by providing fresh answers to issues that traditional ML techniques are unable to solve [5].

1.8.2.6 Integration of Quantum AI

Figure 1.6 depicts the integration of ML with AI. As QML is increasingly incorporated into current AI infrastructure and systems, Businesses and researchers will have access to quantum advantages for better data processing and decision-making.

The nexus of neural networks (AI) and computers, specifically in the context of quantum data mining, is a field that holds tremendous potential for transformation. Even though there are still obstacles to overcome, further study and funding in quantum technology will influence AI and data analysis in the future by opening up new avenues and providing answers to challenging issues. The use of quantum computers has the potential to totally transform technology in the future.

Central to this evolution is the quest to scale up qubits while developing robust error-correction methods, ensuring more reliable and powerful quantum systems. Innovative qubit technologies—such as topological, photonic, and neutral atom qubits—are being explored to enhance coherence and scalability. The potential of quantum computing to revolutionize.

Fields like optimization, cryptography, and material science in terms of algorithms. The significance of the technology would be further increased if secure

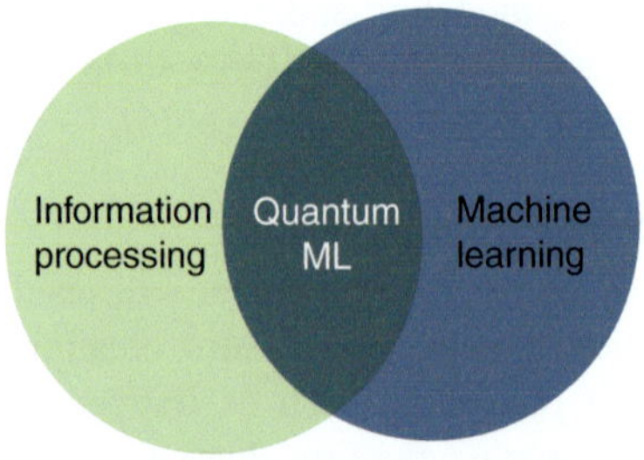

FIGURE 1.6 Integration.

worldwide communication were made possible by the envisaged quantum network and its development. Additionally, democratization access and accelerating real-world applications are two benefits of combining dynamic and conventional systems, especially through cloud-based quantum platforms [4].

1.9 CONCLUSION

The combination of artificial neural networks and quantum technology gave rise to the fascinating and innovative field of quantum learning through machines. As we have navigated the complex web of quantum physics, traditional computing, and ML, we have looked at the origins, applications, and challenges of this creative partnership [15].

The special properties of qubits, such as entanglement and superposition, are used in the learning of quantum machines to evaluate data in ways that conventional machines cannot. By accelerating challenging ML tasks, these quantum properties have the capacity to revolutionize a variety of scientific domains and businesses.

From medication discovery to financial modeling, Practical issues are already being significantly impacted by using QML. Dynamic databases have the power to fundamentally alter how we handle and analyze data, and quantum algorithms are already showing their value in data analysis, grouping, and optimization.

However, scalability, correction of errors, and revolutionary technology's constraints are some of the difficulties that come with QML are still major issues that require constant study and development. Workforce development, ethical issues, and standardization initiatives are also essential for the field's responsible expansion.

QML offers the ability to address problems that were previously intractable as ML and quantum computing advance. Scientific progress might be accelerated, decision-making streamlined, and our understanding of the world enhanced. Science, technology, and society as a whole will be influenced by study and creation in the cutting-edge domains of quantum technology and AI [3].

In this age of tremendous technical advancement, quantum algorithms for learning is a brilliant example showing the path to innovative solutions, solving the enigmas of quantum phenomena, and using AI to improve understanding and productivity.

This convergence encourages us to seize the chances and challenges it offers as we go forward, paving the way for quantum improvements in the analysis of data and AI in the future.

REFERENCES

1. Wisker, Zazli Lily, and Athanasios Poulis. "Emotional intelligence and sales performance. A myth or reality?." *International Journal of Business and Society* 16, no. 2 (2015): 1–12.
2. Mesplomb, F. G. "Three new "gray zones" through the prism of socio-technical developments in cinema: economy of notoriety, uncertainty and tailing phenomena. Some epistemological considerations." *Focus. Notebooks of the French association of teachers and researchers in cinema and audiovisual* 4 (2012).

3. Muniswamaiah, Manoj, Tilak Agerwala, and Charles C. Tappert. "Approximate query processing for big data in heterogeneous databases." *In 2020 IEEE International Conference On Big Data (Big Data)*, pp. 5765–5767. IEEE, 2020.
4. Panigyrakis, G. George, and G. Athanasios Poulis. "Men and women as public relation managers in Greece and Turkey: A comparison study of background variables, job-related factors and activities." *EuroMed Journal of Business* 4, no. 3 (2009): 287–303.
5. Poulis, Athanasios, George Panigyrakis, and Anastasios Panos Panopoulos. "Antecedents and consequents of brand managers' role." *Marketing Intelligence & Planning* 31, no. 6 (2013): 654–673.
6. Poulis, Athanasios, and Zazli Wisker. "Modeling employee-based brand equity (EBBE) and perceived environmental uncertainty (PEU) on a firm's performance." *Journal of Product & Brand Management* 25, no. 5 (2016): 490–503.
7. Vanderschelden, I. "The French film industry: funding, policies, debates." *Studies in French Cinema* 16, no. 2 (2006): 89–94.
8. Abdelgaber, Nahed, and Chris Nikolopoulos. "Overview on quantum computing and its applications in artificial intelligence." In *2020 IEEE Third International Conference on Artificial Intelligence and Knowledge Engineering (AIKE)*, pp. 198–199. IEEE, 2020.
9. Shuford, Jeff. "Quantum computing and artificial intelligence: synergies and challenges." *Journal of Artificial Intelligence General Science (JAIGS)* 1, no. 1 (2024): 1–10.
10. Papakonstantinidis, Stavros, Athanasios Poulis, and Prokopis Theodoridis. *RU# SoLoMo ready?: Consumers and brands in the digital era*. Business Expert Press, 2016.
11. Trivedi, Sandeep, Nikhil Patel, and Nuruzzaman Faruqui. "A novel lightweight lung cancer classifier through hybridization of DNN and comparative feature optimizer." In *International Conference on Hybrid Intelligent Systems*, pp. 188–197. Cham: Springer Nature Switzerland, 2022.
12. Cuong, Nguyen Manh, and Farshad Badie. "International relations and global politics: Germany's cultural diplomacy: A political-logical case study of Friedrich-Ebert-Stiftung in Vietnam." *Russian Law Journal* 11, no. 3 (2023): 1966–1973.
13. Wisker, Zazli Lily, and Athanasios Poulis. "Emotional intelligence–sales performance relationship: A mediating role of adaptive selling behaviour." *International Journal of Management and Economics* 43, no. 1 (2014): 32–52.
14. Hemachandran, K., Areej Alasiry, Mehrez Marzougui, Shahid Mohammad Ganie, Anil Audumbar Pise, M. Turki-Hadj Alouane, and Channabasava Chola. "Performance analysis of deep learning algorithms in diagnosis of malaria disease." *Diagnostics* 13, no. 3 (2023): 534.
15. Ganie, Shahid Mohammad, Majid Bashir Malik, and Tasleem Arif. "Machine learning techniques for diagnosis of type 2 diabetes using lifestyle data." In *International Conference on Innovative Computing and Communications: Proceedings of ICICC 2021*, Volume 3, pp. 487–497. Singapore: Springer Singapore, 2021.

2 Quantum Computing Transforming Machine Learning

An Overview

N. M. Sivamangai, R. Naveenkumar, N. Madhan Kishore, C. M. Lingesh, A. Napolean, and Umaamaheshvari Annamalai

2.1 INTRODUCTION

The convergence of quantum computing and machine learning (ML) represents a transformative shift in computational science, promising breakthroughs that extend far beyond the capabilities of classical systems. Efficiency constraints and scalability limitations are posing a growing threat to established computing approaches as the need to analyze large and complex data increases. ML applications might be greatly enhanced and accelerated by new processes brought about by the development of quantum computing, which are based on quantum physics.

2.1.1 Defining Quantum Computing

A new computational paradigm called quantum computing uses the ideas of quantum physics to carry out tasks that are either impossible or infeasible for traditional computers. The special behavior of quantum bits, or qubits, which function essentially differently from traditional bits, is what gives them their power [1].

2.1.2 Superposition

A key characteristic of quantum systems is superposition, which allows a qubit to simultaneously exist in a mixture of 0 and 1 states. Quantum computers may assess numerous options at once because of qubits in superposition, unlike conventional bits that can only exist in a binary form. As a result, parallelism and possible computing performance are greatly increased.

DOI: 10.1201/9781003587835-2

2.1.3 Entanglement

The quantum phenomenon known as entanglement occurs when two or more qubits get intertwined to the point that, independent of their distance from one another, the state of one directly dictates the state of the other. For certain quantum algorithms, improved coordination and information exchange within quantum systems are made possible by this non-local correlation.

2.1.4 Quantum Parallelism

Superposition and entanglement combine to produce quantum parallelism. Quantum computers can handle many potential solutions at once by taking advantage of these two phenomena. Because of this parallelism, quantum systems are much more effective than conventional computers in solving complicated tasks, such as factoring big numbers, optimizing systems, and simulating quantum processes [2].

2.2 THE SIGNIFICANCE FOR ML

The goal of the data-driven field of ML is to create algorithms that can identify patterns in big, often high-dimensional datasets. The scale and complexity of these databases make standard computing techniques increasingly constrained. Deep neural network (DNN) training and tackling large-scale optimization issues are two examples of tasks that may need a significant amount of time and computer power, and they can sometimes grow exponentially with the quantity of data. Quantum machine learning (QML) has emerged as a potential area of artificial intelligence (AI) study because quantum computing offers a revolutionary way to overcome these computational limitations.

2.2.1 Acceleration of Linear Algebra Operations

The majority of ML algorithms, especially those that use neural networks, mostly depend on linear algebra operations, such as matrix multiplication and inversion. It has been shown that quantum algorithms, such as the Harrow–Hassidim–Lloyd (HHL) algorithm, have the ability to do certain matrix calculations 10 times faster than traditional techniques. The amount of time needed for ML model training and inference may be significantly decreased by this acceleration [3].

2.2.2 Efficient Optimization Problem Solving

Many ML activities, such as feature selection, model training, and hyperparameter tweaking, are based on optimization. New techniques brought about by quantum computing, such as variational quantum algorithms and quantum annealing, may solve certain types of optimization problems more quickly than their conventional equivalents. These methods pave the way for quicker and maybe more accurate model convergence.

2.2.3 Exploration of Novel Algorithmic Approaches

In addition to increasing speed, quantum computing makes it possible to learn in fundamentally novel ways that are not possible in traditional frameworks. The capacity to represent and handle data in high-dimensional Hilbert spaces is provided by quantum-enhanced models, such as quantum generative models and quantum kernel approaches, which give higher expressive capability for pattern detection and generalization.

2.2.4 Emergence of QML

The fast-developing area of QML is the result of the convergence of ML and quantum computing. QML investigates how learning processes might be improved by quantum resources, which could redefine the theoretical and applied boundaries of AI. It has the potential to solve issues that are now thought to be computationally unsolvable, and both business and academia are aggressively researching its implications [4].

2.3 SCOPE OF THIS DOCUMENT

This chapter offers a methodical investigation of the ways in which ML is being impacted by quantum computing, with the aim of advancing theoretical knowledge and useful implementation techniques. The document's scope covers a number of important topics, each of which is covered in separate parts.

2.3.1 Fundamentals of Computation

The basic ideas of both conventional and quantum computing are introduced in the first part. The foundation for comprehending the computing benefits provided by quantum systems is laid by this comparison.

2.3.2 QML Algorithms

The fundamental ideas of QML are examined in later talks, along with several algorithmic frameworks and their theoretical foundations.

2.3.3 Real-World and Emerging Applications

The chapter then goes on to discuss the applications of QML in a variety of fields, from optimization and cybersecurity to healthcare and finance. Additionally, experimental use cases and emerging applications are analyzed.

2.3.4 Technical Challenges and Barriers

The theoretical and practical difficulties of incorporating quantum computing into current ML pipelines are also critically examined. This includes a discussion of issues such as algorithmic limits, scalability, noise, and hardware limitations.

2.3.5 Future Research and Societal Impact

The chapter ends by discussing possible future research avenues and the wider social ramifications of quantum-enhanced AI, including moral dilemmas and the possibility of long-term intelligent system change.

The goal of this thorough assessment is to assist scholars, researchers, and business people who are looking for information on one of the most exciting nexus points of contemporary science and technology [5].

2.4 FUNDAMENTALS OF QUANTUM COMPUTING

2.4.1 Qubits: The Quantum Information Unit

The quantum bit, or qubit, is the central component of quantum computing. A qubit is able to exist in a superposition of both states at the same time, unlike a conventional bit, which can only be either 0 or 1. The state of a qubit may be expressed symbolically as follows:

$$|\psi\rangle = \alpha|0\rangle + \beta|1\rangle \tag{2.1}$$

If the complex amplitudes α and β are such that:

$$|\alpha|^2 + |\beta|^2 = 1 \tag{2.2}$$

The probability of the qubit being measured as $|0\rangle$ $|0\rangle$ or $|1\rangle$ $|1\rangle$ is represented by these squared magnitudes, respectively.

Example: Suppose a qubit is prepared in a state where $\alpha = 1/\sqrt{2}$ and $\beta = 1/\sqrt{2}$. Then the state is

$$|\psi\rangle = 1/\sqrt{2}|0\rangle + 1/\sqrt{2}|1\rangle \tag{2.3}$$

This means that measuring the qubit yields 0 or 1 with equal probability (50% each), which is fundamentally different from a classical bit that is always in one definite state (either 0 or 1).

2.4.2 Quantum Gates and Circuits

Classical computation manipulates binary information using logic gates such as AND, OR, and NOT; quantum computation operates on quantum bits (qubits) through quantum gates. These gates are represented mathematically as unitary operators, which transform the state of a qubit in accordance with the laws of quantum mechanics. Unlike classical gates, quantum gates must preserve the norm of the qubit's state vector, ensuring reversibility and coherence in quantum evolution [6, 7].

2.4.2.1 Single-Qubit Gates

Single-qubit gates apply operations to individual qubits and serve as the fundamental building blocks of quantum circuits. The X gate flips a qubit's state and is sometimes referred to as the quantum counterpart of the conventional NOT gate. In particular, it applies the following rule to change the base state from $|0\rangle$ to $|1\rangle$ and vice versa:

$$X|0\rangle = |1\rangle, X|1\rangle = |0\rangle \tag{2.4}$$

A critical quantum gate that induces a superposition state in a qubit is the Hadamard (H) gate. To provide the interference effects necessary for quantum algorithms, it converts $|0\rangle$ into an equal superposition of $|0\rangle$ and $|1\rangle$ and similarly influences $|1\rangle$. The following provides the transformation:

$$H0\rangle = |0\rangle + |1\rangle / \sqrt{2}, \text{and } H1\rangle = |0\rangle - |1\rangle / \sqrt{2} \tag{2.5}$$

By giving the $|1\rangle$ component a negative sign, the Z gate creates a phase shift while maintaining the $|0\rangle$ component unaltered. It is essential to interference-based methods and quantum phase estimation:

$$Z|0\rangle = |0\rangle, Z|1\rangle = -|1\rangle \tag{2.6}$$

More intricate quantum operations are made possible by these single-qubit gates, which allow qubits to be initialized, rotated, and superposed.

2.4.2.2 Multi-Qubit Operations

Multi-qubit gates are used in quantum circuits to achieve entanglement and enable more complex transformations. The most basic of them is the Controlled-NOT (CNOT) gate. One qubit is referred to as the control qubit and the other as the target qubit when using this gate. Only when the control qubit is in the $|1\rangle$ state does the CNOT gate's conditional action flip the target qubit's state. The target qubit does not change if the control qubit is in the $|0\rangle$ state. In contrast, the target qubit goes through a bit-flip operation, shifting from $|0\rangle$ to $|1\rangle$ or from $|1\rangle$ to $|0\rangle$, if the control qubit is in the $|1\rangle$ state.

The generation of quantum entanglement, a fundamental characteristic of quantum systems where the state of one qubit is intrinsically linked to the state of another, depends on this conditional behavior. It is impossible to factor the combined state of entangled qubits into individual qubit states, and they display correlations that cannot be explained traditionally. Because of this occurrence, quantum systems are able to investigate computational avenues that are not available to traditional computers [8].

Single and multi-qubit quantum gates are arranged in exact sequences and combinations to create quantum circuits. Complex quantum algorithms that are computationally demanding or unfeasible for conventional systems may be implemented using these circuits. To fully use the promise of quantum advantage for applications ranging from ML to encryption, multi-qubit gates, such as the CNOT, are essential [9].

2.5 MEASUREMENT AND DECOHERENCE

The procedure that collapses a qubit from its superposed quantum state into a specific classical output is known as measurement in quantum computing. For example,

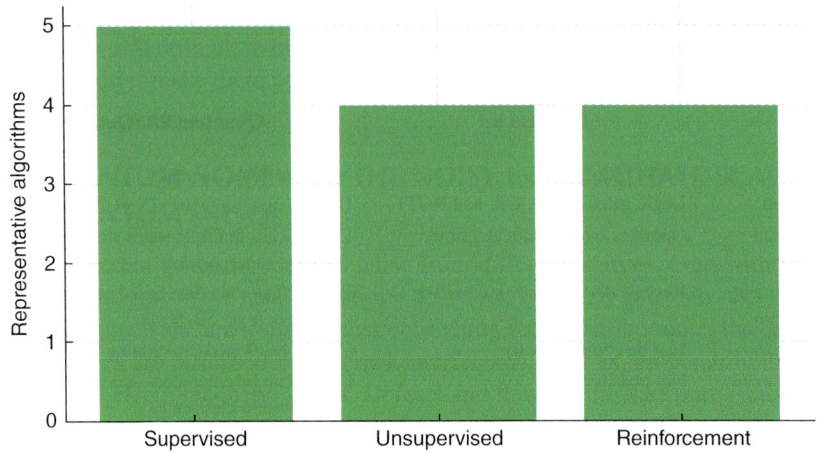

FIGURE 2.2 ML paradigms.

compression and visualization, anomaly detection in cybersecurity, and customer segmentation in marketing.

2.9.3 Reinforcement Learning

A behavioral psychology-inspired goal-driven paradigm known as reinforcement learning (RL) teaches an agent to make choices by interacting with its surroundings and getting feedback in the form of reward or penalties. Through trial and error, the goal is to determine the best course of action that maximizes cumulative benefits over time. The agent (decision-maker), the environment (external system), the state (representation of the current situation), actions (potential choices), and rewards (performance feedback) are important elements in reinforcement learning. Prominent algorithms in this field include Q-Learning, Deep Q-Networks (DQN), Policy Gradient Methods, and Actor–Critic Methods. Reinforcement learning has practical applications in autonomous driving systems, robotics and industrial automation, game-playing AI (such as AlphaGo and OpenAI Five), and smart resource allocation in networks [14]. Figure 2.2 describes ML paradigms.

2.10 STANDARD ML ALGORITHMS

At the core of ML are foundational algorithms that enable systems to recognize patterns, make accurate predictions, and adapt to new data inputs. Each algorithm offers distinct advantages and is tailored for specific problem types and data characteristics. Some of the most widely adopted ML algorithms are presented in the following.

2.10.1 Linear Regression

Linear regression is among the simplest and most interpretable supervised learning algorithms. It fits a linear equation to the observed data to describe the connection between a dependent variable and one or more independent variables. The formula is written as follows: $y = wx + b$, where b is the bias or intercept factor, w is the weight or slope, x is the input feature, and y is the expected output. This method is often used to forecast continuous outcomes, such as temperature, housing prices, and sales revenue. Its computing efficiency, interpretability, and usefulness as a baseline for regression problems are its main advantages [10].

2.10.2 SVM

Strong supervised learning models called SVM are mostly used for classification; however, they may also be modified to solve regression issues. Finding the best hyperplane in the feature space to optimally divide classes is how SVMs operate. The margin, which is the distance between the hyperplane and the closest data points from each class, also referred to as support vectors, is a key idea in SVM. SVM uses the kernel technique, a mathematical transformation that projects data into a higher dimensional space where a separating hyperplane may be identified, to deal with situations when the data is not linearly separable. SVMs are often used in domains including bioinformatics, image recognition, and text categorization. They work well in high-dimensional spaces, are adaptable since several kernel functions are available, and are resistant to overfitting when properly regularized.

2.10.3 Neural Networks

The biological makeup and operations of the human brain serve as the inspiration for neural networks, which are computer models. They are made up of layers of artificial neurons, which are linked nodes that analyze incoming data and use weighted connections to develop hierarchical representations. Typically, the architecture consists of an output layer that produces the final prediction, many hidden layers that perform non-linear modifications, and an input layer that accepts raw data. DNNs are neural networks with many hidden layers that are particularly good at extracting abstract and sophisticated patterns from big, complicated datasets. In a variety of fields, neural networks have shown cutting-edge performance. applications such as image recognition, natural language processing (NLP), speech recognition, and game AI. Their remarkable capacity to describe non-lincar connections, scalability to enormous datasets, and compatibility with sophisticated computer resources are among their main advantages [14].

2.11 COMPUTATIONAL CHALLENGES IN ML

Large-scale model training and deployment have become much more computationally demanding as ML continues to spread across many domains. These issues, which include hardware constraints, algorithmic efficiency, and data management, pose significant barriers to both academic progress and real-world applications.

2.11.1 Data Volume and Dimensionality

Millions of samples and thousands of characteristics are common datasets used in modern ML. Examples include user activity logs, genetic sequences, and high-resolution photos, all of which produce enormous amounts of high-dimensional data.

2.12.4 Quantum Feature Spaces

Hilbert spaces, the mathematical underpinnings of quantum physics, are high-dimensional complex vector spaces in which quantum computers function natively. These areas provide a vibrant and expressive setting for manipulating and representing data. In the field of QML, complex patterns, correlations, and structures that could be obscured in traditional, lower-dimensional classical settings can be found by embedding classical data into such quantum feature spaces. QML models are capable of performing complex learning tasks with improved expressiveness and generalization by using the special characteristics of Hilbert spaces. Applications using complicated or non-linearly separable data benefit greatly from this feature [11].

2.12.4.1 Quantum Kernels

Key elements of many QML algorithms are quantum kernels. They extend the concept of classical similarity measures by computing the inner product (overlap) between quantum states that encode classical data. Given two input vectors, the quantum kernel function evaluates how similar their corresponding quantum states are in Hilbert space. This quantum approach enables robust performance in classification, clustering, and regression tasks, particularly in high-dimensional feature spaces where classical kernel methods may become computationally infeasible or lose effectiveness. Quantum kernels inherently exploit quantum parallelism and interference to encode and compare data more effectively.

2.12.4.2 Non-Linear Feature Mapping via Quantum Circuits

One of the major advantages of quantum feature spaces is the ability to perform complex, non-linear transformations of data through unitary operations implemented by quantum circuits. These circuits apply sequences of quantum gates that evolve the quantum state in a way that corresponds to embedding the input data into a highly expressive feature space. Unlike classical methods, which often require the explicit computation of kernel matrices, an operation that becomes costly with increasing data size, quantum circuits can implicitly realize these transformations efficiently. This makes quantum feature mapping highly scalable and expressive, allowing QML models to capture non-linear relationships in data with significantly greater efficiency and depth [10].

2.12.5 Information-Theoretic Considerations

Understanding the underlying boundaries of data processing, learning, and generalization is made possible by the combination of ML and quantum information theory. Quantum bits (qubits), which take advantage of coherence, entanglement, and superposition, are used to represent quantum information as opposed to binary bits, which are used to store and modify conventional information. These characteristics provide quantum computers the ability to interpret data in ways that go against conventional wisdom and might lead to new ML efficiency advantages. From an information-theoretic perspective, QML opens up new options for feature correlation modeling, query optimization, and sample efficiency.

2.12.5.1 Sample Complexity

Quantum learning algorithms have the potential to reduce the sample complexity, the number of training examples required to achieve a certain level of generalization performance. Under specific conditions and for certain classes of problems, quantum models may learn with fewer examples than their classical counterparts. However, the extent and universality of this advantage remain areas of active theoretical and empirical research. The potential gains are highly problem-dependent and may vary based on the encoding scheme, noise tolerance, and data structure [2].

2.12.5.2 Query Complexity

One of the well-studied advantages in quantum learning lies in query complexity, which refers to the number of oracle calls or data queries needed to learn or infer hidden information. Quantum algorithms have demonstrated exponential improvements in query complexity for specific tasks. For instance, learning hidden structures, solving Boolean function identification, or estimating properties of Hamiltonians can be significantly accelerated through quantum approaches. This reduction in required queries translates directly into more efficient learning, particularly in settings where data acquisition is expensive or limited.

2.12.5.3 Entanglement and Correlations

Quantum systems can exploit entanglement to represent and manipulate complex correlations between features, surpassing classical probabilistic models. Capturing feature dependencies in classical ML often requires explicit modeling and high computing costs. In contrast, QML models may naturally learn complex, high-order relationships because entangled quantum states can naturally express joint feature distributions. This capacity is particularly important in fields such as quantum chemistry, finance, and NLP that deal with structured or interconnected data [9].

2.13 CORE QML ALGORITHMS

2.13.1 Quantum Support Vector Machine (QSVM)

By integrating quantum-enhanced kernel techniques, the QSVM expands the conventional SVM framework into the quantum realm. SVM's fundamental idea is to identify the hyperplane that maximally separates classes in a high-dimensional feature space, a process which hinges critically on the computation of inner products and kernel evaluations between data points.

2.13.1.1 Quantum Advantage and Mathematical Underpinnings

When working with big datasets or intricate feature changes, classical SVMs may become computationally demanding. The time required for training increases exponentially with the complexity of the input space and polynomially with the number of data points. By encoding conventional data vectors into quantum states via Hilbert space embeddings, quantum computing presents a convincing substitute. The squared inner product between two quantum states serves as the representation of the kernel function in this quantum framework that assesses input similarity. Assuming that the quantum states can be effectively synthesized, quantum circuits can estimate these overlaps exponentially more quickly than conventional techniques. The core of the QSVM's ability to perform better than its classical equivalent is this quantum advantage [15].

2.13.1.2 Basic Circuit Design

The swap test, a quantum circuit used to evaluate the overlap (similarity) between two quantum states, is a key part of the QSVM. The following components are part of the swap test's standard configuration.

2.13.1.2.1 Control Qubit Initialization

A control qubit is initialized in a superposition state at the start of the circuit. Usually, to do this, a Hadamard gate (H) is applied to the control qubit, which is initially in the $|0\rangle$ state $1/\sqrt{2}(|0\rangle + |1\rangle)$.

2.13.1.2.2 Data Registers

The encoded data states, $|x\rangle$ and $|x'\rangle$, are stored in two distinct quantum registers, and it is necessary to determine how similar they are. These registers use an encoding strategy appropriate for the QSVM algorithm to represent the classical data embedded into quantum states.

2.13.1.2.3 Interference and Measurement

The swap test employs a controlled-swap (Fredkin) gate, conditioned on the control qubit, which swaps the two data registers if the control qubit is $|1\rangle$. Following this, another Hadamard gate is applied to the control qubit, and the measurement outcome of the control qubit reveals the overlap between $|x\rangle$ and $|x'\rangle$. The probability of measuring the control qubit in $|0\rangle$ is related to the squared inner product $|\langle x|x'\rangle|^2$, thus providing a similarity measure [17].

A fundamental component of QSVM is the swap test, a quantum circuit used to estimate the overlap between two quantum states. The standard configuration involves.

2.13.1.3 Theoretical Complexity and Experimental Status

Theoretically, for certain specially structured quantum kernels and efficiently encodable data, the QSVM can achieve exponential speedups over classical SVMs. Harrow and Montanaro (2017) surveyed cases where quantum kernel estimation costs scale logarithmically with input size, whereas classical methods remain polynomial or worse.

Experimentally, recent implementations on superconducting qubit processors (International Business Machines [IBM], Rigetti) and trapped-ion systems have demonstrated QSVMs on *toy datasets* (2–4 qubits), showing quantum-enhanced feature separation in practice. However, real-world scalability is hampered by noise and data loading bottlenecks.

2.13.2 QPCA

The QPCA algorithm, introduced by Lloyd, Mohseni, and Rebentrost (2014), provides a quantum analogue to classical PCA—a vital technique in dimensionality reduction and feature extraction. Classical PCA computes eigenvectors of the covariance matrix, a process that can become prohibitive for very high-dimensional data [10].

2.13.2.1 Quantum Advantage and Mathematical Foundations

In the quantum setting, the covariance matrix is encoded as a quantum density matrix, a construct that captures the statistical properties of quantum states. The primary goal of QPCA is to extract the principal eigenvectors and eigenvalues of this matrix, which correspond to the dominant patterns or directions of variance in the data. To achieve this, QPCA employs quantum phase estimation algorithms, which allow the extraction of eigenvalues and their associated eigenvectors directly from the density matrix. This approach is efficient because quantum systems may use a logarithmic number of qubits to process exponentially huge state spaces. Compared to traditional PCA, QPCA provides a possible exponential speedup. If the quantum state preparation and access to the density matrix are efficient, the quantum approach can estimate principal components with a runtime that scales logarithmically with the input dimension, whereas classical methods frequently require time that scales quadratically (or worse) with the number of data points [9].

2.13.2.2 Basic Circuit Design

Key quantum subroutines and data preparation techniques are at the heart of designing quantum circuits for QPCA. The need to extract the eigenvalues and eigenvectors of a density matrix ρ, which contains the statistical characteristics of a quantum dataset, is at the heart of QPCA. The following crucial elements are included in the basic circuit design.

2.13.2.2.1 Quantum Phase Estimation (QPE)

The fundamental subroutine for obtaining the eigenvalues of the density matrix ρ is quantum phase estimation. Calculating the phases associated with the eigenstates of ρ, it allows the quantum circuit to determine the major components. The QPE method requires the capacity to execute controlled unitary operations resulting from which may be approximated in practice using simulation techniques or existing oracles.

2.13.2.2.2 Preparation of Multiple Copies of the Density Matrix

The QPCA algorithm requires access to multiple identical copies of the density matrix ρ. This necessitates efficient state preparation, where quantum states are initialized according to the underlying data distribution. The data is embedded into quantum states, and repeated preparations are used to approximate ρ as an ensemble average. This step is crucial for enabling quantum operations, such as QPE, and subsequent measurement to extract meaningful principal component information. Together, these elements form the backbone of QPCA circuit architecture. The practical implementation depends heavily on the fidelity of state preparation and the precision of quantum phase estimation, both of which are key challenges in current and near-term quantum hardware [13].

2.13.2.3 Theoretical Complexity and Experimental Status

The QPCA algorithm's complexity is polylogarithmic in the data dimension for sparse matrices, under idealized assumptions of efficient state and density matrix preparation (see Lloyd et al.). Today, full-scale QPCA has not been demonstrated experimentally due to challenges in preparing numerous copies of quantum states representing large classical datasets. Proof-of-concept implementations, however, have demonstrated key steps on small devices and for synthetic data.

2.13.2.3.1 Quantum k-Means

The quantum k-Means algorithm is designed to accelerate the unsupervised clustering of data into *k* groups based on geometric proximity (e.g., Euclidean distance). The classical k-means repeatedly computes distances between data points and cluster centroids—an operations-intensive process for large, high-dimensional datasets.

2.13.2.3.2 Quantum Speedup and Mathematical Structure

Quantum versions of k-means, pioneered by Lloyd and colleagues in 2013, introduce a fundamentally different approach by encoding classical data into quantum states using amplitude encoding. These quantum representations, combined with quantum random access memory (QRAM), enable the algorithm to process and compare large volumes of data in parallel. At the heart of the quantum k-means algorithm is a quantum distance estimation circuit, which calculates the squared Euclidean distance between a data point and a centroid in a highly efficient manner. Unlike the classical method, which requires evaluating every point-centroid pair individually, the quantum approach uses quantum parallelism to estimate these distances simultaneously across all combinations. This parallelism results in a quadratic speedup: while the classical algorithm has a complexity of O (N, k, M) where N is the number of data points, k is the number of clusters, and M is the feature dimension the quantum algorithm can achieve a reduced complexity on the order of O(k• polylog(N, M)), assuming efficient state preparation and data access via QRAM [16].

By reducing one of the primary computational bottlenecks in clustering, quantum k-means holds promise for scaling unsupervised learning to datasets that are currently impractical for classical methods.

2.13.2.3.3 Circuit Design

The quantum k-means circuit design comprises two main components. First, state preparation circuits efficiently encode all data points into quantum memory, allowing compact representation of the dataset within the quantum system. Second, interference-based circuits, including the swap test and quantum distance estimation circuits, enable simultaneous measurement of the similarity between data points and centroids. This parallel processing is fundamental to the algorithm's ability to achieve speedup over classical methods.

2.13.2.3.4 Theoretical Complexity and Experimental Status

For QRAM-accessible datasets and well-posed encoding, quantum k-means promises quadratic speedup. However, QRAM remains theoretical; no scalable, physical realization exists, and true quantum clustering has so far been demonstrated only on tiny datasets using current NISQ hardware. Research into efficient circuits for state preparation is ongoing and pivotal for practical benefits.

2.13.3 Quantum Neural Networks (QNNs) and Variational Algorithms

2.13.3.1 QNNs: The Quantum Analog of Neural Systems

QNNs are quantum counterparts of classical neural networks, designed to harness the properties of quantum computation, most notably superposition and entanglement, for tasks, such as pattern recognition, classification, and generative modeling.

A direct translation of classical neurons into quantum circuits is challenging due to the no-cloning theorem and the linearity inherent in quantum mechanics. However, several paradigms approximate neural behavior within the quantum domain.

2.13.3.1.1 Quantum Perceptrons

Inspired by the classical perceptron, the foundational element of neural networks, quantum perceptrons exploit unitary operations to apply weighted transformations and measurements to qubits. Early quantum perceptron models utilize quantum gates to process quantum-encoded data. Due to the absence of classical non-linear activation functions, these models rely on creative quantum alternatives such as measurement-induced non-linearity or mappings into higherdimensional Hilbert spaces [2].

2.13.3.1.2 Parametrized Quantum Circuits

Most QNN architectures employ parametrized quantum circuits consisting of quantum gates with tunable parameters (e.g., rotation angles). The network's "layers" are formed by sequences of these gates, where each layer acts analogously to layers in a classical neural network, enabling trainable transformations on quantum states.

2.13.3.2 Variational Quantum Circuits (VQCs): Foundations and Workflow

VQCs form the backbone of practical QML and quantum neural network models, especially on NISQ devices. A VQC creates a hybrid quantum–classical workflow by using a quantum circuit with configurable (variational) parameters that are optimized by a classical computer.

2.13.3.2.1 Preparation

An initial quantum circuit sets the scene for further processing by encoding classical data into a quantum state.

2.13.3.2.2 Parameterization

The behavior of the circuit is defined by a series of quantum gates, often including rotation and entangling gates, applied with changeable parameters such as rotation angles θ_i.

2.13.3.2.3 Measurement

Depending on the settings used, probabilistic results are obtained by measuring the circuit's ultimate quantum state.

2.13.3.2.4 Optimization

To minimize or maximize a predetermined cost function—such as the loss or error in a supervised learning task a classical optimizer repeatedly modifies the circuit's parameters.

2.13.3.3 Applications of QNNs and VQCs in Deep Learning Tasks

2.13.3.3.1 Classification

VQCs are used in quantum classifiers to develop parameterized measurement techniques for data class distinction. Effective categorization in the quantum realm is made possible by this method, which is comparable to soft max layers in traditional deep neural networks.

2.13.3.3.2 Regression

VQCs can model continuous target functions by adjusting gate parameters to minimize loss functions such as mean squared error, allowing the fitting of data in regression tasks.

2.13.3.3.3 Quantum Generative Models

Quantum circuits are explored for generative tasks, including quantum Generative Adversarial Networks (GANs), where the goal is to generate quantum or classical data distributions through parameterized measurements.

2.13.3.3.4 Feature Embedding

QNNs can embed data into complex quantum feature spaces, supporting quantum kernel methods and providing non-linear feature extraction techniques that are not available in classical ML.

Pioneering experiments have demonstrated that QNN- and VQC-based models can classify small datasets (such as handwritten digits from the Modified National Institute of Standards and Technology [MNIST]) and learn quantum states. However, these successes remain at a relatively small, proof-of-concept scale due to current hardware limitations.

2.13.3.4 Training Challenges: Barren Plateaus and Parameter Optimization

2.13.3.4.1 Barren Plateaus

A major challenge in training VQCs is the barren plateau phenomenon, where the gradient magnitudes of the cost function shrink exponentially with the number of qubits or the depth of the circuit. This results in a nearly flat optimization landscape where standard gradient-based methods struggle to find meaningful parameter updates. The root cause lies in the high-dimensional unitary space that the quantum circuit explores, leading to concentration of measure effects that cause gradients to vanish almost everywhere. This makes scaling QNNs to large sizes particularly difficult. Recent studies have identified certain circuit architectures and initialization schemes that can reduce the likelihood of barren plateaus, such as local cost functions and shallow circuits.

2.13.3.4.2 Vanishing and Exploding Gradients

Just as in classical deep learning, quantum models can experience vanishing or exploding gradients during training. However, due to the entangled nature of quantum states and the unitary constraints of quantum gates, these phenomena manifest differently. Instability during optimization may result from the gradient signal's unpredictable oscillation or saturation due to the intricate interactions between parameters. Moreover, quantum gradients are calculated indirectly via repeated measurements, which makes them more susceptible to noise and complicates gradient magnitude management, in contrast to conventional networks [16].

2.13.3.4.3 Stochastic Measurement Noise

Quantum computing is inherently prone to measurement noise. Since quantum measurements are probabilistic, it takes many runs (shots) to precisely predict expectation values for each evaluation of the circuit's output. For deep circuits or when the cost function includes minute variations in measurement results, this statistical noise may overpower faint gradient signals. Noisy gradients and unstable training dynamics are also caused by readout mistakes, decoherence, and gate flaws in existing NISQ systems. Methods including adaptive shot allocation, noise-aware optimization, and error mitigation are being developed to counteract these impacts.

2.13.4 Strategies to Mitigate Training Challenges

2.13.4.1 Circuit Design and Ansatz Selection

It's crucial to choose the appropriate parameterized or ansatz circuit structure. The training landscapes of shallow circuits with localized entanglement patterns are often more favorable because they avoid arid plateaus and minimize noise buildup. Trainability may be increased, and the parameter search space can be decreased by using problem-inspired ansätze, which take into account past knowledge about the task or data. Additionally, layer-wise growth methodologies aid in maintaining controllable gradients by progressively increasing the circuit depth throughout training.

2.13.4.2 Gradient-Free and Alternative Optimization Methods

Gradient-free optimization techniques, including Bayesian optimization, particle swarm optimization, and evolutionary algorithms, have been used for quantum model training since gradient estimations may be inaccurate. Because these techniques do not depend on gradient information, they can withstand flat and noisy environments. Furthermore, quantum natural gradient techniques have shown promise in accelerating convergence and avoiding barren plateaus by using the shape of the parameter space to assist optimization.

2.13.4.3 Modular and Layer-Wise Training Methods

Layer-wise training, which was inspired by traditional deep learning methods, optimizes components of the circuit one at a time rather than all at once. This method may lessen gradient problems and make the optimization problem simpler. Likewise, modular quantum circuits—which train sub-circuits separately before combining them—enable faster debugging and greater scalability.

2.13.4.4 Parameter Initialization and Regularization

The training dynamics may be greatly impacted by properly initializing the parameters. The chance of a barren plateau is decreased by random initializations derived from distributions that start near identity operations or retain gradient magnitudes. Furthermore, overfitting is avoided and generalization is enhanced by regularization strategies tailored to quantum circuits, such as penalty terms on parameter values or entanglement limitations [7].

2.14 APPLICATIONS: QML IN PRACTICE

2.14.1 Overview of Practical and Experimental QML

QML is making its way from theory into practice through experimental demonstrations and emerging prototype applications. While current devices known as NISQ processors are restricted by limited qubit count and noise, recent progress has showcased the real-world impact of QML in diverse domains. These applications span quantum chemistry, finance, drug discovery, materials science, and cryptography. Here, we highlight the most influential proof-of-principle experiments and prototype deployments, referencing major studies and key industry initiatives.

2.14.2 Quantum Chemistry and Materials Science

Quantum chemistry is a flagship application area for quantum computing and QML. Accurately simulating molecular energies, reaction dynamics, and electronic structures becomes computationally intractable for classical computers as system complexity increases. QML models, especially Variational Quantum Eigensolvers (VQE) and QNNs, are being developed to improve quantum simulation tasks.

2.14.2.1 VQE-Based Molecular Simulations

Pioneering experiments have demonstrated quantum circuits calculating the ground-state energies of molecules such as hydrogen (H_2), lithium hydride (LiH), and beryllium hydride (BeH_2). Notably, Kandala et al. (Nature 2017) experimentally proved VQE for simple molecules using a superconducting quantum processor, which is a significant proof of principle. To minimize the molecular energy estimate, the VQE method uses a hybrid quantum–classical optimization loop in which a classical optimizer repeatedly refines parameters while a parameterized quantum circuit creates trial wave functions. By using this approach, the exponential scaling that accurate diagonalization on classical computers faces is avoided [12].

2.14.2.2 ML for Quantum State Classification

Recently, small-scale QML-based classifiers have been built on actual quantum hardware to differentiate between quantum phases of matter, such as topological states (Rocchetto et al., 2019). These classifiers extract tiny patterns that are difficult for classical algorithms to identify by encoding complicated quantum states into high-dimensional Hilbert spaces using quantum feature maps. These developments point to interesting avenues for automated phase identification in condensed matter physics and materials research.

2.14.2.3 Materials Discovery

To predict material characteristics and find novel compounds, quantum Boltzmann machines, or QBMs, have been investigated; representative prototypes have operated on high-fidelity simulators and real quantum processors. These generative models may speed up the process of identifying materials with desired electrical, magnetic, or optical properties by using quantum processes such as entanglement and superposition to describe and sample from complicated distributions across material configurations. Combining QBM with traditional materials databases and density functional theory (DFT) simulations is an active research frontier aimed at hybrid workflows for accelerated materials design.

2.14.3 Finance and Optimization

Completing high-dimensional, computationally demanding optimization issues is necessary for financial modeling's intricate activities, which include risk analysis, portfolio optimization, and derivatives pricing. Potential accelerations and unique modeling dynamics are provided by quantum algorithms and QML, which hold promise for increases in speed and solution quality.

2.14.3.1 Portfolio Optimization Using QAOA

Combinatorial optimization issues may be resolved using the variational hybrid quantum–classical technique known as the QAOA. Portfolio optimization, where the objective is to choose the best subset of assets to maximize returns while minimizing risk within limitations, has been experimentally implemented.

To solve tiny issue cases, Egger et al. (2020, IBM) developed a portfolio selection process based on QAOA using an NISQ device. For small-scale cases, this experiment demonstrated how QAOA circuits may approximate solutions with performance competitive to conventional heuristics, highlighting the practical viability of quantum optimization techniques for finance.

Due to its capacity to adapt to NISQ devices, QAOA is a strong contender for near-term quantum finance applications, even if large-scale implementations are still difficult because of hardware constraints [17].

2.14.3.2 QML for Financial Forecasting

Using quantum-enhanced regression and classification circuits to represent time series and market behavior, QML approaches have also been investigated for financial forecasting. Using tiny datasets, prototype QML algorithms have shown performance equivalent to traditional baselines in binary classification tasks, including trend identification and market movement prediction. To effectively capture intricate non-linear patterns and correlations that classical models can find difficult to depict, these models make use of quantum feature maps and VQCs. This field of study is still in its infancy, but it suggests that quantum-accelerated trading strategies and risk models may be developed that may adjust to changing market conditions more quickly than conventional techniques.

2.14.3.3 Quantum Optimization Beyond Finance

Quantum optimization techniques, such as QAOA and quantum annealing, are being researched for use in fields other than finance, such as resource allocation, logistics, and supply chain management, where equally challenging combinatorial issues occur. These initiatives seek to more effectively explore vast solution areas than traditional heuristics by using the quantum parallelism and probabilistic sampling capabilities of quantum devices.

2.14.4 Drug Discovery and Bioinformatics

The process of finding new drugs is a difficult and resource-intensive one that includes estimating the safety and effectiveness of potential drugs, modeling molecular interactions, and screening large molecular libraries. Large amounts of chemical and biological data, which often show intricate non-linear interactions, must be managed and analyzed for these activities. Rapid pattern recognition and modeling of complex quantum states are two promising capabilities of QML, which might speed up several stages of the drug development process.

2.14.4.1 QNNs for Molecular Classification

VQCs and QNNs have been investigated for molecular property prediction tasks, such as determining biological activity, binding affinity, or solubility from chemical data that has been recorded.

Notably, IBM's partnerships with pharmaceutical firms such as Merck and Roche have produced innovative case studies that show how molecular fingerprints may be encoded into quantum states and how molecular activity can be categorized on NISQ devices. By converting molecular descriptors into high-dimensional quantum feature spaces via quantum feature maps, these prototypes allow QNNs to identify minute chemical patterns that may be missed by conventional models. These initiatives demonstrate how QML may increase the precision of early-stage drug candidate screening, but they are still in their infancy.

2.14.4.2 Hybrid Classical-Quantum Pipelines

A number of experimental pipelines improve tasks, such as drug candidate classification and clustering, by combining quantum feature mapping or quantum kernel techniques with traditional deep learning models. Molecular pictures or descriptors, for instance, may be pre-processed using conventional convolutional neural networks (CNNs) before being encoded into quantum states to take advantage of quantum-enhanced non-linear transformations. Improved prediction accuracy and resilience in bioinformatics applications may result from this hybrid technique, which combines the advantages of quantum computing for exploring complicated feature spaces with the strengths of conventional computation for feature extraction.

2.14.5 Cryptography and Security

A common perspective on the nexus between quantum computing and cryptography is that of quantum threats to traditional cryptosystems, such as Shor's algorithm, which breaks RSA and ECC. But in ways that traditional techniques cannot match, QML also provides new ways to improve security monitoring and cryptographic primitives.

2.14.5.1 Quantum-Based Anomaly Detection

For quantum-enhanced anomaly and fraud detection in large datasets, such as network traffic or financial transactions, QML algorithms have been created and prototyped. QSVMs, for example, have been used to more accurately and efficiently detect patterns suggestive of network infiltration and credit card fraud on certain benchmarks. Such quantum classifiers may be able to identify tiny, non-linear abnormalities that are difficult for conventional algorithms to detect, as Pérez-Salinas et al. (2021) showed. The inherent capability of QML models to function in high-dimensional quantum feature spaces facilitates the more efficient differentiation of suspicious from regular behavior.

2.14.5.2 Quantum Data Hiding and Secure Learning

Additionally, QML makes it possible for cutting-edge cryptography protocols, such as quantum data hiding, in which private data is encoded into quantum states such that it cannot be retrieved by unauthorized parties without the use of certain quantum keys or operations. This idea facilitates the creation of private data categorization and safe multi-party quantum learning, where data privacy is maintained while learning collaboratively over dispersed quantum computers.

By using the special qualities of entanglement and quantum no-cloning, these methods protect the secrecy of data and provide novel approaches to secure pattern recognition and privacy-preserving ML that are hard or impossible to do by traditional means.

2.14.5.3 QML for Quantum-Resistant Cryptography

QML is being investigated as a tool for designing and analyzing quantum-resistant cryptography methods in addition to traditional risks. By providing a dynamic feedback loop between cryptanalysis and cryptosystem design, ML models trained on quantum data might help detect possible flaws and improve post-quantum cryptographic protocols.

2.14.6 Major Case Studies and Proof-of-Principle Experiments

2.14.6.1 Prototype Applications Using NISQ Devices

QML applications have been experimentally proven on both synthetic and small real-world datasets, despite the intrinsic constraints of NISQ devices. As quantum hardware advances, these prototype demonstrations provide the groundwork for future scaling and offer important insights. By fusing conventional optimization and data processing with quantum state preparation and measurement, current hybrid quantum–classical workflows aim to optimize the use of available quantum technology. This method successfully overcomes the limitations caused by noise and finite qubit counts. Table 2.2 depicts major case studies and proof-of-principle experiments.

Although there are still major obstacles that prevent quick real-world effect, such as experimental noise and data encoding bottlenecks, the small-scale demonstrations have shown themselves to be reliable and repeatable, making them crucial proofs of concept for QML techniques. Furthermore, the acceleration of the transfer of QML

TABLE 2.2
Major Case Studies and Proof-of-Principle Experiments

Domain	Experiment/Study	Key Contribution
Quantum chemistry	Kandala et al., Nature 2017	VQE simulation of small molecules on IBM quantum hardware
Optimization	Egger et al., 2020	Portfolio optimization using QAOA on NISQ device
Drug Discovery	Khoshaman et al., 2018	QSVM for molecular property prediction
Materials Science	Rocchetto et al., 2019	Quantum classifier for phase-of-matter detection
Cryptography	Pérez-Salinas et al., 2021	Fraud detection via quantum kernel methods

from theoretical frameworks to real-world applications has been greatly aided by cross-disciplinary partnerships, particularly those combining university research institutes and industry giants, such as IBM, Google, and IonQ. These collaborations provide a thriving environment for QML research by advancing hardware development, algorithm design, and application deployment.

2.15 HARDWARE PLATFORMS AND QUANTUM ML DEVELOPMENT TOOLS

2.15.1 Quantum Hardware Platforms for ML

Developments in quantum hardware are strongly related to the possibility of QML. For ML applications, there are many physical qubit implementations that provide different benefits, each with its own trade-offs in terms of coherence time, connection, scalability, and operational integrity. Among the top platforms for quantum hardware are.

2.15.1.1 Superconducting Qubits

This is the most commercially advanced platform, employed by IBM Quantum, Google Quantum AI, and Rigetti. Qubits are realized through superconducting circuits cooled near absolute zero. They provide fast gate operations and deep integration with cloud-based tools, making them central to executing QML experiments.

2.15.1.2 Trapped Ions

Used by companies such as IonQ and Honeywell, trapped-ion qubits consist of charged atoms suspended by electromagnetic fields. Their long coherence times and high-fidelity suit error-sensitive algorithms, including QML protocols requiring precise quantum control.

2.15.1.3 Photonic Quantum Computers

Providers, such as Xanadu and Psi Quantum, leverage photons to encode and process quantum information at room temperature. Photonic platforms are promising for scalable, low-noise architectures, with distinct applications in quantum-enhanced ML and quantum communication. Other emerging platforms include quantum dots, neutral atoms (e.g., Cold Quanta, PASQAL), and topological qubits (under exploration by Microsoft). These remain primarily at the experimental or pre-commercial stages. The choice of hardware significantly affects both the accessibility for ML practitioners and the types of QML models that can be effectively implemented. Integration with quantum cloud platforms such as IBM Quantum Experience, Amazon Braket, and Azure Quantum provides global access to state-of-the-art quantum devices, facilitating broad experimentation in QML. Figure 2.4 depicts quantum hardware platforms.

2.15.2 Leading QML Software Tools

Quantum ML development is supported by a growing ecosystem of open-source and commercial libraries, which abstract the underlying hardware complexity and provide ready-to-use modules for constructing, training, and benchmarking models. Key tools include.

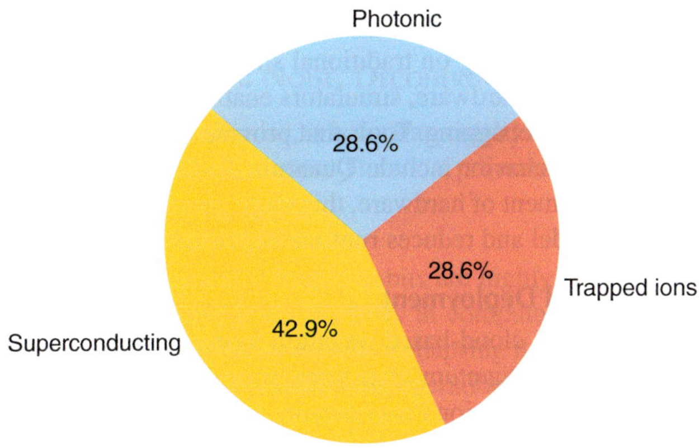

FIGURE 2.4 Quantum hardware platforms.

2.15.2.1 Qiskit ML

Developed by IBM, this extends Qiskit's quantum programming framework with modules for variational classifiers, quantum kernels, and quantum neural network (QNN) architectures.

2.15.2.2 PennyLane

Created by Xanadu, PennyLane focuses on hybrid quantum–classical ML, offering automatic differentiation and seamless integration with deep learning frameworks such as PyTorch and TensorFlow.

2.15.2.3 TensorFlow Quantum

Built by Google, this tool combines TensorFlow's deep learning toolkit with Cirq for defining quantum circuits and hybrid models, especially aimed at research in QNNs.

2.15.2.4 Cirq

A Python library for creating, simulating, and running quantum circuits, primarily designed for Google's quantum processors but widely used for QML prototyping. Other noteworthy libraries include Ocean SDK (from D-Wave, which focuses on quantum annealing-based ML), Strawberry Fields (photonic ML), and QuTiP (for quantum simulations).

2.15.3 Developing and Deploying QML Models

2.15.3.1 Model Design

Using programs, such as Penny Lane or Qiskit, a hybrid quantum–classical model, is first designed. Developers construct parameterized gates, choose quantum circuit layout, and pick data encoding techniques (such as amplitude or angle encoding). Cross-entropy and MSE are examples of classical cost functions that are integrated. Steps for pre-processing and post-processing are also covered. This lays the groundwork for learning strategies and model conduct.

2.16.3 Algorithmic Limits: Speedup, Learnability, and Generalization

2.16.3.1 Speedup Is Not Universal

Only certain classes of QML algorithms are mathematically proven or conjectured to yield *provable* speedups over classical ML. For example, quantum linear algebra routines (HHL algorithm) and certain quantum kernel methods offer exponential or quadratic advantages but only under strict data and model access assumptions.

2.16.3.2 Limited Speedup for Most ML Tasks

For many core ML problems (such as typical regression or image classification on classical data), rigorous analyses show that quantum speedup may be polynomial at best or non-existent given data encoding costs, measurement overhead, and unverifiable algorithmic assumptions.

2.16.3.3 Theoretical Uncertainty in Quantum Learnability

The fundamental learnability of complex distributions by QML algorithms is still being investigated. Open questions surround the sample complexity (amount of training data needed) and the generalization capacity (how well quantum models predict unseen data). For some QML circuits, there exist theoretical obstacles in defining and proving generalization bounds, analogous to classical Vapnik–Chervonenkis (VC)-dimension results.

2.16.3.4 Algorithmic Lower Bounds

It remains an open theoretical question whether quantum models outperform classical algorithms generically, or if there exist fundamental lower bounds precluding exponential quantum speedups for practical ML tasks.

2.16.4 Open Research Directions

The field of QML is evolving rapidly, with several active open problems and research frontiers.

2.16.4.1 Efficient Data Loading

Can new protocols or hardware architectures (even partial QRAM models) minimize the time to encode large, high-dimensional datasets as quantum states without losing theoretical speedup?

2.16.4.2 Error Mitigation and Fault Tolerance in QML

What are optimal strategies to mitigate the impact of noise, readout errors, and decoherence on model accuracy and trainability? Hybrid error mitigation approaches are being developed, but their effectiveness in deep, large-scale QML is not yet established.

2.16.4.3 Barren Plateaus and Trainability

What circuit architectures or initialization strategies can systematically avoid exponentially vanishing gradients in deep QNNs? Can we characterize "trainable" QML circuit families for scalable learning?

2.16.4.4 Quantum Generalization Theory

How can we mathematically characterize and guarantee the generalization performance of quantum models? Are there quantum generalizations of classical concepts, such as the VC-dimension or Rademacher complexity?

2.16.4.5 Classical Simulation Boundaries

As classical hardware and algorithms (e.g., tensor networks, quantum-inspired neural nets) improve, where do quantum advantages remain unassailable?

2.16.4.6 Scalable Quantum-Enhanced Data Structures

Beyond QRAM, can we create physically plausible architectures for "quantum data lakes" or distributed quantum memory, revolutionizing large-scale QML.

2.16.5 Potential Breakthroughs on the Horizon

Despite formidable obstacles, several future breakthroughs could bridge the gap between theory and impactful practice in QML.

2.16.5.1 Demonstration of Quantum Advantage in Practical ML

The first unambiguous real-world demonstration of quantum advantage on a significant ML task beyond synthetic benchmarks will mark a watershed moment for the field.

2.16.5.2 Advances in Quantum Hardware

Progress in scalable, error-corrected quantum processors will enable the implementation and testing of large, complex QML models that are considered impossible today.

2.16.5.3 Efficient Hybrid and Quantum-Inspired Classifiers

Hybrid strategies and quantum-inspired algorithms, such as tensorized neural networks, provide unexpected classical performance gains that may be linked to quantum principles even when full-scale quantum advantage is not present.

2.16.5.4 Novel Quantum Learning Paradigms

Pattern recognition and reasoning might be completely reimagined by using whole new learning frameworks that make use of intrinsic quantum phenomena such as contextuality and entanglement. These frameworks could enable ML capabilities that are not possible on classical machines.

2.17 ETHICAL, SOCIETAL, AND INDUSTRIAL IMPLICATIONS

2.17.1 Ethical Concerns in QML

There are significant ethical issues raised by the development of QML. Quantum computing-powered algorithms may increase the complexity and opacity of decision-making, raising the possibility of inadvertent bias or discrimination. As the underlying mechanics of quantum models become increasingly difficult to understand, it becomes more difficult to ensure fairness and explainability. To prevent prejudice from becoming entrenched and to make sure that quantum-enhanced ML systems are in accordance with social norms, responsible development and strict ethical standards are required.

2.17.2 Data Privacy and Security

The ability of quantum computers to handle and analyzes large datasets presents new data privacy issues. From data sets that were previously believed to be safe, quantum algorithms could be able to recover sensitive information or identify trends. Simultaneously, quantum cryptography innovations, such as quantum key distribution, provide unmatched data security techniques. These technologies' dual-use nature calls for new legal frameworks and meticulous standards for access control and data processing.

2.17.3 Industrial and Societal Disruption

2.17.3.1 Job Market and Skills

Automating intricate analytical procedures via the widespread use of QML might increase demand for specialized knowledge in data science, algorithm design, and quantum engineering. It is essential to have the workforce ready for this change.

2.17.3.2 Industrial Standards and Consortia

To promote the appropriate integration of quantum technology, industry organizations, such as IEEE Quantum, the European Quantum Industry Consortium (QuIC), and the Quantum Economic Development Consortium (QED-C), are actively developing best practices, interoperability standards, and ethical frameworks. Figure 2.6 describes the Global Investment and Research Ecosystem in QML.

2.17.3.3 Regulation

Classical regulatory frameworks are challenged by the speed of quantum development. Harmonizing standards, creating certification criteria, and addressing concerns, such as export restrictions, algorithm transparency, and cryptographic resilience, will all need international cooperation. Global Investment and Research Ecosystem

With nations, such as the United States, China, the European Union (EU), Canada, and Japan, investing billions of dollars in research, infrastructure, and talent pipelines, global investment in quantum computing and QML is rising. Big tech companies, including Alibaba, Google, Microsoft, and IBM Baidu lead industrial research, while startups drive innovation in niche domains. This concentration is promoting multidisciplinary training, fast distribution of innovations, and an expansion of the contact between academia and industry.

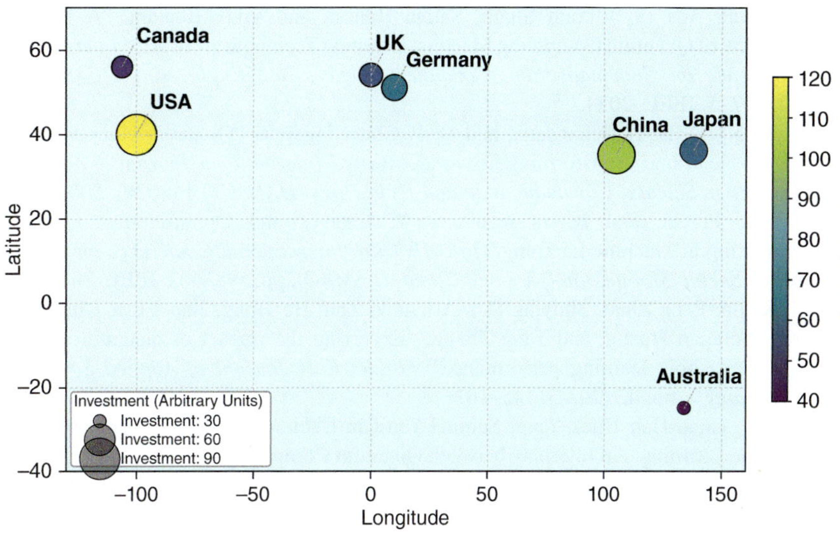

FIGURE 2.6 Global investment and research ecosystem in QML.

2.18 CONCLUSION

QML is an effective amalgamation of ML with quantum computing that holds promise for overcoming traditional constraints in the processing of high-dimensional, complicated data. Emerging algorithms, such as VQCs and QSVMs, which make use of quantum concepts, such as superposition, entanglement, and quantum parallelism, hold promise for a variety of applications, from cybersecurity to molecular modeling. The practicality of QML is gradually increasing due to advancements in hardware, hybrid models, and cloud-based platforms, even if technical issues, such as noise, coherence time, and data encoding, still exist. The creation of robust, scalable quantum algorithms and fault–tolerant quantum computers is anticipated to open up revolutionary possibilities in the fields of science, industry, and AI. In an increasingly digital and data-driven society, QML is at the forefront of computational science and has the potential to completely transform the way we derive insight from complicated data.

REFERENCES

1. Saju, B., M.K. Gopal, B. Nithya, V. Asha, and V. Kumar. "Analysis on role of quantum computing in machine learning." In *2022 Fourth International Conference on Cognitive Computing and Information Processing (CCIP)*, pp. 1–8, 2022. https://doi.org/10.1109/CCIP57447.2022.10058679
2. Nguyen, Thien, Tuomo Sipola, and Jari Hautamäki. "Machine learning applications of quantum computing: A review." arXiv preprint arXiv: 2406.13262 (2024).

3. Aggarwal, Ada, S. Vikram Singh, Saloni Bansal, and Vijay Bhutani. "A Detailed Overview of Quantum Computing Machine Learning Techniques." In *2024 International Conference on Communication, Computer Sciences and Engineering (IC3SE)*, pp. 1721–1725. IEEE, 2024.
4. Shaik, N., D. B. Harichandana, and D. P. Chitralingappa. "Quantum computing and machine learning: Transforming network security." *International Journal of Advanced Research in Science, Communication and Technology (IJARSCT)* 1 (2024): 500–509.
5. Sajwan, Prachi, and N. Jayapandian. "Challenges and Opportunities: Quantum Computing in Machine Learning." In *2019 Third International Conference on I-SMAC (IoT in Social, Mobile, Analytics and Cloud) (I-SMAC)*, pp. 598–602. IEEE, 2019.
6. Li, Keqin, Peng Zhao, Shuying Dai, Armando Zhu, Bo Hong, Jiabei Liu, Changsong Wei, Wenqian Huang, and Yang Zhang. "Exploring the impact of quantum computing on machine learning performance." *Middle East Journal of Applied Science & Technology* 7, no. 02 (2024): 145–161.
7. Qi, Jun, Chao-Han Huck Yang, Samuel Yen-Chi Chen, and Pin-Yu Chen. "Quantum Machine Learning: An Interplay between Quantum Computing and Machine Learning." In *2025 IEEE International Symposium on Circuits and Systems (ISCAS)*, pp. 1–5. IEEE, 2025.
8. Marchetti, Laura, Riccardo Nifosì, Pier Luigi Martelli, Eleonora Da Pozzo, Valentina Cappello, Francesco Banterle, Maria Letizia Trincavelli, Claudia Martini, and Massimo D'Elia. "Quantum computing algorithms: Getting closer to critical problems in computational biology." *Briefings in Bioinformatics* 23, no. 6 (2022): bbac437.
9. Schuld, Maria, Ilya Sinayskiy, and Francesco Petruccione. "An introduction to quantum machine learning." *Contemporary Physics* 56, no. 2 (2015): 172–185.
10. Rebentrost, Patrick, Masoud Mohseni, and Seth Lloyd. "Quantum support vector machine for big data classification." *Physical Review Letters* 113, no. 13 (2014): 130503.
11. Peral-García, David, Juan Cruz-Benito, and Francisco José García-Peñalvo. "Systematic literature review: Quantum machine learning and its applications." *Computer Science Review* 51 (2024): 100619.
12. Sharma, Siddharth. "Qeml (quantum enhanced machine learning): Using quantum computing to enhance ml classifiers and feature spaces." arXiv preprint arXiv:2002.10453 (2020).
13. Algorithms Chaiyathorn, N., and P. Anuwat. "The role of quantum computing in optimizing machine learning." *International Journal of Computer Technology and Science*, 1, no. 2 (2022): 64–70. https://doi.org/10.62951/ijcts.v1i2.64
14. Dunjko, Vedran, Jacob M. Taylor, and Hans J. Briegel. "Quantum-enhanced machine learning." *Physical Review Letters* 117, no. 13 (2016): 130501.
15. S. B. Ramezani, A. Sommers, H. K. Manchukonda, S. Rahimi, and A. Amirlatifi, "Machine Learning Algorithms in Quantum Computing: A Survey." In *2020 International Joint Conference on Neural Networks (IJCNN)*, Glasgow, UK, pp. 1–8, 2020. https://doi.org/10.1109/IJCNN48605.2020.9207714
16. Alchieri, L., Badalotti, D., Bonardi, P. et al. "An introduction to quantum machine learning: from quantum logic to quantum deep learning." *Quantum Mach. Intell.* 3, 28 (2021). https://doi.org/10.1007/s42484-021-00056-8
17. Ciliberto, Carlo, Mark Herbster, Alessandro Davide Ialongo, Massimiliano Pontil, Andrea Rocchetto, Simone Severini, and Leonard Wossnig. "Quantum machine learning: A classical perspective." *Proceedings of the Royal Society A: Mathematical, Physical and Engineering Sciences* 474, no. 2209 (2018): 20170551.

3 Quantum Computing in Machine Learning

N. Sanjana, R. Immanual, J. David Rathnaraj, and G. Mahesh Gopal

3.1 INTRODUCTION

As artificial intelligence (AI) systems grow, classical computing architectures are facing fundamental scaling barriers that threaten to constrain future progress in machine learning (ML) and AI development. The exponential computational demands of modern deep learning models, combined with the curse of dimensionality and energy sustainability challenges, have created a critical bottleneck that incremental improvements cannot overcome. Quantum computing gives an innovative solution to these limitations, and has some advantages through quantum mechanical phenomena like superposition and entanglement that enable fundamentally different approaches to computation. The convergence of quantum computing and ML represents a new way that not only addresses classical computing's limitations but gives entirely new limits for computational intelligence and scientific discovery.

3.1.1 The Classical Computing Bottleneck in Modern AI

The achievements of AI are remarkable in recent years, but it has come with a higher computational cost. As ML models grow and datasets expand exponentially, classical computing architectures face fundamental limitations that threaten to constrain future progress. Understanding this hold reveals why quantum computing represents not merely an incremental improvement, but a necessary move beyond current limitations and embracing new ways of thinking about AI's capabilities and its role in society for the continued advancement of artificial intelligence.

Classical ML algorithms have some severe scaling challenges that grow exponentially with problem complexity. Consider the fundamental task of principal component analysis (PCA), a cornerstone technique for dimensionality reduction and pattern recognition. Classical algorithms for performing PCA requires computational complexity of $O(d^2)$, where d represents the dimensionality of the data space.

The challenge goes further than individual algorithms to entire ML pipelines. Deep neural networks, which have driven recent innovation in image recognition, natural language processing (NLP), and game-playing AI, require massive computational resources for training. Modern language models contain hundreds of billions of parameters, and training them demands computational clusters consuming megawatts of power over extended periods. This exponential growth in

DOI: 10.1201/9781003587835-3

The frontier nature of quantum computing becomes particularly evident when examining concrete examples of quantum supremacy in learning tasks. Recent experimental work has demonstrated that quantum-enhanced experiments can learn properties of physical systems using fewer experiments than conventional approaches exponentially. For instance, quantum machines can learn from exponentially fewer experiments when predicting properties of physical systems, performing quantum PCA on noisy states, and learning approximate models of physical dynamics. In some cases, the quantum processing needed to achieve exponential advantage can be remarkably modest—for example, simultaneously learning about many non-commuting observables by processing only two copies of a quantum system.

This quantum advantage has been experimentally validated using superconducting quantum processors with up to 40 qubits and 1,300 quantum gates, showing that substantial quantum advantages can be achieved even with today's relatively noisy quantum processors. Such experimental results prove that quantum computing's boundary is not only theoretical but represents a practical computational prototype that is already delivering measurable advantages over classical approaches.

The importance of quantum computing as the next step is boosted by its ability to overcome the basic limitations facing classical computing. As Moore's Law approaches its physical limits and classical algorithms face exponential overhead for certain problem classes, quantum computing offers another alternative pathway. The quantum basic linear algebra subroutines (qBLAS) provide more speed over their normal equivalent for operations such as Fourier transforms, eigenvalue decomposition, and solving linear systems of equations—fundamental building blocks for numerous computational applications.

3.1.3 Transformative Applications Already Emerging

The transformative impact of quantum computing will show across diverse application domains, with quantum machine learning (QML) leading the charge in demonstrating practical quantum advantages. These emerging applications showcase solid examples where quantum algorithms provide measurable improvements over classical approaches, more than theoretical potential to practical implementation.

Experimental implementations of QML algorithms have been successfully demonstrated on various quantum platforms. Nuclear magnetic resonance testbeds have been used to implement quantum support vector machines for handwritten digit recognition tasks, while quantum Boltzmann machines have been realized on quantum annealing systems with over a thousand qubits. These demonstrations prove that QML is changing from a theoretical possibility to a practical implementation. The pharmaceutical and molecular simulation sector represents another domain where transformative applications are emerging. Quantum computers can naturally represent and manipulate the quantum states of molecular systems, enabling exponentially more efficient simulation of molecular interactions compared to classical approaches. This capability is particularly valuable for drug discovery, where quantum algorithms can predict molecular behavior, drug-target interactions, and chemical reaction pathways with high accuracy. The ability to imitate quantum systems using quantum computers gives a basic advantage over the normal systems, regardless of their computational power. Financial optimization and risk analysis present convincing use cases where quantum algorithms show some advantages. Quantum approximate optimization algorithms (QAOA) and quantum strong approaches can solve complex portfolio optimization problems, risk situations, and fraud detection tasks more efficiently than classical methods. The inherent parallelism of quantum computation allows parallel research, implying that many solutions in high-dimensional optimization landscapes, giving advantages for financial modeling problems that have many variables and constraints. The emergence of quantum cloud computing platforms is giving access to quantum technologies and accelerating the development of transformative applications. Companies like IBM, Google, and Rigetti provide cloud-based access to quantum processors, allowing researchers worldwide to experiment with quantum algorithms and develop practical quantum applications without any specialized quantum hardware expertise.

3.1.4 The Convergence of Two Revolutionary Technologies

The convergence of quantum computing and ML represents a fundamental transformation that combines the exponential computational advantages of quantum systems with the pattern recognition and optimization capabilities of ML algorithms. This combination creates QML as a different computational discipline that leverages quantum mechanical properties to enhance learning algorithms while simultaneously employing ML techniques to advance quantum computing technologies.

The theoretical foundation for this intersection rests on the basic advantages that quantum systems provide for linear algebraic operations that form the core of ML algorithms. The Harrow–Hassidim–Lloyd (HHL) algorithm for solving linear systems of equations shows that quantum computers can achieve rapid speedups for problems central to ML, such as least-squares fitting, PCA, and support vector machine training. These qBLAS provide the computational foundation for QML algorithms that can process high-dimensional data exponentially more efficiently than classical approaches.

Experimental evidence validates the practical significance of this convergence. Quantum-enhanced experiments have demonstrated exponential advantages in learning tasks, with quantum strategies requiring only constant or polynomial numbers of experiments to achieve learning objectives that require exponential numbers of experiments using classical approaches. For instance, quantum machines can predict properties of exponentially many non-commuting observables using only polynomial numbers of quantum measurements, while classical approaches require exponential scaling. These experimental demonstrations using superconducting quantum processors prove that the convergence provides measurable advantages even with current noisy intermediate-scale quantum (NISQ) devices.

3.2 QML Algorithms

3.2.1 Introduction to QML

QML represents a significant change in quantum computing and AI, fundamentally reimagining the approach to computational learning tasks [1]. At its essence, QML exploits the unique properties of quantum systems—superposition, entanglement, and quantum interference—to potentially achieve exponential advantages over classical ML algorithms. The core QML algorithms form the foundation of this emerging discipline, each addressing specific aspects of learning while leveraging quantum facts to enhance computational capabilities beyond what is achievable with classical computers [2]. The mathematical foundation of QML algorithms rests on the representation of classical data in quantum Hilbert spaces, where the exponential dimensionality of quantum systems enables the encoding and manipulation of vast amounts of information using relatively few quantum bits [3]. This encoding process, known as quantum feature mapping, transforms data vectors into quantum states through parameterized quantum circuits, creating high-dimensional feature spaces that capture complex non-linear fundamentals in the data. The quantum algorithms then operate directly on these quantum representations, utilizing quantum gates and measurements to perform learning tasks that would be computationally difficult for classical systems when dealing with exponentially large feature spaces.

3.2.2 Variational Quantum Algorithms (VQAs) for ML

VQAs represent a foundation close to QML, offering a practical pathway to achieve quantum computational advantages with current NISQ devices [2]. These algorithms support a hybrid classical–quantum approach, where quantum circuits perform computations in high-dimensional Hilbert spaces while classical optimizers handle parameter updates.

Figure 3.1 shows the hybrid quantum–classical approach where a quantum computer estimates the cost function while a classical optimizer trains the parameters. The parameterized quantum circuit (ansatz) is similar to a neural network, demonstrating the iterative optimization process that forms the foundation of QML algorithms.

The variational quantum eigensolver (VQE) has emerged as a fundamental framework for optimization problems in ML, particularly in finding ground state energies and solving combinatorial optimization challenges [2]. Building upon these principles, the QAOA has found extensive applications in ML optimization problems, particularly in clustering, feature selection, and graph-based learning tasks [2]. This algorithm alternates between problem-specific cost Hamiltonians and mixing Hamiltonians,

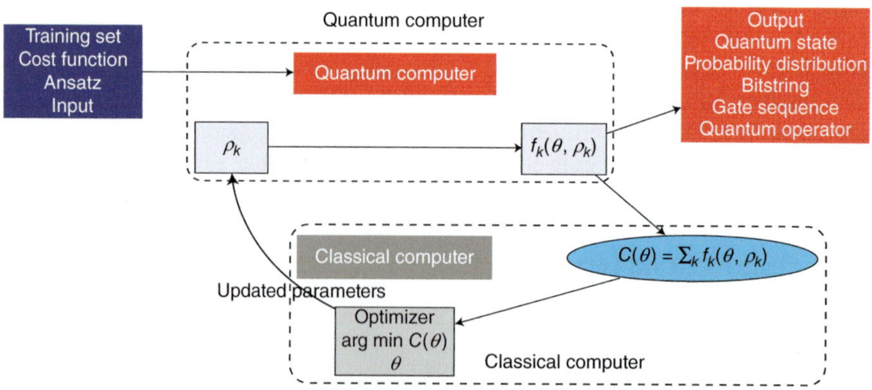

FIGURE 3.1 Schematic diagram of a variational quantum algorithm (VQA).

creating a variational ansatz that can approximate solutions to computationally hard problems commonly encountered in ML. Recent applications include quantum-enhanced portfolio optimization for financial ML, quantum clustering algorithms for unsupervised learning tasks, and quantum approximate solutions to graph partitioning problems for community detection in social networks.

Variational quantum classifiers represent a growth of classical ML to the quantum domain, using parameterized quantum circuits to learn complex decision boundaries in high-dimensional feature spaces [2]. These classifiers encode classical data into quantum states through various embedding strategies, including basis encoding, where data are represented as computational basis states, amplitude encoding, where data vectors are embedded in quantum state amplitudes, and angle encoding, where features are encoded as rotation angles [3]. The data re-uploading technique has already been demonstrated to be particularly effective, allowing the same qubits to process different data points arranged in a particular order, thereby increasing the effective dimensionality of the quantum feature space without requiring additional qubits. This approach enables quantum classifiers to achieve universal function approximation capabilities while maintaining hardware efficiency for current quantum devices.

Parameter optimization strategies in VQAs need a refined approaches that account for the unique challenges of quantum systems, including measurement noise, gate errors, and barren plateaus, which refers to a process where the optimization landscape becomes extremely flat and featureless as the number of qubits (problem size) increases in the optimization [2]. Gradient-based methods have been adapted for quantum circuits through parameter-shift rules and finite-difference techniques, which enable the computation of exact gradients for quantum expectation values. Natural gradient descent and quantum natural gradient methods have shown good results in accelerating convergence by including the geometric structure of the quantum parameter space. Additionally, gradient-free optimization methods such as evolutionary algorithms, simultaneous perturbation stochastic approximation, and Bayesian optimization have proven effective for QML tasks where gradient computation is challenging or when dealing with discrete optimization variables.

3.2.3 Quantum Neural Networks

Quantum neural networks represent a change in neural computation, utilizing quantum mechanical principles to process information in ways that are different from classical neural networks [1]. At their core, quantum neural networks utilize parameterized quantum circuits as universal function approximators, capable of representing arbitrary functions through appropriate choice of circuit architecture and parameters. These circuits have layers of quantum gates with trainable parameters, creating a quantum analog to classical neural network weights and biases. The key advantage is the exponential dimensionality of quantum Hilbert spaces, allowing quantum neural networks to represent and define vastly more complex functions than their classical counterparts using the same number of parameters [2].

Quantum convolutional neural networks extend the successful architecture of convolutional neural networks to the quantum domain, maintaining the needed feature extraction and translation-invariance properties while leveraging quantum superposition and entanglement for enhanced computational power [2]. These networks implement quantum convolution operations through localized quantum circuits that scan across quantum data structures, applying the same parameterized transformation to different spatial regions of the input quantum state. The quantum pooling operations, implemented through incomplete measurements or controlled quantum operations, reduce the dimensionality while storing the quantum information that is needed. This architecture has shown some effective image processing tasks, quantum state classification, and pattern recognition in quantum data, demonstrating the ability to identify phase transitions in quantum many-body systems and classify different quantum states of matter.

Feedforward quantum neural networks with qudits exceed the traditional two-level qubit systems used for higher dimensional quantum systems, resulting in increased computational capacity per quantum unit. Qudits, or multi-level quantum systems, provide a natural extension to classical neural networks where each quantum node can represent more complex probability distributions and computational states. The implementation of feedforward architectures with qudits involves quantum gates that work on higher dimensional Hilbert spaces, which work on more complex transformations and reduce the number of quantum units required for some computational tasks. Recent experimental implementations have demonstrated qudit-based quantum neural networks using trapped ions and superconducting circuits, showing promise for QML applications that require high-dimensional feature spaces and complex pattern recognition capabilities.

Quantum autoencoders represent a quantum approach to unsupervised learning and dimensionality reduction, mostly to compress quantum information while keeping essential features of the input quantum states. These systems consist of an encoder circuit that maps input quantum states to a smaller dimensional latent space and a decoder circuit that reconstructs the original state from the compressed representation. The training process minimizes the rebuilding error between input and output quantum states, learning to capture the most important features in the reduced-dimensional quantum representation. Quantum autoencoders have demonstrated remarkable capabilities in quantum error correction, quantum data compression, and feature extraction from quantum datasets, showing potential advantages over classical dimensionality reduction techniques when dealing with quantum data that cannot be efficiently represented classically.

3.2.4 Quantum Kernel Methods and Support Vector Machines

Quantum kernel methods represent a sophisticated approach to QML that leverages the geometric structure of quantum Hilbert spaces to enhance classical learning algorithms [4]. The basic idea of quantum computing is surprisingly similar to that of kernel methods in ML: efficiently performing computations in an intractably large Hilbert space. Quantum Support Vector Machines uses quantum computing to evaluate kernels that are difficult to handle, potentially providing exponential speedups for certain ML tasks [5]. The foundation of quantum kernel methods lies in the quantum feature map, which encodes classical data into quantum states through carefully designed parameterized quantum circuits.

These quantum feature maps can create large feature spaces that have complex non-linear patterns in the original data, allowing quantum kernels to perform well when compared to classical kernels for specific datasets and problems [4]. The implementation of quantum support vector machines and support vector kernels involves sufficient quantum circuit designs that compute inner products between quantum states representing different data points. Fidelity-based quantum kernels measure the overlap between quantum states, providing a natural distance metric in quantum Hilbert space, while projected kernels focus on specific subspaces of the quantum feature space to increase computational efficiency and reduce quantum resource requirements.

Recent experimental results on quantum processors have shown that the designed quantum kernels are carefully designed and can achieve superior performance compared to classical kernels on synthetic datasets, particularly when the quantum feature map is tailored to the specific structure of the learning problem [4]. Quantum kernel ridge regression and classification enhance the quantum kernel framework for supervised tasks given by quantum algorithms for kernel matrix computations, potentially offering advantages over classical methods in high-dimensional spaces while integrating quantum kernels into classical support vector machine frameworks for training and evaluation.

Quantum kernel alignment and parameter optimization represent important aspects of making quantum kernel methods practical and effective for real-world ML applications [5]. Kernel alignment techniques measure how well a particular quantum kernel matches the target learning task, guiding the design and optimization of quantum feature maps for specific datasets and problems. Parameter optimization in quantum kernels involves tuning the parameters of the quantum circuits that implement the feature map, requiring sophisticated optimization strategies that account for the outliers in the current quantum devices and the complex optimization landscape of parameterized quantum circuits. Experimental demonstrations and performance benchmarks have been established across various quantum computing platforms, providing insights into the practical advantages and limitations of quantum kernel methods compared to their classical counterparts.

3.2.5 Quantum Reinforcement Learning

Quantum reinforcement learning shows an emerging frontier that combines quantum computing principles with sequential decision-making frameworks, giving potential advantages in achieving efficiency, policy representation, and computational speedup for complex reinforcement learning tasks [2]. The integration of quantum mechanics into reinforcement learning leverages quantum superposition to explore multiple actions simultaneously, quantum entanglement to capture complex state-action correlations, and quantum interference to enhance learning efficiency through constructive and destructive interference of probability amplitudes. These quantum advantages are particularly important for reinforcement learning problems with large

3.4.5 Materials Science and Optimization

Materials science represents one of the most natural application domains for QML, given the inherently quantum nature of material properties and the exponential complexity of many-body quantum systems. QML approaches have demonstrated exceptional capabilities in materials discovery and characterization, leveraging quantum algorithms to predict materials properties, design novel compounds, and optimize synthesis pathways. Recent experimental implementations have shown that quantum-enhanced models can achieve superior accuracy in predicting electronic band structures, mechanical properties, and catalytic activities compared to classical density functional theory calculations, while requiring significantly less computational time and resources [8].

3.5 CURRENT CHALLENGES AND LIMITATIONS

The interaction between quantum computing and ML is one of the most promising but also challenging horizons of computational science. However, while theoretical benefits exist for these QML algorithms, their practical implementation suffers from numerous challenges, including hardware constraints, algorithmic development, scaling factor issues, and software development (see Figure 3.4). It is important to know these limitations to have a clear expectation and guide the path forward for QML.

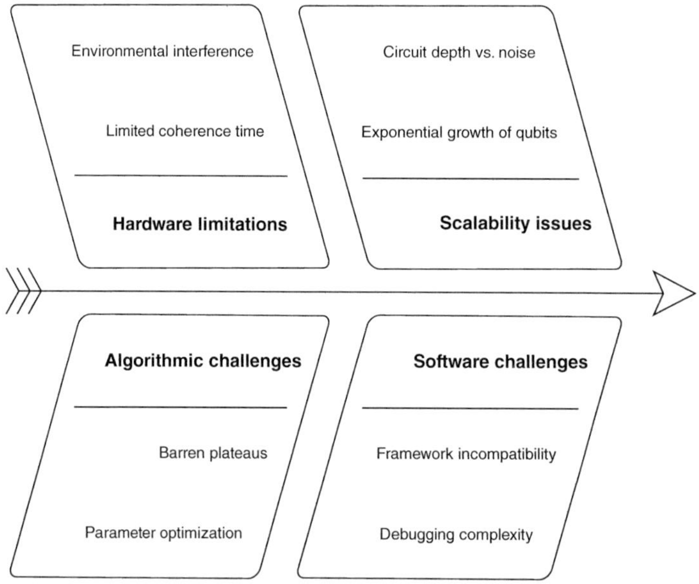

FIGURE 3.4 Major challenges impeding quantum machine learning (QML) implementation.

3.5.1 Hardware Limitations and Noise Issues

We are now in an era of quantum devices where very primitive devices are available, sometimes called NISQ devices, that have fundamental limitations that play a significant role in ML problems. These are devices with relatively small coherence times, in general on the order of µs to ms, which limits the depth of quantum circuits that can be reliably run. Gate fidelities in today's systems are getting better, but still introduce errors at a pace that can rapidly accumulate in ML algorithms that have many quantum operations. Moreover, the connectivity restrictions of many quantum architectures further restrict the type of quantum circuits that can be done efficiently and usually demand SWAPs, which compromise performance even more and add more noise.

3.5.2 Algorithmic Challenges

The barren plateau problem has emerged as one of the most significant algorithmic challenges in QML, particularly affecting VQAs that form the backbone of many quantum ML approaches. As described in the seminal work by McClean et al., random parameterized quantum circuits with sufficient depth exhibit exponentially vanishing gradients, creating vast regions of parameter space where optimization becomes ineffective. This phenomenon occurs because the high-dimensional Hilbert space of quantum systems leads to concentration-of-measure effects, in which most quantum states become approximately uniformly distributed, resulting in flat cost function landscapes that provide no guidance for optimization algorithms.

Recent theoretical advances have begun to address the barren plateau problem through several innovative approaches. Structured design, which includes problem-specific structure into quantum circuits rather than using random parameterizations, has shown good results in maintaining trainable gradients. Local cost function design shows another development, where instead of using global observables that average over the entire quantum system, researchers design cost functions that focus on local subsystems, which avoids the rapid scaling that leads to barren plateaus. These approaches show that circuit design and cost function engineering can preserve trainability even in larger quantum systems.

Parameter initialization and optimization strategies have become critical areas of research as the QML community struggles with the unique challenges of quantum optimization landscapes. Different classical neural networks, where random initialization often meets requirements, quantum circuits need more advanced initialization schemes that take into account the underlying quantum geometry. Novel optimization techniques that support quantum-specific properties, such as natural gradients computed using the quantum Fisher information metric, have shown improved performance compared to classical optimizers. Additionally, hybrid classical–quantum optimization approaches that use classical preprocessing to identify promising regions of parameter space before quantum refinement are emerging as practical solutions to these challenges.

The theoretical foundations of QML are compelling and mathematically rigorous. Quantum algorithms such as the HHL algorithm for linear systems, quantum kernel methods, and VQAs demonstrate clear pathways to exponential speedups for specific problem classes. The ability of quantum systems to naturally represent exponentially large feature spaces through superposition and to capture complex correlations through a trap that provides genuine advantages for certain ML tasks that are fundamentally intractable for classical computers. The examination done for quantum neural networks, quantum generative models, and quantum reinforcement learning algorithms reveals sophisticated approaches that leverage these quantum mechanical properties to enhance learning capabilities beyond classical limits.

The systematic examination of challenges presented in this chapter—from hardware limitations and algorithmic difficulties to scalability and software issues—illustrates the interconnected nature of QML, which faces errors during implementation. The barren plateau problem, environmental decoherence, exponential qubit scaling requirements, and framework incompatibilities collectively create a challenging barrier for practical deployment that cannot be addressed through single technological improvements but requires coordinated advances across multiple fronts. The journey toward practical QML may be longer and more challenging than initial optimism suggested, but the destination—a world where quantum-enhanced intelligence transforms industries, gives scientific discovery, and solves previously intractable problems—remains a goal worthy of sustained pursuit. As this chapter has demonstrated, the convergence of quantum computing and ML offers some opportunities to overcome traditional computational limitations and unlock new boundaries of AI that will shape the future of technology and human knowledge.

REFERENCES

1. Biamonte, Jacob, Peter Wittek, Nicola Pancotti, Patrick Rebentrost, Nathan Wiebe, and Seth Lloyd. "Quantum machine learning." *Nature* 549, no. 7671 (2017): 195–202.
2. Cerezo, Marco, Andrew Arrasmith, Ryan Babbush, Simon C. Benjamin, Suguru Endo, Keisuke Fujii, Jarrod R. McClean et al. "Variational quantum algorithms." *Nature Reviews Physics* 3, no. 9 (2021): 625–644.
3. Preskill, John. "Quantum computing in the NISQ era and beyond." *Quantum* 2 (2018): 79.
4. Schuld, Maria, and Nathan Killoran. "Quantum machine learning in feature Hilbert spaces." *Physical review letters* 122, no. 4 (2019): 040504.
5. Suzuki, Yudai, Hiroshi Yano, Qi Gao, Shumpei Uno, Tomoki Tanaka, Manato Akiyama, and Naoki Yamamoto. "Analysis and synthesis of feature map for kernel-based quantum classifier." *Quantum Machine Intelligence* 2, no. 1 (2020): 9.
6. Kandala, Abhinav, Kristan Temme, Antonio D. Corcoles, Antonio Mezzacapo, Jerry M. Chow, and Jay M. Gambetta. "Extending the computational reach of a noisy superconducting quantum processor." arXiv preprint arXiv:1805.04492 (2018).
7. Huang, Hsin-Yuan, Michael Broughton, Jordan Cotler, Sitan Chen, Jerry Li, Masoud Mohseni, Hartmut Neven et al. "Quantum advantage in learning from experiments." *Science* 376, no. 6598 (2022): 1182–1186.
8. Smaldone, Anthony M., Yu Shee, Gregory W. Kyro, Chuzhi Xu, Nam P. Vu, Rishab Dutta, Marwa H. Farag et al. "Quantum machine learning in drug discovery: Applications in academia and pharmaceutical industries." *Chemical Reviews* 125, no. 12 (2025): 5436–5460.

9. Senokosov, Arsenii, Alexandr Sedykh, Asel Sagingalieva, Basil Kyriacou, and Alexey Melnikov. "Quantum machine learning for image classification." *Machine Learning: Science and Technology* 5, no. 1 (2024): 015040.
10. Widdows, Dominic, Willie Aboumrad, Dohun Kim, Sayonee Ray, and Jonathan Mei. "Quantum natural language processing." *KI-Künstliche Intelligenz* 38, no. 4 (2024): 293–310.
11. Devitt, Simon J., William J. Munro, and Kae Nemoto. "Quantum error correction for beginners." *Reports on Progress in Physics* 76, no. 7 (2013): 076001.
12. McClean, Jarrod R., Sergio Boixo, Vadim N. Smelyanskiy, Ryan Babbush, and Hartmut Neven. "Barren plateaus in quantum neural network training landscapes." *Nature communications* 9, no. 1 (2018): 4812.
13. Łodyga, Justyna, Paweł Mazurek, Andrzej Grudka, and Michał Horodecki. "Simple scheme for encoding and decoding a qubit in unknown state for various topological codes." *Scientific reports* 5, no. 1 (2015): 8975.
14. Li, Weijia, Yawen Lai, Linning Xu, Yuanbo Xiangli, Jinhua Yu, Conghui He, Gui-Song Xia, and Dahua Lin. "Omnicity: Omnipotent city understanding with multi-level and multi-view images." In *Proceedings of the IEEE/CVF Conference on Computer Vision and Pattern Recognition*, pp. 17397–17407. 2023.
15. Zaman, Kamila, Alberto Marchisio, Muhammad Abdullah Hanif, and Muhammad Shafique. "A survey on quantum machine learning: Current trends, challenges, opportunities, and the road ahead." arXiv preprint arXiv:2310.10315 (2023).

4 Harnessing Quantum Computing for Predictive Analysis

Understanding the Social Media Impact on Stock Market Investment

Talla Shirisha and M. Rajyalaxmi

4.1 INTRODUCTION

A number of factors, such as technological development, the rise of algorithmic trading, integration, and the increased influence of individual investors, have brought about a sea change in the investment environment in the stock market over the last couple of decades. Employers, bankers, and other institutions used to make most stock market investment decisions with a focus on companies' stock financial analysis, fundamentals of the market, and having to make reasonable profits consistently over the long run. A growing number of people, especially those with the so-called long tail effect, are getting more involved in the stock market due to the democratization of finance, which is a result of easy access to the financial markets through the Internet, and have access to a lot of additional information. Through space–time optimization, this revelation is a technological savior for fields such as healthcare, economics, and chemistry [1].

How societal mass media platforms such as Facebook, Reddit, and Twitter are influencing the behavior of stock markets is illustrated with so-called "meme-stock," such as GameStop and AMC. Earnings volatility driven by emotions, rather than actual figures, is one of the typical effects of a retail investor's ability to manipulate stock prices through online forums. Stock market prediction is known to forecast the future movement of stock prices or the whole stock arcade [2], and high-frequency trading (HFT) and algorithmic trading have become the main components of today's stock market. With these parts, refined algorithms respond to data, such as mood in social networks, and conduct transactions in milliseconds.

Originating in quantum mechanics, quantum computing (QC) is a computational method [3]. Moreover, exchange-traded funds (ETFs) have emerged in the investment industry and appear to have changed the existing approach to portfolio

 DOI: 10.1201/9781003587835-4

diversification, which is available only to major investors at a moderately low cost. The growth of artificial intelligence (AI) and machine learning (ML) in recent financial forecasting practices has revised the manner in which market trends are forecast. With the prospect of QC, they may have even deeper impacts on stock market investments and an increased ability to analyze large datasets from tweets, news feeds, and worldwide financial markets.

The environment in which investors invest has been changing, and is becoming even more inclined toward sentiment, data analysis, and some of the best innovations. This landscape is the result of a balanced relationship between traditional financial concepts and recent technologies. QC is one of the many fields that can potentially spur technological advancement in the next decade [4].

A game-changing tool for forecasting using QC defines a new generation compared to the existing technology that can entirely transform various fields, including "predictive analytics wherein applications such as finance, stock exchange, and big data have big difficult problems" [5]. An innovative instrument for forecasting through QC, since computing is a topic that grows quickly, new, futuristic research that consolidates existing and newly developed knowledge and examines possibilities is needed [6]. These qubits are based on superposition, entanglement, and quantum interference, which means that a qubit can be in more than one state at the same time and can process more than one computation at a time. This feature makes quantum computers ideal for predictive analytics, where massive amounts of data need to be analyzed quickly and accurately. It also guarantees that quantum computers can handle large datasets in ways that are unthinkable for classical computers.

QC may improve AI and ML [7]. Regarding traditional forecasting and analytical approaches within finance and stock market industries, the processing power of the former has been a bottleneck. Classical algorithms are known to be restricted by their processing methods, where tasks are sequentially processed. However, quantum computers, by means of superposition, can handle many options simultaneously. This parallelism could extend to quantum computers, considering all possible outcomes and trends of a stock market simultaneously, which will help improve the accuracy of the forecasts as well as the time taken for the same. For instance, when trading stocks, one must draw conclusions based on price chemistry, trends, buzz phrases, social media topics, rates, and occurrences. Quantum computers can examine all these parameters simultaneously, thereby creating a much more diverse and dynamic prediction model.

The second element of QC, which makes it particularly powerful for predictive analysis, is quantum entanglement. QC develops principles of quantum mechanics to set and process their mechanisms [8]. This phenomenon enables distinct entangled qubits to be connected, irrespective of the gap between them. This is because altering one of the qubit particles will, in effect, flip its partner instantly, thus significantly enhancing data transfer and communication. As such, it may be particularly useful in financial management, where timeliness in readjusting responses to continually developing world events can be critical for making or losing money [9]. It also generates extensive networks that the existing economy will allow financial institutions to study interconnected worldwide markets. Table 4.1 describes the function of QC in social media influence and stock market predictive analysis.

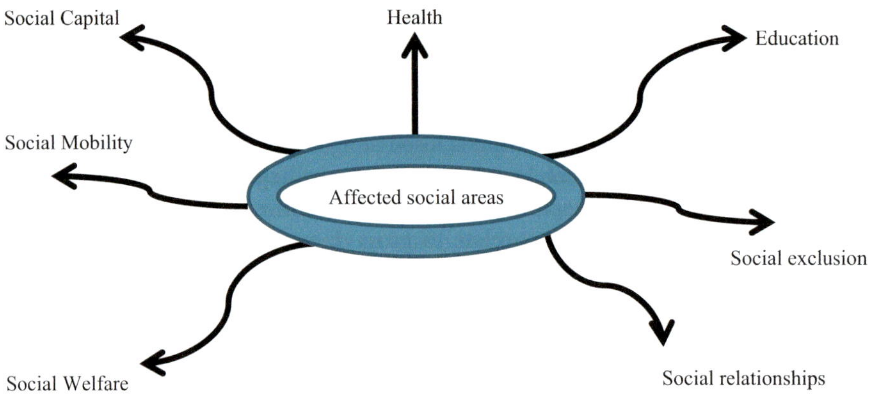

FIGURE 4.1 Authors' own compliance with the social domain impacts of COVID-19.

embodies physical and "mental health" difficulties arising from the crisis. "Education" draws attention to the disruption of learning continuity and accessibility, and growing inequalities. Such social concepts as "social mobility" and "social exclusion" are aimed at the economic standstill and vulnerable individuals' isolation, respectively. "Social welfare" refers to the pressure on the community infrastructures; in contrast, "social relationships" focus on how restrictions have also affected the interpersonal associations, negatively.

On the diagram discussed, all these aspects intersect, and crisis management implies considering these fragments interconnected. Consequently, this chapter highlights the need to combat these challenges in one concerted effort to facilitate the rebuilding of societies in the post-pandemic world.

4.2.1 Analysis of User Sentiment and Investor Behavior from Financial Forums and Social Media Platforms Such As Reddit and Twitter

Since they provide a window into the collective psychology of institutional and retail investors, investor behavior and sentiment analysis from sites such as Reddit, Twitter, and economic forums have grown to be essential parts of contemporary market analysis. Social media has transformed the way investors gather information, share thoughts, and execute investment strategies. Platforms such as Twitter, Reddit (particularly subreddits such as Wall Street Bets), and various financial forums provide real-time discussions, opinions, and insights that can drastically affect investor behavior [20]. Unlike traditional financial analysis, which is largely rooted in historical data, earnings reports, and economic indicators, sentiment analysis taps into the emotional and psychological factors that drive decision-making, especially among retail investors. Positive sentiment, such as optimism about a company's growth prospects or excitement over a product launch, can spur buying activity, while negative sentiment, such as concerns about regulatory scrutiny or product failures, can trigger sell-offs. The collective behavior driven by these emotional and psychological factors can significantly impact stock prices, particularly when social media amplifies opinions and actions across a vast audience. Because the time people spend on their work has been reduced due to COVID-19 crisis, they have had enough time to focus on the stock market [21].

COVID-19 was a great global health concern that occurred in 2020, affecting human life and health adversely [22]. With such types of social networks, the speed at which information on the social networks reaches investors has greatly changed their reaction to the market news. On websites such as Twitter, for instance, mere breaking news, rumor, or speculation spreads to millions in minutes, triggering an instant reaction in the stock market. Since utilizing real-time information from social media allows investors to act faster than carrying out normal market news monitoring or waiting for volunteered financial statements, the investor using social media information will be made to stand a better chance in a market where speed is of the essence. This real-time feature can lead to herd behavior typified by situations whereby large numbers of investors mimic a few important typical users or commenters, thereby creating feedback loops that can swiftly alter the intrinsic value of stocks. Just the whim of one celebrity, for example, Elon Musk, on the Twitter platform is enough to cause dramatic fluctuations in stocks as well as entire categories of assets such as cryptocurrencies. With regard to Musk, we have observed that public figures with sizable social media followings possess the capacity to influence investor sentiment and, consequently, market outcomes in ways that are wholly unpredictable.

According to a study discussed in Ref. [23], there has been a lot of research and analysis on the stability of investors' attitudes in the financial market. Sentiment analysis technologies for analyzing social media content are crucial for interpreting changes in investor behavior. Through tracking the post, comment, hashtags, and emojis, sentiment analysis algorithms can assess the tone of the talks and find the patterns that have not been reflected in stock prices yet. Figure 4.2 depicts the authors' own compliance platform-derived sentiment analysis and investor behavior.

Investor behavior and sentiment analysis derived from Platforms centers on social media platforms, including YouTube, Stocktwits, Reddit, and Twitter, are essential in the subject analysis of investors' behavior and sentiments. It demonstrates the fact that such sites are active centers of discussion of various financial issues, as well as the factors affecting the development of markets and decision-making. Each medium is treated equally, which is important since all of them play a role in the creation of investors' perception.

YouTube offers detailed video breakdowns and instructions, which appeal to both green and experienced traders, who are always interested in a deeper comprehension of changes in the market. Stocktwits functions as a specific media where users can discuss the financial market and share current moods and opinions of various

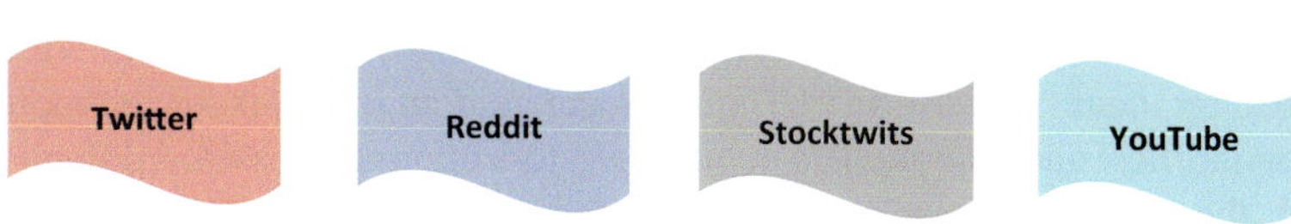

FIGURE 4.2 The authors' own compliance platform-derived sentiment analysis and investor behavior.

communities. Reddit is a social media platform of forums that captures collective opinion and, many times, highlights unusual investing trends, such as "meme stocks." Twitter also acts as a fast-moving news aggregator, and because news travels fast, it can be used to relay relevant market information and opinions.

The diagram builds on the fact that data from such platforms as Twitter, Facebook, and LinkedIn can be captured and used in financial forecasting and "strategic management" to accommodate sentiment data. They reflect the fact that this community-based approach becomes paramount in the current discussion of the stock market fundamental shifts from traditional informative tools to digital mainstays. To get a complete picture of a given market, the visualization advises analysts and investors to base their analyses on social media activity.

4.2.2 Challenges in Traditional Methods of Analyzing Social Media Impact on Stock Markets

Conventional methods for assessing how social media affects stock exchanges. The unconventional, disorganized, and unpredictable nature of social media data presents a number of significant challenges for markets. The websites such as Twitter, Facebook, LinkedIn help in getting medical information for millions of their members, which has been explored in many research studies [24]. One of the biggest issues is the sheer volume and velocity of information created on social media, including Twitter, Reddit, or Facebook. Each second, millions of posts, comments, and replies are created, and conventional methods of analyzing data are insufficient in processing data in real time without using advanced computing resources.

The Table 4.2, explains that social media had a big influence on stock market movements between 2020 and 2024, and QC was essential to the investing strategy. Electric vehicle stocks, such as Tesla and Nio, saw exponential growth in 2020 as a result of Twitter hashtags such as #EVStocks. Early detection of this trend using quantum algorithms allowed investors to generate profits that were above average. Meme companies such as GameStop (GME) and AMC had significant increases in 2021 thanks to Reddit's r/Wall Street Bets, but these were followed by sharp declines. By identifying these unsustainable surges, quantum techniques helped investors avoid suffering significant losses. By 2022, the excitement on LinkedIn about green energy stocks helped firms such as First Solar expand steadily. For investors who prioritized sustainable assets, quantum portfolio optimization further increased profits. Viral TikTok videos endorsing AI businesses propelled huge increases in stocks such as NVIDIA in 2023. Investors were able to time their transactions to optimize earnings with the use of quantum sentiment analysis. Lastly, Instagram and X (previously Twitter) highlighted AR/VR and metaverse stocks in 2024. Smaller speculative stocks were erratic, while major corporations such as Meta Platforms witnessed increases. By identifying overhyped equities and guiding investors toward more reliable possibilities, quantum models helped investors minimize losses. All things considered, the combination of social media sentiment and QC enabled investors to make wise choices and enhance

TABLE 4.2
The Stock Market's Dynamics, Social Media, and Quantum Computing (QC) from 2020 to 2024

Year	Social Media Trend	Stock Market Impact	Role of Quantum Computing	Investment Outcome
2020	Surge in Twitter hashtags for #EVStocks (e.g., Tesla and Nio)	(Tesla: 700%; Nio: 300%) The stock market for electric vehicles (EVs) grew exponentially.	Using social sentiment analysis, quantum algorithms forecasted strong momentum in EV trends.	Early acting investors had returns that were up to 20% higher than the market average.
2021	Reddit's/ WallStreetBets movement on meme stocks such as GME and AMC	Corrections followed massive short squeezes, which caused strong gains (for example, GME went up to 1,600% before falling 70%).	Unsustainable surges were identified two weeks ahead of time via quantum anomaly detection.	By leaving early during declines, investors were able to avoid suffering large losses.
2022	Positive LinkedIn sentiment for green energy stocks	Stocks in renewable energy companies (such as First Solar and Plug Power) increased at a rate of 30% each year.	Sustainable investing options were advised using quantum-driven portfolio optimization.	Portfolios with a concentration on green energy did better than others by around 15%.
2023	Viral TikTok videos promoting AI-focused startups	AI stocks (such as NVIDIA and Palantir) had a 50% increase in value, peaking in value during viral periods.	The optimal timings to enter and depart were determined via quantum sentiment analysis.	By using quantum predictions to time their transactions, investors were able to increase their earnings by 10–12%.
2024	High engagement on Instagram and X (formerly Twitter) for Metaverse and AR/VR stocks	Performance was mixed; smaller augmented reality/virtual reality (AR/VR) companies underperformed and displayed volatility, whereas Meta Platforms saw a 20% rise.	The market's overconfidence in speculative equities was exposed by quantum forecasting models.	By concentrating on bigger, more reliable metaverse players such as Meta, investors were able to avoid speculative losses of around 18%.

Another complicated factor is the time factor. Being in the superfast social media era, the opinion about a stock or market may change in a streak of lightning. Social media results in opinion changes every minute, whereas traditional finance research methodologies, which possibly rely on quarterly and annual reports and figures, cannot capture [25]. Conventional analytical tools are inherently more rigid and, as such, there is always a time-lag between the actual real-time sentiment in the market and these analytical tools. If, for instance, a given social media campaign emerges in the period immediately after a certain business has released a favorable earnings report, indicating a scandal or failure in a certain product, then there will be a decline in the stock price of the concerned business. This shift in the market sentiment generated by the information from the social network accounts would be invisible to the quantitative research tools that would center only on the earnings announcement. Market participants who solely rely on standard methods are at a disadvantage in that they cannot capture emotion in real-time. Figure 4.3 describes tracking sentiment trends over time for each platform.

Figure 4.3 displays the distribution of sentiment on Facebook, Instagram, and Twitter, three social media platforms. The sentiment categories are labeled as "Negative" (dark blue), "Neutral" (lighter blue), and "Positive" (orange). Facebook: There is a large portion of negative sentiments (dark blue), with very little neutral and almost no positive sentiments. Instagram: There is a similar distribution of negative sentiment, but as it moves toward Twitter, the negative sentiment tapers off, and the neutral sentiment (red) increases on Twitter: this platform has a higher proportion of neutral and positive sentiments (red and dark blue). Positive sentiment (orange) also appears here, but at a lower proportion compared to Facebook; overall, the graph shows that Facebook has a predominantly negative sentiment, Instagram transitions between negative and neutral, and Twitter leans more toward neutral and positive sentiment. The sum of sentiments by month across these platforms varied, indicating a shift in user sentiment across time.

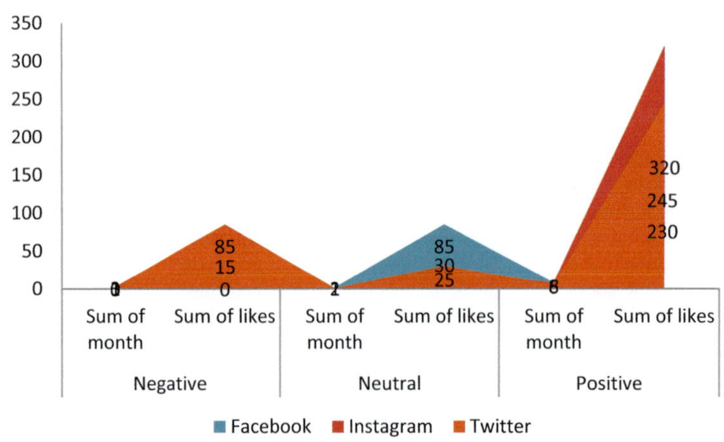

FIGURE 4.3 Tracking sentiment trends over time for each platform.

The global and diverse nature of social media also poses challenges. Social media platforms bring together investors from all over the world, each with their own perspectives, biases, and levels of financial literacy [26]. Traditional analysis models, which are often tailored to specific markets or regions, may not be well-suited to analyze the global sentiment that can emerge from social media. Moreover, discussions about stocks on social media often cross language barriers, with conversations occurring in multiple languages and cultural contexts simultaneously. Because traditional sentiment analysis tools may be limited by language or cultural understanding, this diversity makes it challenging for them to accurately assess the general sentiment of the market. Furthermore, local events, trends, or market conditions frequently influence social media conversations in ways that traditional analysts might not notice right away.

Therefore, mainstream research faces serious challenges examining social media on stock markets, including the overwhelming quantity of data, reliability and context challenges, time-dependency, market manipulation and group behavior appearance, the inequality of key players, global nature of social media, and regulatory uncertainty. Methods that have been used tend to be traditional in the study of fundamental market trends and business, and therefore, need to be complemented by the abrupt, unpredictable, and highly emotionally charged nature of stocks influenced heavily by social media platforms. Table 4.3 describes the total number of months per sentiment, which is grouped by platform.

The Table 4.3 sums up the sentiment and related likes distribution for each month across three societal broadcasting platforms, including Facebook, Instagram, and Twitter. Specifically for Facebook, 2 negative sentiment months with 85 likes, 8 neutral sentiment months with 230 likes, and no positive sentiment months with any influence on likes were noted. When it comes to the sentiment Analysis for Instagram, it consists of the following: 1 Negative month with 15 likes, 1 Neutral month with 25 likes, and 8 positive months with 320 likes, which makes Instagram the most Positive platform among all of these. The 3 negative sentiment month data shows 85 likes, 1 neutral sentiment month from 30 likes, and 6 positive sentiment months from 245 likes. In general, Instagram indicated a higher positivity level than any other platform, while the situation with Twitter was relatively neutral.

TABLE 4.3
Count of Sum of Month Per Sentiment Grouped by Platform

	Negative		Neutral		Positive	
Sentiment Platform	**Sum of Month**	**Sum of Likes**	**Sum of Month**	**Sum of Likes**	**Sum of Month**	**Sum of Likes**
Facebook			2	85	8	230
Instagram	1	15	1	25	8	320
Twitter	3	85	1	30	6	245

4.3 INTRODUCTION TO QC

An up-and-coming area of study, QC uses calculations based on quantum physics, which may be more efficient than conventional computing for certain tasks. Multiple states can be processed simultaneously because qubits can live in superposition states, which are the fundamental building blocks of quantum information. Because they can represent two states at once rather than just one, quantum bits, or qubits, enable quantum parallelism [27, 28]. It has been noted that QC, which integrates several science disciplines such as quantum physics and quantum mechanics, is a novel approach to handling information.

In conclusion, QC is one of the revolutionary approaches in data processing technology that will prove useful in many application areas that including such areas as AI, cryptography, filtering, and analyzing big data [29]. As progress in this field of study continues to move ahead, the use of QC is predicted to change numerous industries and solve problems that are unsolvable by current computing methods.

Quantum mechanics is the basis of operation for a quantum computer. To completely grasp quantum principles—including concepts such as superposition, entanglement, and decoherence—a new lexicon of terminology is necessary. What follows is an explanation of these ideas.

4.3.1 Superposition

Superposition states that, as classical physics suggests, the combination of two or more states results in another legal state; it also applies to quantum conditions. The idea of state-vector superposition, in contrast, states that any significant state can be represented as the sum of two or more separate states. Because qubits are in a state of parallelism, which is essential to quantum computers, millions of operations can be performed simultaneously.

4.3.2 Entanglement

Quantum entanglement is said to exist between two systems in a manner considered to achieve a state of interdependence whereby knowledge of one system holds direct knowledge of the other even when they are far apart. Interestingly, quantum computers may reason about one particle by determining another particle [30]. For instance, they may discover that if one qubit is oriented in the upward direction, the second one will always be oriented downward, and if the second is in the upward direction, the first will be in the downward direction. Quantum connectivity is a phenomenon that permits quantum computers to solve multifaceted problems in a shorter time.

4.3.3 Decoherence

Damage to a qubit's coherence state is known as dephasing. The state of affairs of qubits may collapse at the quantum level due to certain contextual factors, such as radiation. The design of structures that avoid the decoherence issue, which necessitates the creation of structures that isolate the qubit from outside forces, is one of the main technical challenges with quantum computer hardware.

ML: Machine learning, or ML for short, is a method for teaching computers to make better judgments by analyzing massive amounts of data. Advancements in quantum physics are being considered as part of the study of the inevitable limits of information operations in QC. Numerous fields, including chemistry, optimization, and molecular modeling, benefit from the present study. While the industrial sector seeks methods to boost efficiency, the financial services sector seeks instruments to foretell potential market upheavals.

Optimization: QC is likely to revolutionize research and development, create better supply-chain and manufacturing processes. QC may be applied for minimizing the costs of comprehensiveness of manufacturing processes as well as cycle times by identifying, for example, the best routes in complicated procedures. Another is quantum optimization of loans to help lenders unlock cash, lower or improve their services and interest rates on their portfolios. Figure 4.4 depicts the authors' own creation, exploring QC on Amazon Braket.

The above Figure 4.4 depicts the features of Amazon Braket, a service meant to enable users to initiate and experiment with QC. It is an overview of a complete developer's journey from creating quantum algorithms, simulators for testing them, and finally executing them on any preferred quantum computer. The output of these computations is then stored in another bucket of Amazon S3 for further analysis. This integrated environment makes it possible to construct, examine, and analyze quantum algorithms, which enhance the connection between model-based quantum technologies and practical implementations. Amazon Braket enables researchers and developers to learn about and test QC capabilities through access to their multiple resource offerings.

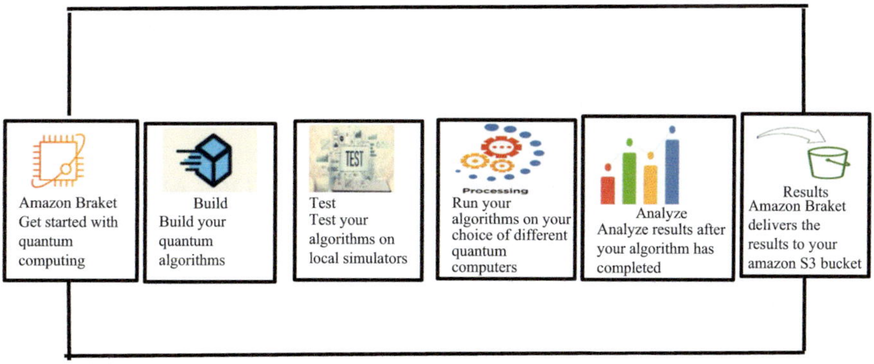

FIGURE 4.4 Authors' own creation exploring quantum computing (QC) on Amazon Braket.

4.4 GATHERING AND USING DATA

4.4.1 Real-time Data Feeds, Web Scraping, and APIs Are Some Techniques for Gathering Societal Broadcasting Facts

Some of the methods for extracting facts from societal broadcasting are APIs, web scraping, and real-time data streaming. The availability of platform-specific information through API and application programming interfaces is widely appreciated by users of social media data [31]. Nonetheless, they also have verification requirements and rate constraints when it comes to retrieving data, despite their standardization [32].

In contrast, web scraping is a technique of data collection other than using APIs; it involves the recovery of information from websites more effectively and flexibly than APIs [10]. Such scrapers could grant access to data that is sometimes unavailable through application programming interfaces, is sensitive to changes in website architecture, and can raise issues of ethical and legal concern [33, 34]. When focusing on current events or trends, researchers may greatly benefit from real-time data feeds, such as for instance Twitter's streaming API, to get hold of extremely large quantities of data in real time [35].

In their study, [36] have established that many university academics are noting increased difficulties in collecting social media data, particularly from Facebook and Instagram, due to changes in the availability of API, recently enacted. For this reason, the research methodologies have evolved, and novel questions about the course of social media research have been brought to light. As such, it is considered that researchers focus on novel methods of data collection and developing such criteria that enhance the reliability of online-based surveys [37].

Getting social media data through APIs, web scraping, and real-time feeds are different approaches, each with its own strengths and weaknesses. APIs, while offering a strictly formatted compliant access pathway, suffer from having rate limit restrictions. This flexibility comes at the cost of legal and technical challenges that web scraping experiences. Immediate data access is possible with real-time feeds; however, they necessitate a sound, architecturally strong framework and can be expensive. Both methods are useful in their own right, depending on the kind of evaluation and objectives of the data gathered. Since many branches rely on opinions, markets, or trends that can all be seen on social media, the ability to gather, analyze, and process the data collected from social media platforms will remain significant.

4.5 QUANTUM SENTIMENT ANALYSIS AND STOCK MARKET PREDICTIONS

Twelve of the articles that are available do not even think about using quantum sentiment analysis to forecast future stock market trends. The articles focus on natural language processing, the deep learning method, and standard ML in relation to sentiment analysis and the stock market. When forecasting algorithms are applied, the ML and deep learning models for stock market prediction have yielded favorable results. Among the deep learning models, long short-term memory (LSTM) yielded the best results with an accuracy of 92% [38].

It has been discovered that sentiment analysis of data from social network sites such as Stock Twits and Twitter can significantly improve the performance of the models used in stock price forecasting. For example, Mas Diyasa et al. found that their models with Twitter sentiment analysis and LSTM models for Tesla stock price prediction were relatively small, but their models with no sentiment data had higher mean squared error (MSE) and (root mean squared error (RMSE) [39]. According to a different study that used data from StockTwits, sentiment analysis improved the forecast of stock prices for major information technology (IT) companies such as Apple, Amazon, and Microsoft.

Although it is not explicitly explained in this article, the articles generally highlight the need to combine quantum sentiment analysis with other funding sources, traditional financial data, and sophisticated ML techniques to improve stock market forecasts [40]. While congruent textual and numerical data analysis is based on deep learning models, the collection of market emotions and the forecasting of stock movements are quite promising.

4.5.1 Conclusion

QC for Predictive Analysis: Understanding how Social Media Affects Stock Market Investments provides a look at using QC in the field of financial markets, with emphasis on the stock market in particular. It illustrates how new stocks, such as AMC and GameStop, in which the combined actions of ordinary traders shifted the features of the market, show how social platforms influence stock prices. Financial predictive analytics translates very well to the thought of processing through qubits, superposition, as well as entanglement, since a quantum computer works through instant analysis of large datasets.

Two of the quantum algorithms discussed are Grover and Shor, which aid in sentiment research and risk. It helps to enhance the predictive ability and control the fluctuation because of social media influences. However, there are challenges that we have not yet observed in the QC environment, but they are all connected with the primary physical limitations of the hardware and regulation issues for the implementation of superior data analysis and sentiment analysis for the better management of risks associated with stock exchange prediction. Nevertheless, they contain a lot of authority in future investment decisions.

REFERENCES

1. Yu, Jae Yong, Woo Seob Sim, Jae Yeob Jung, Si Heon Park, Han Sang Kim, and Yu Rang Park. "Evaluation of conventional and quantum computing for predicting mortality based on small early-onset colorectal cancer data." *Applied Soft Computing* 162 (2024): 111781.
2. Gandhudi, Manoranjan, P. J. A. Alphonse, Ugo Fiore, and G. R. Gangadharan. "Explainable hybrid quantum neural networks for analyzing the influence of tweets on stock price prediction." *Computers and Electrical Engineering* 118 (2024): 109302.

3. Ukpabi, Dandison, Heikki Karjaluoto, Astrid Bötticher, Anastasija Nikiforova, Dragoş Petrescu, Paulina Schindler, Visvaldis Valtenbergs, and Lennard Lehmann. "Framework for understanding quantum computing use cases from a multidisciplinary perspective and future research directions." *Futures* 154 (2023): 103277.
4. Kar, Arpan Kumar, Wu He, Fay Cobb Payton, Varun Grover, Adil S. Al-Busaidi, and Yogesh K. Dwivedi. "How could quantum computing shape information systems research–An editorial perspective and future research directions." *International Journal of Information Management* 80 (2025): 102776.
5. Dwivedi, Yogesh K., D. Elvira Ismagilova, Laurie Hughes, Jamie Carlson, Raffaele Filieri, Jenna Jacobson, Varsha Jain et al. "Setting the future of digital and social media marketing research: Perspectives and research propositions." *International Journal of Information Management* 59 (2021): 102168.
6. Sukhpal Singh, Gill, Huaming Wu, Panos Patros, Carlo Ottaviani, Priyansh Arora, Victor Casamayor Pujol, David Haunschild et al. "Modern computing: Vision and challenges." *Telematics and Informatics Reports* 13 (2024): 100116.
7. Hassanzadeh, Parichehr. "Towards the quantum-enabled technologies for development of drugs or delivery systems." *Journal of Controlled Release* 324 (2020): 260–279.
8. Woerner, Stefan, and Daniel J. Egger. "Quantum risk analysis." *npj Quantum Information* 5, no. 1 (2019): 15.
9. Aljaafari, Mohammed. "Quantum computing for social business optimization: a practitioner's perspective." *Soft Computing* 1 (2023): 1–23.
10. Jain, Prateek, and Alberto Garcia Garcia. "Quantum classical hybrid neural networks for continuous variable prediction." arXiv preprint arXiv:2212.04209 (2022).
11. Moussa, Faten, Olfa BenOuda, and Ezzeddine Delhoumi. "The use of open source internet to analysis and predict stock market trading volume." *Research in International Business and Finance* 41 (2017): 399–411.
12. Carrascal, Gines, Beatriz Roman, Alberto del Barrio, and Guillermo Botella. "Differential evolution VQE for crypto-currency arbitrage. Quantum optimization with many local minima." *Digital Signal Processing* 148 (2024): 104464.
13. Hacioglu, Umit, Hasan Dincer, Mustafa Kemal Yilmaz, Serhat Yüksel, Mariama Sonko, and Dursun Delen. "Optimizing sustainable industry investment selection: A golden cut-enhanced quantum spherical fuzzy decision-making approach." *Applied Soft Computing* 148 (2023): 110853.
14. Altares-López, Sergio, Juan José García-Ripoll, and Angela Ribeiro. "Optimal quantum circuit generation for pixel segmentation in multiband images." *Applied Soft Computing* 166 (2024): 112175.
15. Guo, Hong, Juheng Zhang, and Gary J. Koehler. "A survey of quantum games." *Decision Support Systems* 46, no. 1 (2008): 318–332.
16. Saquete, Estela, Jose Zubcoff, Yoan Gutiérrez, Patricio Martínez-Barco, and Javi Fernández. "Why are some social-media contents more popular than others? Opinion and association rules mining applied to virality patterns discovery." *Expert Systems with Applications* 197 (2022): 116676.
17. Pei, Zongrui, Yilun Gong, Xianglin Liu, and Junqi Yin. "Designing complex concentrated alloys with quantum machine learning and language modeling." *Matter* 7, no. 10 (2024): 3433–3446.
18. Nyakurukwa, Kingstone, and Yudhvir Seetharam. "Sentimental showdown: News media vs. social media in stock markets." *Heliyon* 10, no. 9 (2024): 2468–2476.
19. Nyakurukwa, Kingstone, and Yudhvir Seetharam. "The evolution of studies on social media sentiment in the stock market: Insights from bibliometric analysis." *Scientific African* 20 (2023): e01596.

20. Shunza, Justus, Mary Akinyemi, and Chika Yinka-Banjo. "Application of quantum computing in discrete portfolio optimization." *Journal of Management Science and Engineering* 8, no. 4 (2023): 453–464.
21. Kwak, Jun Hee. "Individual investor trading and stock returns after the Covid-19 pandemic: Evidence from Korea." *Finance Research Letters* 61 (2024): 105027.
22. Jin, Xiu, Yueli Liu, Jinming Yu, and Weiqiang Huang. "COVID-19 and extreme risk spillovers between oil and BRICS stock markets: A multiscale perspective." *The North American Journal of Economics and Finance* 68 (2023): 101967.
23. Song, Ziyu, Xiaomin Gong, Cheng Zhang, and Changrui Yu. "Investor sentiment based on scaled PCA method: A powerful predictor of realized volatility in the Chinese stock market." *International Review of Economics & Finance* 83 (2023): 528–545.
24. Zhang, Xi, Jiawei Shi, Di Wang, and Binxing Fang. "Exploiting investors social network for stock prediction in China's market." *Journal of Computational Science* 28 (2018): 294–303.
25. Liao, Weidong, and Robert Chhoeut. "Using social networking APIs to collect real-time data for analytics." *Proceedings of the West Virginia Academy of Science* 89, no. 1 (2017): 1–12.
26. Kwak, Jun Hee. "Individual investor trading and stock returns after the Covid-19 pandemic: Evidence from Korea." *Finance Research Letters* 61 (2024): 105027.
27. Fu, Kui, and Yanbin Zhang. "Incorporating multi-source market sentiment and price data for stock price prediction." *Mathematics* 12, no. 10 (2024): 1572.
28. Lelisho, Mesfin Esayas, Digvijay Pandey, Bizuwork Derebew Alemu, Binay Kumar Pandey, and Seid Ali Tareke. "The negative impact of social media during COVID-19 pandemic." *Trends in Psychology* 31, no. 1 (2023): 123–142.
29. Uehara, Glen S., Andreas Spanias, and William Clark. "Quantum information processing algorithms with emphasis on machine learning." In *2021 12th International Conference on Information, Intelligence, Systems & Applications (IISA)*, pp. 1–11. IEEE, 2021.
30. Uehara, Glen S., Andreas Spanias, and William Clark. "Quantum information processing algorithms with emphasis on machine learning." In *2021 12th International Conference on Information, Intelligence, Systems & Applications (IISA)*, pp. 1–11. IEEE, 2021.
31. Batrinca, Bogdan, and Philip C. Treleaven. "Social media analytics: A survey of techniques, tools and platforms." *Ai & Society* 30, no. 1 (2015): 89–116.
32. Boegershausen, Johannes, Hannes Datta, Abhishek Borah, and Andrew T. Stephen. "Fields of gold: Scraping web data for marketing insights." *Journal of Marketing* 86, no. 5 (2022): 1–20.
33. Boegershausen, Johannes, Hannes Datta, Abhishek Borah, and Andrew T. Stephen. "Fields of gold: Web scraping and APIs for impactful marketing insights." *Journal of Marketing* 86, no. 5 (2022): 1–20.
34. Cao, Jian, Nicholas Adams-Cohen, and R. Michael Alvarez. "Reliable and efficient long-term social media monitoring." arXiv preprint arXiv:2005.02442 (2020).
35. Tyagi et al., 2024. Stock price prediction using sentiment analysis. *International Journal for Research in Applied Science and Engineering Technology*, 12(1), 1301–1305. https://doi.org/10.22214/ijraset.2024.58167
36. Agnihotri, Raj, Khashayar Afshar Bakeshloo, and Sudha Mani. "Social media analytics for business-to-business marketing." *Industrial Marketing Management* 115 (2023): 110–126.
37. Raut, Vishranti, and Prafulla Patil. "Use of social media in education: Positive and negative impact on the students." *International Journal on Recent and Innovation Trends in Computing and Communication* 4, no. 1 (2016): 281–285.

38. Song, Ziyu, Xiaomin Gong, Cheng Zhang, and Changrui Yu. "Investor sentiment based on scaled PCA method: A powerful predictor of realized volatility in the Chinese stock market." *International Review of Economics & Finance* 83 (2023): 528–545.
39. Zhang, Xi, Jiawei Shi, Di Wang, and Binxing Fang. "Exploiting investors social network for stock prediction in China's market." *Journal of Computational Science* 28 (2018): 294–303.
40. Agnihotri, Raj, Khashayar Afshar Bakeshloo, and Sudha Mani. "Social media analytics for business-to-business marketing." *Industrial Marketing Management* 115 (2023): 110–126.

5 Quantum-Powered Fraud Detection

Revolutionizing Financial Security

Koteswara Rao Veginati, Kafila, and Kudali Prasanthi

5.1 INTRODUCTION

The financial sector continues to grow rapidly, and cybersecurity and fraud detection are becoming increasingly important. With the rise in financial digitization, systems have become vulnerable to a variety of threats. These include advanced cyberattack, data leak, identity theft, and financial fraud. Currently, these threats affect most financial institutions. The launch of tools such as online banking, digital payments, and decentralized finance (DeFi) has augmented the possibility of financial services. Simultaneously, new security threats emerged.

Since its implementation, India has made significant strides in quantum technologies. The cabinet approved the National Quantum Mission (NQM) on April 19, 2023, totaling 6003.65 crores from 2023–2024 to 2030–2031. The NQM was fundamentally designed to address highly complex computational problems, thereby surpassing the capabilities of conventional supercomputers. Quantum computers are game-changers. India's technology strategy focuses on problem-solving application sectors such as defense, finance, healthcare, manufacturing, and social welfare (NQM), among others [1]. Although quantum computing (QC) exhibits potential, machine learning (ML) methods remain essential for fraud detection.

The quantum support vector classifier (QSVC), utilizing Z-feature mapping and linear entanglements, achieved a prediction of 1.0 in a study examining various quantum algorithms for classification. This demonstrates a significant decrease in false-positive results [2]. This highlights the potential of hybrid methodologies that combine the quantum and classical techniques. The combination of these two models yields remarkable results. They can detect fraud 98.5% of the time, and reduce and achieve a 40% in false positives relative to the traditional approach [3].

DOI: 10.1201/9781003587835-5

5.1.1 Objective

The important aim of this study is to study the potential of ML QC to aid in the identification of financial fraud across industries.

5.1.2 Research Question

How can the security and effectiveness of financial systems be enhanced by quantum-enhanced fraud detection tools? Table 5.1 describes the literature survey.

TABLE 5.1
Literature Survey

Category	Source	Year	Key Findings	Estimated Impact
QC in finance	Gartner Research	2024	Financial institutions were early adopters of quantum technologies, focusing on quantum cryptography to ensure transaction integrity.	Post-quantum encryption method may reduce data breaches by 40%.
	International Business Machines (IBM) Quantum Computing	2022	The quantum optimization used for managing portfolios resulted in a 15% increase in productivity.	This ensures the practicality of finance-related quantum use cases.
	Deloitte Insights	2024	By 2030, the combination of QC is expected to enhance fraud detection capabilities, potentially achieving twice the current speed.	It would save billions of dollars worldwide in fraud losses.
Fraud detection technology	KPMG Global Fraud Reports	2021	Global financial fraud has increased by 19%, with cyber-related fraud being the leading cause.	Increased regulatory pressure on AI-based fraud detection systems.
	The Association of Certified Fraud Examiners (ACFE) Global Fraud Study	2022	Fraud consumes 5% of an organization's revenue, resulting in $4.7 trillion in annual global losses.	This emphasizes the critical need for scalable fraud detection systems.
	Nasdaq Verafin	2023	AI- and ML-based fraud detection successfully reduced false positive alerts by 32%.	Increased efficiency in transaction monitoring and investigation.

(Continued)

TABLE 5.1 (Continued)

Category	Source	Year	Key Findings	Estimated Impact
Quantum in fraud detection	MC Kincy & Company	2023	Pilots using quantum-enhanced fraud detection have achieved a 25% improvement in anomaly detection.	Initial evidence suggests that quantum technology can improve financial security.
Impact of COVID-19 Fraud	PwC Economic Crime Report	2020–2024	There was an increase in fraud cases during the pandemic, particularly for online banking and digital transactions.	The focus has shifted to fraud detection in both remote and digital ecosystems.

5.1.3 Overview of the Financial Cybersecurity Threats

Financial technology has rapidly improved, and the financial sector has integrated technology into financial services. Evaluation of financial technology has influenced the financial sector. This enhances productivity, availability, and improvement. The rise of cybersecurity risk as a critical threat to the financial sector has led researchers and analysts to examine the issue from multiple viewpoints. Figure 5.1 presents an overview of financial cybersecurity threats.

Financial Technology, a significant entity in the global economy and financial sector, prioritizes technological innovations designed to automate finance, a domain

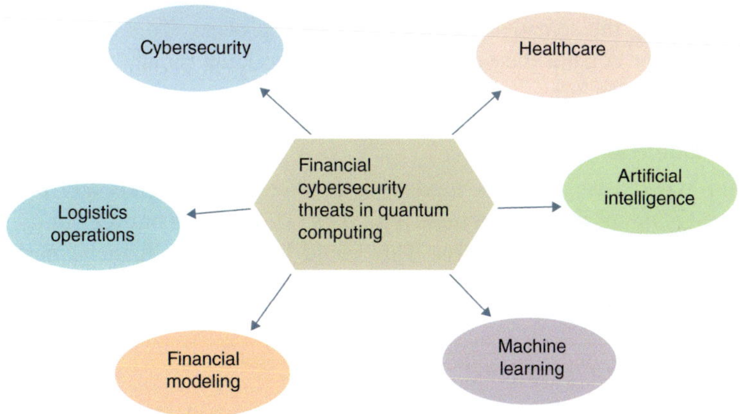

FIGURE 5.1 Overview of financial cybersecurity threats.

(Authors' own compliance.)

particularly vulnerable to cyberattacks and cyber espionage. The financial sector is a segment of the low-cost sector. It comprises public and private companies, institutions, insurance companies, and retail customers. It encompasses a wide range of real estate, banking, and exchange investments. These financial institutions are concerned about cyberattacks [4].

5.1.3.1 Cybersecurity

Our current Internet security, such as how online banking is protected, relies on incredibly strong encryption. Quantum computers could break these existing codes, making our financial systems vulnerable to cyberattacks that steal money or sensitive data. This means our cybersecurity defenses need a complete overhaul to stay ahead of this new quantum threat.

5.1.3.2 Healthcare

Healthcare systems hold large amounts of valuable financial data, ranging from patient billing records to insurance information. If these systems are affected by quantum attacks, all private financial information could be stolen or compromised. We need to ensure that the security of patient records and billing systems in healthcare is ready for quantum threats.

5.1.3.3 Artificial Intelligence (AI)

Financial companies are using AI to make important decisions, such as approving loans or detecting fraud. QC could potentially hack these AI models by how they work or by secretly changing the data they use. This could lead to bad financial decisions or even widespread fraud, making it possible to protect AI systems from quantum interference.

5.1.3.4 ML

ML is used for things such as noticing unusual patterns in credit card transactions to detect fraud. Quantum systems can find ways to achieve these ML algorithms, targeting the sensitive financial data they process. This could lead to big data breaches or corrupt the very models meant to keep money safe, so we need stronger security for ML.

5.1.3.5 Financial Modeling

Financial experts use complex models to predict market trends and investment decisions. Quantum attacks can mess with these simulations or even subtly change the numbers in financial forecasts. This could lead to big financial mistakes or create opportunities for fraud, making it crucial to develop quantum-safe tools for financial modeling.

5.1.3.6 Logistics Operations

The financial aspects of how goods move around the world, including supply chain transactions and inventory data, can also be disrupted by quantum cyberattacks. If these systems are compromised, they can throw global trade into chaos, thereby affecting financial settlements and operational flow. We must ensure that the connections between logistics and finances are secure against these future threats.

5.1.4 The Future Development of Fraud Detection Technology

Future advancements in fraud detection technology will likely incorporate erudite technologies, such as AI and ML, and blockchain, to create more robust and adaptable systems. Currently, cyberattacks are more common, and fraud detection is quick. Fraudsters have begun to improve their technology for hacking information from different sources, such as AI and ML. In comparison, AI tools and QC are capable of identifying large datasets and analyzing fraudulent activities. Fraud detection activities increasingly affect both individual and organizational financial sector services [5].

The digital age improved from 2016 to 2024. The explosion of digital transactions, online payments, e-commerce, and banking services has created new opportunities for fraudsters in the financial system. AI and big data technologies offer innovative solutions for identifying financial fraud, overcoming the shortcomings of predictable methods in managing promptly evolving fraudulent activities [6]. We used ML algorithms such as logistic curve fitting, random forest, and decision trees to expand the precision of fraud-detection models.

5.1.5 QC Enters Finance

Most financial services and sectors significantly rely on technology. Quantum computing outperforms conventional computers in terms of precision and the quick processing of large amounts of data. Traditional computers rely on binary systems that are either zero or one. To solve these problems, these computers use step-by-step algorithms and logical operations. QC depends on the qubits that exist concurrently in numerous states. Portfolio optimization results in increased profits and reduced fraud detection. Traditional computers are mean-variance optimization algorithms. QC solves this problem with high accuracy. Different variants can solve this QC superposition formula based on work at different times [7].

5.2 THE GROWTH OF FRAUD DETECTION METHODS IN FINANCE

5.2.1 Traditional Fraud Detection Methods

Cyberattacks have plagued the financial services sector for several years. Governments and private organizations have developed protection technologies related to detecting fraudulent financial activities. These methods are rule-based and statistical.

5.2.1.1 Rule-Driven Systems

This system has certain restrictions and parameters based on its workings. Example: There is a customer account with significant transactions, and the system immediately alerts us to the red flag.

5.5 QUANTUM-ENHANCED FRAUD DETECTION TECHNIQUES IN FINANCE

QC is gaining popularity owing to its high speed and accuracy, which are crucial for fraud detection in the modern era of finance. According to research, it has been confirmed that a quantum-assisted SVM outperforms in the assessment of fraudulent statistics, especially for extremely skewed time-series data.

5.6 CONCLUSION

In summary, amalgamating QC with ML can revolutionize fraud detection in the financial industry by achieving better accuracy and efficiency than classical techniques.

FUTURE SCOPE

In future work, the functionality of quantum-classical hybrid systems at financial institutions should be investigated, including the improvement of quantum algorithms and issues related to the security of electronic data.

REFERENCES

1. "National Quantum Missions (NQM)." Gov.in, n.d., https://dst.gov.in/national-quantum-mission-nqm. Accessed 1 Oct. 2024.
2. Ghernaouti-Hélie, Solange, and Mohamed Ali Sfaxi. "Guaranteerring security of financial transaction by using quantum cryptography in banking environment." In *International Conference on E-Business and Telecommunication Networks*, pp. 139–149. Berlin, Heidelberg: Springer Berlin Heidelberg, 2005.
3. Abdulrazzaq, Mohammed Aqeel. "Quantum-assisted machine learning for enhanced fraud detection in cybersecurity." *International Research Journal of Innovations in Engineering and Technology*, 8, no. 5 (2024): 319.
4. Javaheri, Danial, Mahdi Fahmideh, Hassan Chizari, Pooia Lalbakhsh, and Junbeom Hur. "Cybersecurity threats in FinTech: A systematic review." *Expert Systems with Applications* 241 (2024): 122697.
5. Al-Jumeily, Dhiya, Abir Hussain, Áine MacDermott, Hissam Tawfik, Gemma Seeckts, and Jan Lunn. "The development of fraud detection systems for detection of potentially fraudulent applications." In *2015 International Conference on Developments of E-Systems Engineering (DeSE)*, pp. 7–13. IEEE, 2015.
6. Wang, Ziyue. "Research on the application of artificial intelligence and big data technology in financial fraud detection." *Journal of Theory and Practice of Engineering Science* 4, no. 03 (2024): 216–219.
7. Kasedullah, Mohammad, Shuvo Karmaker, Md Saeelan Arafat, Sal Sabil, Md Shahabul Islam Sarker, and Apurba Afiat. "Energizing blockchain and Artificial Intelligence for enhanced fraud detection in modern banking systems." *International Journal of Science and Research Archive* 16, no. 1 (2025): 613–621.
8. Bao, Yang, Gilles Hilary, and Bin Ke. "Artificial intelligence and fraud detection." In *Innovative Technology at the Interface of Finance and Operations*: Volume I, pp. 223–247. Cham: Springer International Publishing, 2022.
9. Orús, Román, Samuel Mugel, and Enrique Lizaso. "Quantum computing for finance: Overview and prospects." *Reviews in Physics* 4 (2019): 100028.

10. Biamonte, Jacob, Peter Wittek, Nicola Pancotti, Patrick Rebentrost, Nathan Wiebe, and Seth Lloyd. "Quantum machine learning." *Nature* 549, no. 7671 (2017): 195–202.
11. Montanaro, Ashley. "Quantum speedup of Monte Carlo methods." *Proceedings of the Royal Society A: Mathematical, Physical and Engineering Sciences* 471, no. 2181 (2015): 20150301.
12. Low, Guang Hao, Theodore J. Yoder, and Isaac L. Chuang. "Quantum inference on Bayesian networks." *Physical Review A* 89, no. 6 (2014): 062315.
13. Wiebe, Nathan, and Christopher Granade. "Can small quantum systems learn?." arXiv preprint arXiv:1512.03145 (2015).
14. Kapoor, Ashish, Nathan Wiebe, and Krysta Svore. "Quantum perceptron mode." *Advances in Neural Information Processing Systems* 29 (2016): 1–29.
15. Wiebe, Nathan, Daniel Braun, and Seth Lloyd. "Quantum algorithm for data fitting." *Physical Review Letters* 109, no. 5 (2012): 050505.
16. Wiebe, Nathan, Ashish Kapoor, and Krysta M. Svore. "Quantum deep learning." arXiv preprint arXiv:1412.3489 (2014).
17. Amin, Mohammad H., Evgeny Andriyash, Jason Rolfe, Bohdan Kulchytskyy, and Roger Melko. "Quantum boltzmann machine." *Physical Review X* 8, no. 2 (2018): 021050.
18. Kieferova, Maria, and Nathan Wiebe. "Tomography and generative data modeling via quantum Boltzmann training." arXiv preprint arXiv:1612.05204 (2016).
19. Lloyd, Seth, Masoud Mohseni, and Patrick Rebentrost. "Quantum principal component analysis." *Nature Physics* 10, no. 9 (2014): 631–633.
20. Rebentrost, Patrick, Masoud Mohseni, and Seth Lloyd. "Quantum support vector machine for big data classification." *Physical Review Letters* 113, no. 13 (2014): 130503.
21. Mellaerts, Julien. "Quantum-inspired anomaly detection, a QUBO formulation." arXiv preprint arXiv:2311.03227 (2023).
22. Leon, De, P. Nathalie, Kohei M. Itoh, Dohun Kim, Karan K. Mehta, Tracy E. Northup, Hanhee Paik, B. S. Palmer, Nitin Samarth, Sorawis Sangtawesin, and David W. Steuerman. "Materials challenges and opportunities for quantum computing hardware." *Science* 372, no. 6539 (2021): eabb2823.
23. Salam, Masaud, and Muhammad Ilyas. "Quantum computing challenges and solutions in software industry—A multivocal literature review." *IET Quantum Communication* 5, no. 4 (2024): 462–485.
24. Stırbu, Vlad, Majid Haghparast, Muhammad Waseem, Niraj Dayama, and Tommi Mikkonen. "Full-stack quantum software in practice: Ecosystem, stakeholders and challenges." In *2023 IEEE International Conference on Quantum Computing and Engineering (QCE)*, vol. 2, pp. 177–180. IEEE, 2023.
25. Yao, Xing-Can, Tian-Xiong Wang, Hao-Ze Chen, Wei-Bo Gao, Austin G. Fowler, Robert Raussendorf, Zeng-Bing Chen et al. "Experimental demonstration of topological error correction." *Nature* 482, no. 7386 (2012): 489–494.
26. Chatterjee, Avimita, Subrata Das, and Swaroop Ghosh. "Q-pandora unboxed: Characterizing noise resilience of quantum error correction codes." arXiv preprint arXiv:2308.02769 (2023).
27. Grossi, Michele, Luca Crippa, Antonello Aita, Giacomo Bartoli, Vito Sammarco, Eleonora Picca, Najla Said, Filippo Tramonto, and Federico Mattei. "A serverless cloud integration for quantum computing." arXiv preprint arXiv:2107.02007 (2021).
28. Yalla, S. P., A. Uriti, A. Sethy, and V. Sathishkumar. "Secure method of communication using Quantum Key Distribution." *Applied and Computational Engineering* 30 (2024): 32–37.
29. Ponnuviji, N. P., and M. Vigilson Prem. "Morphic computing with machine learning for enhanced fraud detection in financial applications." *ICTACT Journal on Soft Computing* 15, no. 2 (2024): 1–15.

30. Atadoga, A., C. U. Ike, O. F. Asuzu, B. S. Ayinla, N. L. Ndubuisi, and R. A. Adeleye. "The intersection of AI and quantum computing in financial markets: A critical review." *Computer Science & IT Research Journal* 5, no. 2 (2024): 461–472.
31. Collins, Robert J., Ryan Amiri, Mikio Fujiwara, Toshimori Honjo, Kaoru Shimizu, Kiyoshi Tamaki, Masahiro Takeoka, Erika Andersson, Gerald S. Buller, and Masahide Sasaki. "Experimental transmission of quantum digital signatures over 90 km of installed optical fiber using a differential phase shift quantum key distribution system." *Optics Letters* 41, no. 21 (2016): 4883–4886.

6 Quantum Computing in Healthcare

S. V. K. R. Rajeswari and Govind Kumar Pandey

6.1 INTRODUCTION

The quantum computing statistics are predicted to rise to USD 949 million by 2025 from USD 89 million in 2016 [1]. The benefit of quantum computing over regular computers is that all the information can be looked at the same time, which leads to faster computing. This is on account of the fundamentals of quantum mechanics, which enable us to perform complex calculations [2]. Quantum computing finds its application in making healthcare better by finding new medicines, genome research, understanding, diagnostics, with treatment and intervention [3]. Quantum computing adapts the foundational theories of quantum mechanics, such as superposition, entanglement, and tunneling, offering an unparalleled computational power compared to classical systems. This increases the performance potential to address challenges in healthcare by reducing the computational costs, and enhancing data, and overcoming the challenges of delay and latencies [4]. Bits are implemented in regular transistors in traditional computers, whereas qubits are used in quantum computers. Qubits can exist in several states simultaneously; that is, they can be both "0" and "1" at the same time. This property of qubits enhances the power of quantum computers and is unique from classical computers [5, 6]. Qubits are organized on a superconducting chip in a chessboard pattern. They are made of tiny niobium capacitors where the charges oscillate as a part of the quantum property, and the small antennae respond to microwaves for communication in the quantum system. Parallel computation in classical computers takes a long time, whereas in quantum computers, programming executes multiple tasks simultaneously.

Given the properties and advancements of quantum computing over classical computers, the determination behind this chapter is driven by the necessity to advance healthcare facilities, especially in the areas of precision medicine, drug discovery, diagnosis, bioinformatics, smart decision-making and devices, medical imaging, and genetics, aligning with the Sustainable Development Goals (SDG) 3 [6–8].

6.2 QUANTUM COMPUTING IN HEALTHCARE SYSTEMS

This section explores a transformative technology of quantum computing that has made an impact in several fields of healthcare research. Employing the formerly discussed principles of superposition and entanglement, quantum computing delivers massive processing power when compared to classical computers. Figure 6.1 depicts a quantum computing architecture.

DOI: 10.1201/9781003587835-6

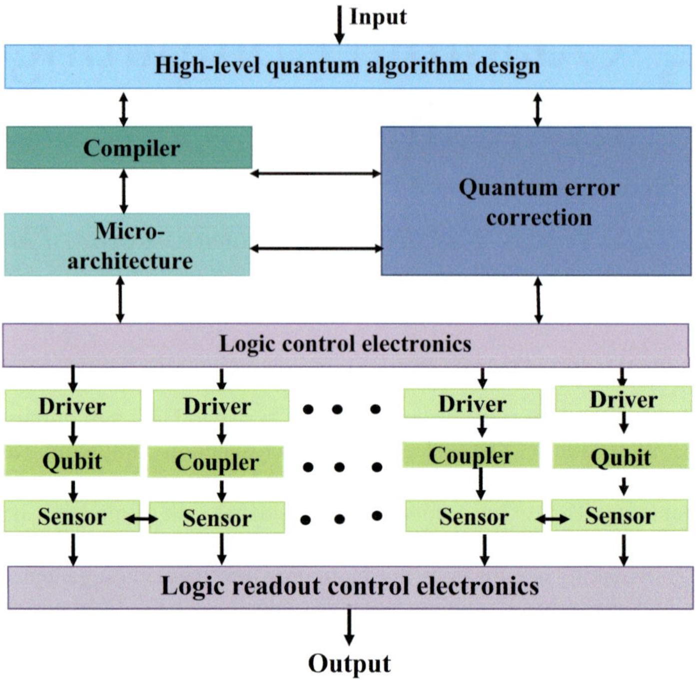

FIGURE 6.1 Quantum computing architecture.

6.2.1 Quantum Computing Architecture

It is evident from the quantum properties that there is a possibility to address the challenges of classical computers, leading to novel revelations and findings. This enhancement can be applied to the applications in healthcare. Few investigations have implemented the breakthroughs pertaining to quantum computing in biomedical research. The quantum computing architecture consists of layers, as illustrated in Figure 6.1. The flow starts from the first, topmost layer composed of "High-Level quantum algorithm design." The quantum-based algorithms exhibit a complex coding language that is hardware-neutral, meaning the program assumes idealistic qubits and operations. These algorithms can be simple machine learning algorithms written in Qiskit. "Compiler" is the second layer, which translates the high-level algorithms into machine-level instructions that the quantum hardware can execute. The concurrent, "quantum error correction (QEC)" layer is responsible for creating fault-tolerant versions, ensuring noise- and error-free algorithms. "Microarchitecture" is the fourth layer, which converts the instructions into low-level commands that hardware understands, which bridges the gap between logical instructions and physical hardware.

Figure 6.2 describes a flowchart of a quantum computing architecture with faster quantum ridge regression. The 'Control/Readout Electronics' is the fifth layer that consists of drivers, couplers, qubits, and sensors to convert the low-level instructions into control waveforms. The quantum computations take place in the qubit layer. Signals are generated by drivers to control the qubits, whereas the couplers are implemented to manage the interactions between qubits for implementing quantum gates

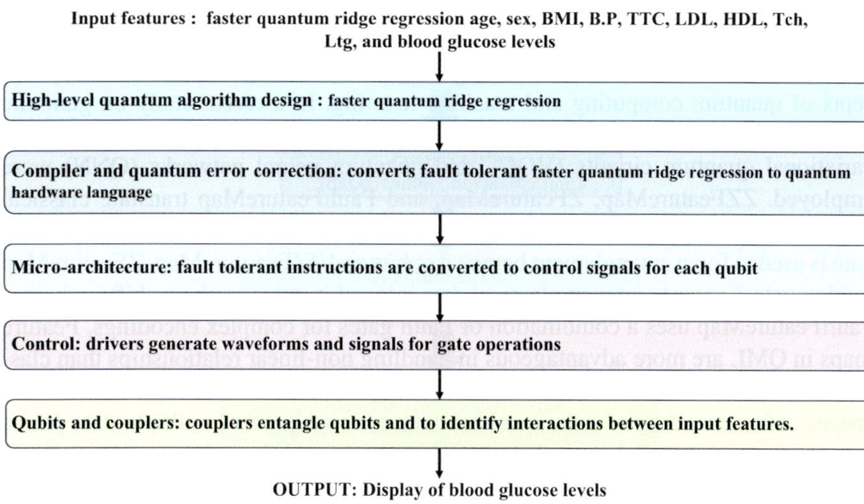

FIGURE 6.2 Flowchart of quantum computing architecture with faster quantum ridge regression.

involving multiple qubits, such as CNOT and entanglement. The sensors are present to detect the quantum states of the qubits, enabling the extraction of classical output data from the quantum system [9–12]. An instance of blood glucose prediction from input features of age, sex, body mass index (BMI), blood pressure (BP), total serum cholesterol (TC), low-density lipoproteins (LDL), high-density lipoproteins (HDL), total cholesterol (Tch), and log of serum triglycerides (Ltg) can be applied on the quantum computing architecture [13]. The flowchart of blood glucose prediction with the integration of quantum computing and a step-by-step process, with a combination of the logical framework and hardware architecture, is presented in Figure 6.2.

At the topmost layer, 'high-level quantum algorithm design," the input features, that is, age, sex, BMI, BP, TTC, LDL, HDL, Tch, Ltg, and blood glucose levels, are pre-processed. At this step, a prediction algorithm example, a faster quantum ridge regression [14] is employed to predict diabetes. The compiler converts the regression to quantum hardware language. The algorithm is fault-tolerantly converted into quantum hardware instructions in the QEC layer. At the hardware layer, the quantum operations are performed to operate qubits using control drivers. Interactions between input features are captured by entangling the couplers with qubits. The final qubit layers are measured by the sensor, and blood glucose levels are predicted.

6.3 QUANTUM COMPUTING IN HEALTHCARE SYSTEMS

Transformative impacts have emerged in healthcare where fundamental concepts of quantum computing and mechanics are explored in the areas of quantum machine learning (QML) (genome analysis, drug discovery, clinical decision-making), quantum sensors and diagnostics (early disease detection and enhanced imaging techniques), and personalized medicine (data-driven treatment plans, continuous monitoring of vitals) [6, 15–20].

TABLE 6.2
Difference between Conventional Sensors and Quantum Sensors

Classical Sensors	Quantum Sensors
The principle of operation is on spin states for measurements, enabling high precision and sensitivity.	The principle of operation is based on changes in resistance, capacitance, or optical properties for measurement.
Highly sensitive to detect changes in nanoscale fields, forces, or particle variations.	Sensitive to macroscopic applications and limited to quantum states.
High cost and complexity due to technology.	Affordable and less complex.

amperometric immunosensor is developed, implementing colloidal quantum dots to detect MPO even in low concentrations. The changes in the biomarker concentration are followed by an electrical response. From 1 pg/mL to 1 ng/mL in the detection range, with a sensitivity of 31.6 fg/mL, the sensor functions [34]. The detection of free radicals in Huntington's Disease (HD) is explored in a study. Diamond quantum sensors are proposed that utilize NV centers to perform nanoscale magnetic resonance imaging. A correlation between PolyQ aggregation and an increase in free radical levels was observed, implying oxidative stress contributing to autolysosomal dysfunction in HD [35]. Quantum biosensors and diagnostics hold transformative potential with the properties of ultra-sensitive, real-time detection of biomarkers for early diagnosis of diseases. The difference between classical and quantum sensors is presented in Table 6.2.

6.3.3 Personalized Medicine

Figure 6.5 describes quantum personalized treatment. Quantum computing finds its application in transforming personalized medicine in the area of genetics, enhancing diagnostics, and drug discovery. Tailored treatment plans can be created for an individual based on the history of diagnosis, medications, and the current scenario. Personalized medicine requires analyzing high volumes of genetic data. As classical computing methods have the drawback of complexity and size of genome data, quantum computing overcomes the challenges with quantum parallelism. The concept of quantum parallelism eases the time required for complex computations [36, 37]. A recent study compared classical computing approaches with quantum computing approaches in genetic sequencing. Gates with multiple controls, such as the Toffoli gate, are implemented to entangle information regarding both the position and value of nucleotides with the sequence. Quantum-based Flexible Representation of Quantum Image (FRQI) algorithm was implemented that enhanced granular composition with high-resolution analysis of genetic sequences, similarity score calculation for mutation detection, and improvement of efficiency [38]. A related study proposed Quantum Tunnel Annealing (QTA) for optimizing challenges of non-convex, large-scale optimization problems for treatment planning in radiotherapy. The QTA algorithm has an additional degree of freedom known as barrier width

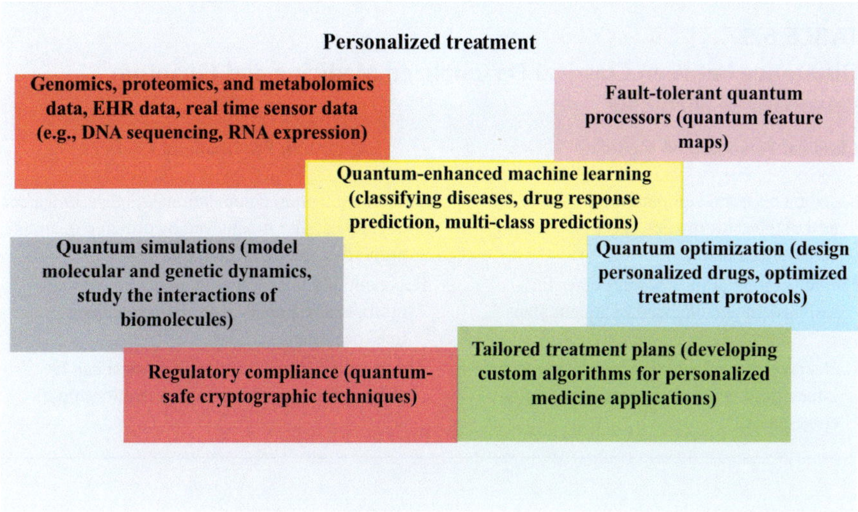

FIGURE 6.5 Quantum personalized treatment.

"w," which is not present in simulated annealing that deploys 46.6% faster convergence in maximizing intensity of beamlet, and 26.8% faster convergence in direct aperture optimization [39]. A parallel study proposed an optimized radiotherapy plan for cancer treatment by optimizing dose distribution. The complexity of the non-convex problem is addressed with a tensor network that employs mathematical models for handling high-dimensional data. The cost function is proposed to represent the contrast between the reference and forecasted dose distribution to the tumor and surrounding tissues. The cost function is mapped to the Ising-like Hamiltonian for interaction over long distances. The Tree Tensor Network algorithm is proposed to handle the base state of Hamiltonian corresponding to optimal dose distribution [40]. In a closer study on diagnosing breast cancer, QSVM is proposed to classify malignant and benign tumors in high-dimensional spaces that potentially provide exponential speedup in training times compared to classical SVM. A 98% accuracy with QSVM is achieved when compared to the 95% accuracy of SVM [41]. The difference between classical personalized medicine and quantum personalized medicine is presented in Table 6.3.

6.3.4 Quantum Resource Management

Cloud computing is in demand for ease of access and data storage. Assessment of resource utilization and performance is key to optimal management of jobs and resources at the client and vendor end. Quantum cloud is employed for handling waiting times and fidelity variations across machines. This is achieved by creating a forecasted model to predict circuit-depth dependent fidelity progressions and errors, and the prediction of queuing times based on execution time estimations [42]. Figure 6.6 depicts quantum resource management.

TABLE 6.3
Difference between Classical Personalized Medicine and Quantum Personalized Medicine

Classical Personalized Medicine	Quantum Personalized Medicine
Based on classical computational models, by utilizing bioinformatics, machine learning, and systems biology.	Based on quantum computational models, enhanced data processing is achieved by utilizing quantum properties and molecular interactions.
Limited computational power delays the response in personalized treatment plans.	Exponentially faster computational power that prompts a response faster in personalized treatment plans.
Lacks precision in handling high-dimensional interactions, such as in protein folding and epigenetics.	The property of quantum entanglement can be utilized for identifying hidden relationships.

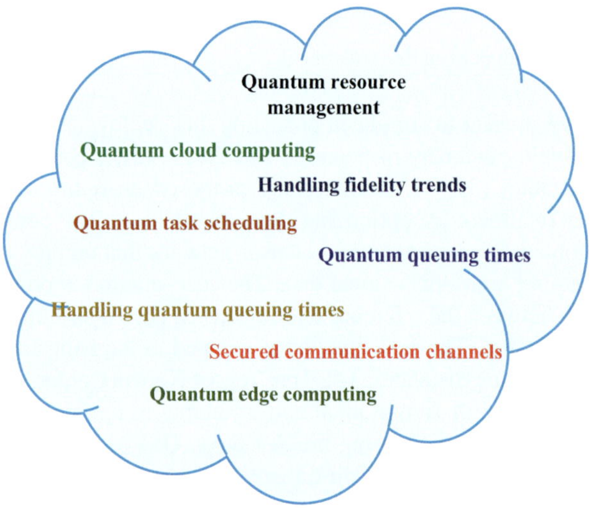

FIGURE 6.6 Quantum resource management.

A study proposed quantum Virtual Private Networks (QVPNs) for enabling secure communication channels over public quantum networks. QVPNs utilize the quantum concepts of entanglement and superposition for securing communication frameworks. The proposed centralized optimization framework allows coordination of resource allocation among multiple organizations with the same quantum network, such as genetic and machine learning algorithms for optimizing path selection and resource allocation [43]. In a parallel study of managing resources and scheduling circuits within distributed quantum computing (DQC), a multi-objective optimization algorithm is proposed. The quantum processing units (QPUs) are assigned to quantum circuits to maximize the number of successfully assigned QCirs by also minimizing errors due to latencies in communication, with a success

TABLE 6.4
Difference between Classical Resource Management and Quantum Resource Management

Classical Resource Management	Quantum Resource Management
It can handle algorithms based on logic states.	It can handle algorithms based on superposition and entanglement.
It cannot handle exponential complexity.	It can handle large-scale, complex issues.
It can be used only in classical hardware.	It is scalable in quantum hardware.
It can handle linearity and moderately complex data.	It can handle exponentially complex data.

rate improvement of 5.25% to 13.75%. Circuit scheduling and Mixed Integer Linear Programming (MILP) are developed to find a solution for the optimization issue and to control the resource allocation decisions [44]. A related study has proposed a Constrained Quantum Optimization Algorithm (CQOA) to enhance the efficiency of Resource Distribution Management Systems (RDMS) by improving the efficiency in parallel processing of data for smart decision-making and minimizing waste [45]. A tutorial on Variational Quantum Algorithms (VAQs) is employed to address the challenges in resource management of cloud and edge computing architectures. An Ising model is formed where Quantum Approximate Optimization Algorithm (QAOA) and Variational Quantum Eigensolver (VQE) are proposed to determine the ground state energy of quantum systems [46]. A recent study has proposed iQuantum, a simulation kit for building prototyping and reviewing system design and scheduling algorithms for quantum and hybrid quantum-classical environments. The toolkit employs Quantum Datacenters (QDatacenter) to identify physical locations, Quantum Computers (QNode) for processing quantum units, Quantum Tasks (QTask) to execute on hardware, and Quantum Broker (QBroker) to allocate tasks to quantum resources [47]. The difference between classical resource management and quantum resource management is presented in Table 6.4.

6.3.5 *In Silico* Clinical Trials with Quantum

Quantum computing finds its application in enhancing the execution of clinical trials for assessing the safety of new treatments and lessening the failure rates and lengthy timelines. Quantum computing has the potential in clinical model development, protocol design, and data management. The vast amount of clinical data, patient responses, and design of trials are the required areas of enhancement. A study proposed quantum optimization and QML algorithms to simulate test cases and enable researchers to determine the best designs and selection processes for trial sites without an issue of bias [48]. A recent study proposed a novel hybrid quantum computing pipeline algorithm by integrating quantum computing into the procedure for drug discovery. The algorithm addresses the criticality of determining Gibbs free energy profiles and simulating covalent bond interactions. The Variational Quantum Eigensolver (VQE) framework was proposed to handle parameterized quantum circuits and classical

6.5 ROADMAP TOWARDS QUANTUM COMPUTING

A roadmap to create and apply quantum solutions is discussed for long-term success and alignment with societal needs. Strategic planning is required to create a significant impact on the healthcare, finance, energy, logistics, and climatic science industries. Funding from the government and private sectors will advance quantum research, infrastructure, and skill development. Multidisciplinary collaboration between physicists, mathematicians, materials scientists, and engineers is essential for designing and improving qubits, cooling systems, and error correction mechanisms. Ethicists and sociologists should come up with quantum solutions. Reskilling and upskilling will improve the quantum projects. Collaboration with national quantum initiatives and the European quantum flagship promotes strategic planning and collaboration. Interdisciplinary research can be fostered by organizations such as QuTech (The Netherlands) and the Institute for Quantum Computing (IQC, Canada). Strategic planning and multidisciplinary collaboration are essential in advancing smart quantum solutions. The technical, ethical, and regulatory challenges can be overcome by aligning goals, pooling resources, and fostering cooperation across disciplines.

6.6 CONCLUSION

Quantum computing possesses the ability to transform healthcare by addressing challenges that surpass the abilities of classical computing. From QML, quantum biosensors and diagnostics, personalized medicine, quantum resource management, and *In Silico* Clinical Trials with Quantum for accelerating the field of healthcare and enhancing medical images, and simulating biological systems, quantum technologies upgrade the current healthcare scenario. As quantum computing is a new field of research, the advantages require overcoming technical, ethical, and accessibility challenges. Multidisciplinary collaboration is required for advancing quantum computing in healthcare. This can be achieved with strategic investment, multidisciplinary collaboration, and a commitment to ethical guidelines, unlocking transformative solutions, driving innovation, and delivering accurate, efficient, and inclusive healthcare solutions globally. Nevertheless, as technology progresses, it offers the promise of shaping a better future in healthcare with advancements and accessibility to all.

REFERENCES

1. Dilmegani, Cem. "Quantum computing statistics: Forecasts & facts [2021]." *Research.aimultiple.com*, 5 Nov. 2020, https://research.aimultiple.com/quantum-computing-stats/
2. Durant, Thomas J.S., Elizabeth Knight, Brent Nelson, Sarah Dudgeon, Seung J. Lee, Dominic Walliman, Hobart P. Young, Lucila Ohno-Machado, and Wade L. Schulz. "A primer for quantum computing and its applications to healthcare and biomedical research." *Journal of the American Medical Informatics Association* 31, no. 8 (2024): 1774–1784.
3. Flöther, Frederik F. "The state of quantum computing applications in health and medicine." *Research Directions: Quantum Technologies* 1 (2023): e10.
4. Biamonte, Jacob, Peter Wittek, Nicola Pancotti, Patrick Rebentrost, Nathan Wiebe, and Seth Lloyd. "Quantum machine learning." *Nature* 549, no. 7671 (2017): 195–202.

5. Biamonte, Jacob, Peter Wittek, Nicola Pancotti, Patrick Rebentrost, Nathan Wiebe, and Seth Lloyd. "Quantum machine learning." *Nature* 549, no. 7671 (2017): 195–202.
6. Ur Rasool, Raihan, Hafiz Farooq Ahmad, Wajid Rafique, Adnan Qayyum, Junaid Qadir, and Zahid Anwar. "Quantum computing for healthcare: A review." *Future Internet* 15, no. 3 (2023): 94.
7. Jeyaraman, Naveen, Madhan Jeyaraman, Sankalp Yadav, Swaminathan Ramasubramanian, and Sangeetha Balaji. "Revolutionizing healthcare: the emerging role of quantum computing in enhancing medical technology and treatment." *Cureus* 16, no. 8 (2024): 1–16.
8. United Nations. "Goal 3: Good Health and Well-Being." *The Global Goals*, 2022, www.globalgoals.org/goals/3-good-health-and-well-being
9. Ryan-Anderson, Ciarán. "Quantum algorithms, architecture, and error correction." PhD diss., The University of New Mexico, 2018.
10. Maronese, Marco, et al. "Quantum Compiling." ArXiv.org, 30 Nov. 2021, arXiv preprint arXiv: 2112.00187.
11. Geck, Lotte, Andre Kruth, Hendrik Bluhm, Stefan van Waasen, and Stefan Heinen. "Control electronics for semiconductor spin qubits." *Quantum Science and Technology* 5, no. 1 (2019): 015004.
12. Priyadarshan, Prasuryya, et al. Quantum Computing-A Review. *JASC: Journal of Applied Science and Computations* 5, no. 7 (13 Dec. 2018): 501–504, www.researchgate.net/publication/329609678_Quantum_Computing-A_Review
13. Chen, Menghan, Chaohua Yu, Gongde Guo, and Song Lin. "Faster quantum ridge regression algorithm for prediction." *International Journal of Machine Learning and Cybernetics* 14, no. 1 (2023): 117–124.
14. Shams, Muhammad, Jinal Choudhari, Katherine Reyes, Sophia Prentzas, Abubakar Gapizov, Abdullah Shehryar, Maryam Affaf et al. "The quantum-medical nexus: Understanding the impact of quantum technologies on healthcare." *Cureus* 15, no. 10 (2023): 1–15.
15. "What Can Quantum Computing Do to Healthcare? - the Medical Futurist." The Medical Futurist, 31 Oct. 2019, https://medicalfuturist.com/quantum-computing-in-healthcare
16. Clinic, Cleveland. "How quantum computing can advance medical research." Cleveland Clinic, Cleveland Clinic, 20 Mar. 2023, https://newsroom.clevelandclinic.org/2023/03/20/how-quantum-computing-can-advance-medical-research
17. Solenov, Dmitry, Jay Brieler, and Jeffrey F. Scherrer. "The potential of quantum computing and machine learning to advance clinical research and change the practice of medicine." *Missouri Medicine* 115, no. 5 (2018): 463.
18. Padalhin, Andrew, Phil-Sang Chung, and Seung Hoon Woo. "Quantum technology: a beacon of light for next-generation healthcare." *Medical Lasers; Engineering, Basic Research, and Clinical Application* 12, no. 4 (2023): 212–219.
19. Singh, Navneet, and Shiva Raj Pokhrel. "An independent implementation of quantum machine learning algorithms in qiskit for genomic data." arXiv preprint arXiv:2405.09781 (2024).
20. Park, Jae-Eun, Brian Quanz, Steve Wood, Heather Higgins, and Ray Harishankar. "Practical application improvement to Quantum SVM: theory to practice." arXiv preprint arXiv:2012.07725 (2020).
21. Gupta, Himanshu, Hirdesh Varshney, Tarun Kumar Sharma, Nikhil Pachauri, and Om Prakash Verma. "Comparative performance analysis of quantum machine learning with deep learning for diabetes prediction." *Complex & Intelligent Systems* 8, no. 4 (2022): 3073–3087.
22. Sierra-Sosa, Daniel, Juan D. Arcila-Moreno, Begonya Garcia-Zapirain, and Adel Elmaghraby. "Diabetes Type 2: Poincaré Data Preprocessing for Quantum Machine Learning." *Computers, Materials & Continua* 67, no. 2 (2021): 1–8.

23. Yue, Chi, Liu Xin, Xia Kewen, and Su Chang. "An intelligent diagnosis to type 2 diabetes based on QPSO algorithm and WLS-SVM." In *2008 International Symposium on Intelligent Information Technology Application Workshops*, pp. 117–121. IEEE, 2008.
24. Maheshwari, Danyal, Begona Garcia-Zapirain, and Daniel Sierra-Soso. "Machine learning applied to diabetes dataset using Quantum versus Classical computation." In *2020 IEEE International Symposium on Signal Processing and Information Technology (ISSPIT)*, pp. 1–6. IEEE, 2020.
25. Jain, Siddhant, Jalal Ziauddin, Paul Leonchyk, Shashibushan Yenkanchi, and Joseph Geraci. "Quantum and classical machine learning for the classification of non-small-cell lung cancer patients." *SN Applied Sciences* 2, no. 6 (2020): 1088.
26. Das, Suparna, Hirak Mazumdar, Kamil Reza Khondakar, Yogendra Kumar Mishra, and Ajeet Kaushik. "Quantum biosensors: principles and applications in medical diagnostics." *ECS Sensors Plus* 3, no. 2 (2024): 025001.
27. Chugh, Vibhas, Adreeja Basu, Ajeet Kaushik, and Aviru Kumar Basu. "Progression in quantum sensing/bio-sensing technologies for healthcare." *ECS Sensors Plus* 2, no. 1 (2023): 015001.
28. Aslam, Nabeel, Hengyun Zhou, Elana K. Urbach, Matthew J. Turner, Ronald L. Walsworth, Mikhail D. Lukin, and Hongkun Park. "Quantum sensors for biomedical applications." *Nature Reviews Physics* 5, no. 3 (2023): 157–169.
29. Gauglitz, Günter. "The new generation: quantum sensors." *Analytical and Bioanalytical Chemistry* 413, no. 23 (2021): 5679–5680.
30. Chugh, Vibhas, Adreeja Basu, Nagendra Kumar Kaushik, Ajeet Kaushik, Yogendra Kumar Mishra, and Aviru Kumar Basu. "Smart nanomaterials to support quantum-sensing electronics." *Materials Today Electronics* 6 (2023): 100067.
31. Kamarchuk, G., A. Pospelov, L. Kamarchuk, V. Belan, A. Herus, A. Savytskyi, V. Vakula, D. Harbuz, V. Gudimenko, and E. Faulques. "Quantum mechanisms for selective detection in complex gas mixtures using conductive sensors." *Scientific Reports* 13, no. 1 (2023): 21432.
32. Oukaira, Aziz, Ouafaa Ettahri, and Ahmed Lakhssassi. "Advancing quantum temperature sensors for ultra-precise measurements (UPMs): a comparative study." *Electronics* 13, no. 18 (2024): 3715.
33. Tao, Yanbing, Yunong Zhao, Le Wang, Jing Huang, Yan Chen, Qing Huang, Boxiang Song, Hua-Yao Li, Jianjun Chen, and Huan Liu. "Flexible amperometric immunosensor based on colloidal quantum dots for detecting the myeloperoxidase (MPO) systemic inflammation biomarker." *Biosensors* 13, no. 2 (2023): 255.
34. Fan, S., L. Nie, Y. Zhang, E. Ustyantseva, W. Woudstra, H. H. Kampinga, and R. Schirhagl. "Diamond quantum sensing revealing the relation between free radicals and huntington's disease." *ACS central science* 9, no. 7 (2023): 1427–1436.
35. Jeyaraman, Naveen, Madhan Jeyaraman, Sankalp Yadav, Swaminathan Ramasubramanian, and Sangeetha Balaji. "Revolutionizing healthcare: the emerging role of quantum computing in enhancing medical technology and treatment." *Cureus* 16, no. 8 (2024): 1–16.
36. Sharma, Muskan, Yash Mahajan, and Abdullah Alzahrani. "Personalized medicine through quantum computing: Tailoring treatments in healthcare." In *Quantum Innovations at the Nexus of Biomedical Intelligence*, pp. 147–166. IGI Global Scientific Publishing, 2024.
37. Kösoglu-Kind, Büsra, Robert Loredo, Michele Grossi, Christian Bernecker, Jody M. Burks, and Rüdiger Buchkremer. "A biological sequence comparison algorithm using quantum computers." *Scientific Reports* 13, no. 1 (2023): 14552.
38. Pakela, Julia M., Huan-Hsin Tseng, Martha M. Matuszak, Randall K. Ten Haken, Daniel L. McShan, and Issam El Naqa. "Quantum-inspired algorithm for radiotherapy planning optimization." *Medical Physics* 47, no. 1 (2020): 5–18.

39. Cavinato, Samuele, Timo Felser, Marco Fusella, Marta Paiusco, and Simone Montangero. "Optimizing radiotherapy plans for cancer treatment with tensor networks." *Physics in Medicine & Biology* 66, no. 12 (2021): 125015.
40. Vashisth, Shubham, Ishika Dhall, and Garima Aggarwal. "Design and analysis of quantum powered support vector machines for malignant breast cancer diagnosis." *Journal of Intelligent Systems* 30, no. 1 (2021): 998–1013.
41. Cloud, Quantum. "EPiQC." *EPiQC*, 2014, www.epiqc.cs.uchicago.edu/quantum-cloud-resource-management. Accessed 19 Dec. 2024.
42. Pouryousef, Shahrooz, Nitish K. Panigrahy, Monimoy Deb Purkayastha, Sabyasachi Mukhopadhyay, Gert Grammel, Domenico Di Mola, and Don Towsley. "Resource Management in Quantum Virtual Private Networks." In *2023 IEEE International Conference on Quantum Computing and Engineering (QCE)*, vol. 2, pp. 393–394. IEEE, 2023.
43. Bahrani, Sima, Romerson D. Oliveira, Juan Marcelo Parra-Ullauri, Rui Wang, and Dimitra Simeonidou. "Resource management and circuit scheduling for distributed quantum computing interconnect networks." arXiv preprint arXiv:2409.12675 (2024).
44. El Gaily, Sara, and Sándor Imre. "Quantum optimization in large resource management systems." In *2019 IEEE 20th International Workshop on Signal Processing Advances in Wireless Communications (SPAWC)*, pp. 1–5. IEEE, 2019.
45. Mastroianni, Carlo, and Andrea Vinci. "Tutorial on Variational Quantum Algorithms for Resource Management in Cloud/Edge Architectures." In *Proceedings of the 33rd International Symposium on High-Performance Parallel and Distributed Computing*, pp. 350–351. 2024.
46. Nguyen, Hoa T., Muhammad Usman, and Rajkumar Buyya. "iQuantum: A case for modeling and simulation of quantum computing environments." In *2023 IEEE International Conference on Quantum Software (QSW)*, pp. 21–30. IEEE, 2023.
47. Doga, Hakan, Aritra Bose, M. Emre Sahin, Joao Bettencourt-Silva, Anh Pham, Eunyoung Kim, Alan Andress et al. "How can quantum computing be applied in clinical trial design and optimization?." *Trends in Pharmacological Sciences* 45, no. 10 (2024): 880–891.
48. Li, Weitang, Zhi Yin, Xiaoran Li, Dongqiang Ma, Shuang Yi, Zhenxing Zhang, Chenji Zou et al. "A hybrid quantum computing pipeline for real world drug discovery." *Scientific Reports* 14, no. 1 (2024): 16942.
49. Gupta, Shivam, Sachin Modgil, Priyanka C. Bhatt, Charbel Jose Chiappetta Jabbour, and Sachin Kamble. "Quantum computing led innovation for achieving a more sustainable Covid-19 healthcare industry." *Technovation* 120 (2023): 102544.

This superposition allows quantum computers to represent and process a combination of many classical states concurrently.

Entanglement is another important quantum feature. This is when qubits become physically separated but become dependent on each other, so that the state of one qubit instantly changes the state of another. Quantum connections, which are needed for powerful computing jobs, cannot be made without this interconnectivity.

7.2.2 Quantum Gates and Circuits

- Quantum processes are done by putting qubits through a series of operations called quantum gates. These gates change the states of qubits using unitary transformations that can be undone. They are similar to classical logic gates in a quantum way [15].

Some common single-qubit gates are:

- **Pauli-X gate**: This flips the qubit state, analogous to classical NOT.
- **Hadamard gate (H)**: This creates superposition by transforming basis states into equal probability states.
- **Phase shift gates**: These modify the relative phase between quantum states, crucial for interference effects.

Multi-qubit gates, such as the **CNOT (Controlled NOT)** gate, introduce entanglement by conditionally flipping the state of a target qubit based on the control qubit's state. Quantum circuits that run complex quantum algorithms can be constructed by placing these gates together in ordered patterns.

7.2.3 Quantum Algorithms

Quantum algorithms use superposition, entanglement, and interference to get better results than traditional algorithms at solving certain types of problems. One well-known example is Shor's Algorithm, which efficiently factors big numbers and poses a challenge to traditional encryption.

- Grover's Algorithm: It makes unorganized search problems four times faster.

VQE stands for variational quantum eigensolver. A mixed classical and quantum method for estimating molecular ground states is very useful for finding new drugs.

These methods show how quantum computers can be used for optimization, simulation, and search tasks that are important in healthcare, similar to molecule modeling and finding patterns in medical data.

7.2.4 Quantum Decoherence and Error Correction

When qubits interact with their surroundings, they lose their quantum behavior. This is called quantum decoherence, and it is one of the biggest technical problems in quantum computers. When decoherence occurs, the delicate superposition and entanglement states break down into classical mixtures. This leads to mistakes and the loss of information.

The no-cloning theorem says that qubits cannot be copied or measured without changing their states. This is different from classical bits. So, regular ways of finding errors are not good enough; you need special quantum error repair techniques to make quantum computing work well.

Quantum error correction methods use linked states to turn logical qubits into multiple physical qubits. This lets mistakes be found and fixed without directly measuring the quantum information. Some examples are the Shor code, the Steane code, and the surface code. These are all important for making quantum computers that can handle errors and do long, complex calculations [16].

7.2.5 Summary of Quantum Computational Power and Challenges

- Quantum computing is very powerful because it can store and handle data in exponentially large Hilbert spaces using superposition and entanglement. This lets many processing paths be explored at the same time. This feature is especially useful for healthcare issues that involve big combinatorial search spaces or complex molecular models [17].

  Still, there are big problems with putting it into practice:

- **Qubit Quality**: Maintaining coherence and minimizing noise is critical but remains technologically challenging.
- **Scalability**: Increasing the number of qubits while preserving entanglement and error rates is nontrivial.
- **Algorithm Development**: Designing efficient quantum algorithms tailored to healthcare data and problems requires multidisciplinary collaboration.

Addressing these challenges is essential for harnessing the full potential of quantum computing in healthcare, paving the way for more accurate simulations, faster optimizations, and breakthroughs in personalized medicine and diagnostics.

7.3 HEALTHCARE DATA AND COMPUTATIONAL CHALLENGES

The healthcare industry creates a huge number of different types of data that keeps growing. These dataset include genetic sequences, medical imaging results, EHRs, and extensive information on clinical trials. Existing classical computing systems find it hard to process, analyze, and come up with useful insights in time frames that are clinically important [16, 18, 19]. This is because each type has its own features and computational needs.

7.3.1 Types of Healthcare Data

- **Genomic Data**: Since high-throughput sequencing methods came out, a lot of genomic datasets have been created. These include whole-genome sequences, transcriptomics, epigenomic profiles, and multi-omics data. These datasets are typically high-dimensional, comprising billions of base pairs and complex interactions across genetic loci. Their scale and intricacy require powerful computational frameworks for alignment, variant calling, functional annotation, and integrative analysis.
- **Medical Imaging**: MRI, computed tomography (CT), positron emission tomography (PET), and ultrasound are all types of diagnostic imaging that give clear, detailed pictures. These images often exist as multidimensional arrays (two dimensional; [2D], 3D, or 4D across time). Medical imaging data are large in volume and are further complicated by noise, artifacts, and heterogeneity among scanners and protocols, posing challenges for storage, processing speed, and accurate image reconstruction.
- **EHRs**: EHRs encapsulate a comprehensive range of patient data, including demographic details, clinical notes, lab results, medication histories, vital signs, and procedural information. This data are highly heterogeneous, structured, semi-structured, and unstructured, and often fragmented across healthcare providers. The variability in data quality, standardization, and completeness complicates longitudinal patient modeling and predictive analytics.
- **Clinical Trial Datasets**: Clinical research generates specialized datasets tracking treatment protocols, patient responses, adverse events, and biomarker measurements over time. Clinical trial data are often longitudinal and involve multi-center data integration. Making sure data are correct, harmonizing them, and handling different forms all add to the complexity of computing.

7.3.2 Problems with Computing with Healthcare Data

Classical computing systems face a lot of tough problems when dealing with the aforementioned data types. These problems are mostly caused by the large amount of data, its complexity, its variety, and the need for fast, accurate research to help doctors make decisions.

7.3.2.1 Data Volume and Storage

The amount of healthcare data are growing very quickly, thanks to improvements in processing speed and image quality. A single whole-genome sequence, for example, has around 200 gigabytes of raw data, and high-resolution image studies can make many gigabytes per scan. Petabyte-scale datasets are created by combining data from big groups or ongoing studies. These datasets need large storage space and fast ways to get the data they contain.

7.3.2.2 Data Heterogeneity and Integration

Multiple data types and models make it difficult to integrate data without. The bioinformatics file formats used for genomic data are FASTQ or VCF files, the Digital Imaging and Communications in Medicine (DICOM) standards are used for image data, and EHRs combine both coded data and free-text clinical reports. For these different types of data to be analyzed together, classical computer systems must performs extensive cleaning and normalization work, which can cause information loss or introduce errors.

7.3.2.3 Complex Data Structures and High Dimensionality

A lot of healthcare records have complex structures and naturally high dimensions, which makes it harder to create algorithms. There are complex networks of gene–gene and gene–environment interactions in genomic data. Imaging data has relationships in both space and time, and EHRs show patient paths over time with random sampling. Classical analytical models often have trouble capturing these complex interdependencies without making assumptions that are too simple [20].

7.3.2.4 Computational Speed and Efficiency

In hospital settings, where quick action can change outcomes, handling data quickly and efficiently is crucial. However, classical computer systems often need a long time to process jobs, such as molecular models, high-resolution picture reconstructions, or large-scale prediction modeling, which limits how useful they are in medicine. As the amount of data gets more complex, standard methods become less scalable, which causes problems.

7.3.2.5 Handling Noise, Uncertainty, and Missing Data

There is a lot of noise, measurement errors, and missing values in clinical data, which makes it less reliable for later studies. Traditional computer methods have trouble to reliably combine noisy, diverse sources while keeping sensitivity and precision. They usually need to be manually curated, or estimation strategies are used over and over again.

7.3.3 Implications for the Development of Quantum Solutions and Classical Computing

These complex issues suggest that traditional healthcare computer frameworks are severely limited. Large-scale heterogeneous data and the exponential growth of biological complexity frequently make classical algorithms ineffective or even unfeasible for some computational tasks, especially those involving combinatorial optimization, nonlinear modeling, or high-fidelity molecular simulations.

One intriguing paradigm to overcome these constraints is quantum computing. Quantum computers offer the ability to improve modeling quality, speed up data processing, and more naturally handle complicated, high-dimensional data by taking advantage of quantum parallelism and special algorithmic characteristics. For instance, quantum algorithms could execute optimization and search operations with exponential speedups, which would allow for the effective investigation of large molecular conformations or patient stratification situations. As a result, a thorough understanding of the unique data properties and computational constraints in the healthcare industry forms the basis for the creation of focused quantum algorithms meant to address the core issues faced by conventional systems [21].

7.4 APPLICATIONS OF QUANTUM COMPUTING IN HEALTHCARE

Quantum computing has the potential to revolutionize several aspects of the healthcare industry by providing new ways to address issues that are now beyond the capabilities of even the most formidable conventional computers. Superposition, entanglement, and quantum tunneling effects are only a few of the special powers of quantum computers that open up new possibilities for machine learning, modeling, and optimization that are very pertinent to both clinical and biological research. This section explores specific applications, showing how quantum computing might provide substantial benefits in fields ranging from the logistical challenges of healthcare delivery to the basic science of drug development.

7.4.1 Drug Development

The promise of quantum computing to transform medication research and discovery is among its most eagerly awaited uses in healthcare.

Finding, creating, and testing novel pharmaceutical compounds is a famously difficult, expensive, and time-consuming process; it sometimes takes more than 10 years and billions of dollars to produce a single effective treatment. Accurately simulating molecular systems and their interactions at the quantum mechanical level is a significant obstacle. When trying to represent molecules with more than a few dozen atoms, the enormous number of conceivable electrical configurations presents an exponential scaling barrier for classical computers. Simulating quantum mechanical systems, such as molecules, is a natural application for quantum computers.

More accurate and efficient algorithms than traditional approaches are being developed to compute molecular ground state energies and other parameters, such as the VQE and Quantum Phase Estimation (QPE). The energy of the ground state is $E_0 = \theta_{min}\langle\psi(\theta)|H|\psi(\theta)\rangle$. Determining these energies precisely is essential for evaluating binding affinities, forecasting molecule stability, and comprehending chemical processes.

Among the specific uses in drug discovery are:

- **Molecular Simulation**: Simulating the electronic structure and dynamics of molecules and proteins to understand their behavior, predict reactivity, and design novel compounds. Reaction pathways and transition states that are not accessible via classical means may be revealed using quantum simulation.
- Predicting the degree to which a possible therapeutic molecule will attach to a target protein or enzyme is known as drug docking and binding affinity prediction. This is a challenging optimization task that entails investigating a wide range of potential conformations and interaction energies. Quantum algorithms have the ability to speed up this search and increase the precision of binding energy estimations when paired with conventional methods in hybrid approaches.
- **Quantum Machine Learning for Predicting Drug Properties**: Predicting traits such as toxicity, solubility, or effectiveness by analyzing vast datasets

of molecule structures and properties using quantum-enhanced machine learning techniques. Quantum neural networks or quantum kernels may be useful for spotting intricate patterns in chemical space.
- Lead optimization is the process of improving potential medication prospects according to desired characteristics. This involves complex multi-parameter optimization problems that could potentially be tackled by quantum optimization algorithms such as Quantum Approximate Optimization Algorithm (QAOA) or Quantum Annealing.

The quantum advantage in this domain stems from the ability to efficiently represent and manipulate the quantum states of electrons within molecules, a task that scales exponentially on classical systems but polynomially on a fault-tolerant quantum computer. While current noisy intermediate-scale quantum (NISQ) devices have limitations, they are already being explored for early stage simulations, providing valuable insights and driving algorithm development toward achieving quantum advantage [22].

7.4.2 Genomics Medicine

Genomics and personalized medicine rely heavily on analyzing vast amounts of genetic and biological data to understand disease susceptibility, predict treatment response, and tailor medical interventions to individual patients. Challenges include processing large-scale sequencing data, identifying complex genetic variations and their interactions, and integrating multi-omics data (genomics, transcriptomics, proteomics, etc.) to build comprehensive patient profiles.

Quantum computing can contribute to these areas through:

- **DNA Sequencing and Alignment**: Accelerating the process of aligning short DNA reads to a reference genome, which is a computationally intensive task. While classical algorithms are efficient, quantum algorithms similar to Grover's search could potentially offer quadratic speedups for specific search tasks within alignment or variant calling.
- Using quantum machine learning algorithms for tasks similar to variant categorization, illness association research, and finding genetic markers that predict treatment response is known as genomic data analysis. In high-dimensional genomic datasets, quantum algorithms could be more capable of identifying minute patterns and correlations. For example, genetic data might be classified and its dimensionality reduced using quantum principal component analysis (QPCA) or quantum support vector machines (QSVMs).
- **Population Genomics and Ancestry Analysis**: Examining big datasets at the population level to comprehend illness prevalence, migration trends, and genetic diversity. Novel approaches to examining these intricate interactions may be offered by quantum algorithms for correlation or grouping.
- **Personalized Treatment Prediction**: Using clinical data and a patient's unique genetic composition, quantum-enhanced models are being developed to forecast how the patient will react to various treatments. This

includes intricate regression and classification issues that could benefit from quantum machine learning or optimization methods to choose the best course of action.

- Drug repurposing is the process of finding current medications that may be useful for novel indications by analyzing molecular databases and disease pathways using quantum algorithms. This entails scouring and contrasting enormous biological and chemical areas.

The ability to rapidly analyze and identify patterns in the vast combinatorial universe of genetic data is the potential quantum edge in genomics. Key analytical processes in genomics might be greatly accelerated by quantum machine learning and search and pattern recognition algorithms, opening the door to quicker and more precise understandings of disease causes and individualized treatment plans [23].

7.4.3 Medical Imaging Enhancement

A vital diagnostic tool, medical imaging generates high-resolution data that needs complex processing for analysis, interpretation, and reconstruction. Image segmentation (finding structures or abnormalities), image registration (aligning numerous pictures), noise reduction, and the extraction of useful characteristics for diagnosis are among the difficulties. Classical methods often involve computationally intensive algorithms and can be limited by processing time or the ability to handle complex noise patterns [24].

The following are some ways that quantum computing might improve medical imaging:

- Image Reconstruction: speeding up the difficult mathematical inverse problems that are required to recreate pictures from unprocessed sensor data (such as in MRI or CT scans). In certain reconstruction circumstances, quantum algorithms based on quantum Fourier transforms or other methods may provide speedups.
- Noise Reduction and Filtering: Creating quantum algorithms for signal processing and noise reduction that use quantum features to better separate signals from noise than traditional filters.
- Image Segmentation and Analysis: Using quantum optimization techniques or quantum machine learning for tasks such as quantitative feature analysis, tumor detection and classification, or automated organ segmentation. It may be possible to increase the precision and speed of recognizing intricate patterns in visual data using quantum algorithms. For instance, various tissue types might be segmented using quantum clustering techniques.

Optimizing the alignment of many photos taken at various times or using various modalities is known as image registration. This is a challenging optimization issue that may be solved more effectively by using quantum optimization methods to determine the ideal transformation parameters.

Managing and evaluating the ever-growing amount of medical image data is known as "processing large imaging datasets." Large-scale data processing jobs, such as identifying for comparable instances in massive picture databases, may be sped up using quantum algorithms. Faster algorithms for linear algebra operations that are essential to image processing, better **optimization** for tasks such as registration, and improved pattern recognition capabilities through quantum machine learning could all contribute to this quantum advantage, which would enable quicker and more precise image analysis and diagnosis [13].

7.4.4 Resource Allocation

Effective resource management is essential to providing healthcare. This includes preparing emergency responses, managing drug and equipment supply chains, scheduling patients and employees, and maximizing hospital capacity. These are often complex, large-scale optimization issues that may be difficult to effectively resolve using traditional computers, particularly when there are more variables and limitations.

Promising methods for solving these combinatorial optimization issues are provided by quantum computing:

- **Appointment Scheduling**: Making the most of patient appointments to reduce wait times and make the most use of available resources (e.g., equipment use and doctor availability).
- **Staff Rostering**: Creating optimal work schedules for doctors, nurses, and support staff, considering various constraints, such as skill sets, availability, and labor regulations.
- **Hospital Resource Management**: Optimizing the allocation of beds, operating rooms, and other limited resources to meet patient demand efficiently.
- **Supply Chain Optimization** is the process of controlling the logistics of the delivery of pharmaceuticals and medical supplies, including inventory control and distribution network optimization, to guarantee prompt availability and save expenses.
- **Emergency Response Planning**: Optimizing the deployment of resources, such as ambulances and medical personnel, during public health emergencies.
- **Facility Location Planning**: Determining optimal locations for new clinics or hospitals based on population needs and existing infrastructure [17].

These kinds of issues are very well-suited to quantum optimization methods, such as Quantum Annealing and QAOA. By embedding the issue into a quantum system and using quantum tunneling or annealing processes to explore the solution space—which may be represented by qubits, these algorithms seek to identify the optimal answer among a large number of potential outcomes. Early experiments on small-scale issues demonstrate the potential of quantum techniques to discover better answers or find solutions quicker than conventional heuristics, but gaining a meaningful quantum edge for big, real-world logistics challenges remains to be an open research challenge.

7.4.5 Disease Modeling

It takes advanced modeling and simulation to comprehend the intricate processes behind illnesses, from the molecular level to epidemics affecting whole populations. This involves modeling the transmission of infectious illnesses, simulating the behavior of proteins implicated in disease processes, and simulating the results of various therapies. To be manageable on traditional computers, these simulations sometimes depend on simplifying assumptions and might be computationally demanding.

Modeling and simulating diseases may be improved by quantum computing via:

- **Protein Folding and Dynamics**: Simulating the complex process by which proteins fold into their functional 3D structures. Many illnesses are associated with misinformation. Protein folding dynamics may be more accurately modeled by quantum simulation than by traditional techniques, providing information on disease processes and possible treatment targets.
- **Enzyme Activity Simulation**: Modeling the principles of catalysis by enzymes is essential for comprehending metabolic pathways and developing medications that block enzymes.
- **Modeling Biological Systems**: Simulating the behavior of larger biological systems, such as cellular processes or biochemical pathways. While highly complex, quantum techniques might offer ways to model certain key interactions or steps more accurately.
- **Epidemiological Modeling**: While large-scale population models are primarily classical, quantum approaches might potentially optimize parameters within complex models or simulate the interaction dynamics of infectious agents and host systems at a finer granularity.
- **Drug–Target Interaction Simulation**: Simulating the detailed quantum mechanical interactions between a drug molecule and its biological target, providing deeper insights than classical docking simulations [14].

The quantum advantage here is primarily in simulating the underlying quantum mechanical reality of biological molecules and interactions. While simulating entire complex biological systems is far beyond current capabilities, simulating key components or interactions with higher accuracy using quantum computers could provide critical inputs for larger, hybrid quantum–classical simulations, leading to a more fundamental understanding of disease processes.

7.4.6 Drug Discovery

Quantum computing has the potential to significantly accelerate drug discovery by enhancing molecular simulations and optimizing drug candidates more efficiently than classical approaches. Simulating the quantum behavior of molecules, including their electronic structures and chemical interactions, is a central challenge in pharmaceutical research. Classical methods suffer from exponential scaling as molecular complexity increases, limiting the accuracy and feasibility of modeling larger compounds and reaction mechanisms.

- Quantum algorithms, such as the VQE and Quantum Phase Estimation (QPE), are made to more accurately predict the ground state energies of molecules and model their electronic structures. VQE works well with NISQ devices because it uses both quantum processors and regular optimization to get closer and closer to the right answer over and over again.

  Because of these programs,
- **Accurate Molecular Simulation**: Capturing electron correlations and complex chemical environments at quantum accuracy, aiding in understanding reaction pathways and molecular stability.
- **Drug Candidate Optimization**: Exploring vast conformational spaces to identify molecular structures with optimal binding affinities and pharmacological profiles.
- **Binding Affinity Prediction**: Figuring out the interaction energies between drug molecules and target proteins to find the most hopeful compounds early in the development process.

In hybrid quantum–classical approaches, quantum processors are used to help traditional computers do jobs such as drug docking and property prediction using machine learning methods that are improved by quantum information. Figure 7.3 depicts quantum applications in drug discovery

Quantum computing provides a technique to get over traditional bottlenecks by effectively modeling quantum states of electrons inside molecules. This might reduce the time and expense of drug development while increasing the success rate of candidate selection.

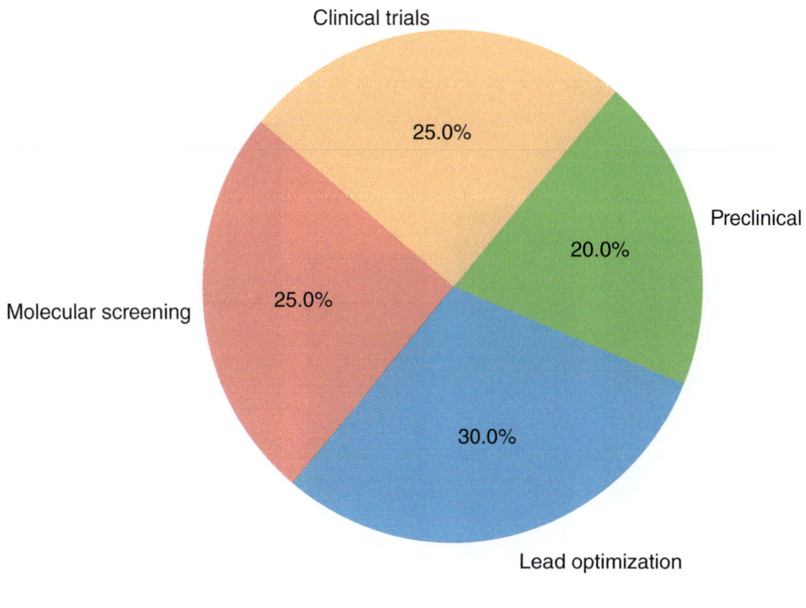

FIGURE 7.3 Quantum applications in drug discovery.

7.4.7 Personalized Medicine

Quantum computing could help genetics and personalized medicine move forward by making it easier to quickly analyze complex genetic data that is hard for regular computers to do. Genetic datasets are very big and have a lot of dimensions. They contain billions of base pairs and millions of variants for each genome. Finding DNA markers, knowing the effects of changes, and making personalized healthcare plans all depend on how well this data are analyzed.

Quantum algorithms can search and optimize in parallel across very large genetic search spaces by using superposition and entanglement. Grover's method, for instance, makes unstructured search problems four times faster, which could make it faster to find genetic differences that are linked to diseases or drug reactions. Quantum machine learning techniques such as QSVM and QPCA may also help with reducing the number of dimensions and classifying data, which makes it possible to find small trends in large collections of multiple omics.

Quantum-enhanced analytics can help choose the best treatment and figure out who is most likely to get a disease by quickly figuring out the complex relationships between genetic markers and changes. This feature helps personalized medicine by making it easier to accurately predict how a patient's treatment will work based on their genetic information. This leads to better plans for how to help them. Quantum computers could also make it easier to combine different types of biological data, such as genomes, transcriptomics, and proteomics, so that a full picture of each patient's biology can be created. This complete understanding helps create personalized treatment plans that take into account DNA traits, environmental factors, and the effectiveness of drugs [9]. Figure 7.4 describes quantum-accelerated genomic pattern recognition.

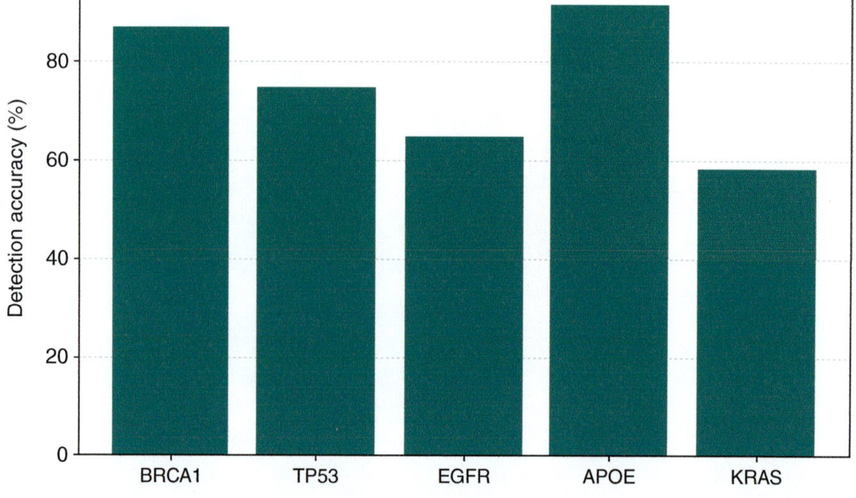

FIGURE 7.4 Quantum-accelerated genomic pattern recognition.

In real life, these benefits will only happen when quantum hardware and algorithms get better. However, the potential quantum speedups in genomic data processing mark the start of a new era for personalized healthcare, promising faster, more accurate genomic interpretation and better outcomes for patients.

7.4.8 Quantum-enhanced Optimization Methods

MRI and CT are two types of medical imaging that produce huge amounts of data that need to be processed using complex algorithms to rebuild images, get rid of noise, and identify features. Even though classical image algorithms work, they often have problems with processing speed and accuracy, especially when dealing with datasets that are noisy or complex. Quantum computing is a revolutionary method that uses quantum parallelism and new mathematical techniques to make it easier to process and understand medical pictures. One big benefit of quantum computing for medical images is that it might make it easier to spot patterns. Quantum machine learning algorithms can look at picture data with a lot of dimensions to find strange patterns and structures that regular methods might miss. For example, quantum filters and grouping algorithms could help with more accurate segmentation of body parts or the edges of tumor's, which would help with early and accurate diagnosis [11].

Getting rid of noise is another interesting use. Quantum algorithms that use quantum Fourier transforms and quantum filtering can better tell the difference between signal and noise in imaging data that is very complex.

These methods could improve diagnostic confidence by using quantum interference and entanglement to get rid of imaging artifacts and make the reconstructed pictures clearer.

Quantum-enhanced optimization methods are also good at solving the opposite problems that come up when reconstructing images. Quantum approximate optimization and other algorithms like it could speed up the process of solving big linear systems or the optimization jobs needed to turn raw sensor data into high-quality pictures. Figure 7.5 describes an enhanced medical image simulated by a heatmap.

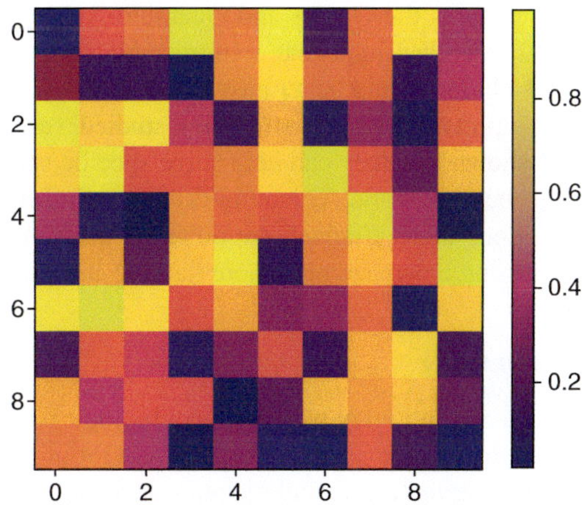

FIGURE 7.5 Enhanced medical image simulated by a heatmap.

All of these quantum-enhanced features promise faster processing times and better image quality, which will help doctors make more accurate diagnoses. As quantum hardware keeps getting better, combining these methods with current medical imaging workflows could make a big difference in diagnostic radiology and personalized patient care.

7.4.9 Optimization of Healthcare Logistics

The level of care for patients, the cost of running the business, and the happiness of the staff are all directly affected by how well planning and resource sharing work. Healthcare centers and hospitals have to create complex schedules for patients, professional staff, operating rooms, testing equipment, and supply lines. These problems get worse as the number and types of services given grow. This means that traditional optimization methods cannot keep up with the combinatorial complexity and changing limits. Quantum computing offers exciting new ways to solve these optimization problems by using quantum parallelism and special algorithms that are better at exploring large solution spaces than traditional methods. Some important areas of use are:

- **Scheduling Patients**: Quantum algorithms can find the best appointments to minimize wait times and make the best use of resources, taking into account things such as how urgent the case is, how long the treatment will last, and the patient's wishes.
- **Staff Allocation**: Making the best staff schedules that take into account labor rules, shift choices, and skill needs, which increases worker output and decreases stress.
- **Supply Chain Logistics**: Improving stocking levels, restart points, and delivery paths so that medicines, supplies, and important tools are always available while lowering costs and waste.
- **Facility Utilization**: Moving beds, operating rooms, and testing services around to accommodate new patients and medical needs while increasing output.

Quantum methods, such as the QAOA and Quantum Annealing, can turn these problems into cost functions that qubits can minimize by "tunneling" through local minima. This could lead to faster and better answers.

While full-scale quantum advantage is still being studied, early mixed quantum–classical models have shown that they can help solve specific scheduling and transportation problems in the real world. Quantum-driven optimization is on track to make healthcare operations more efficient, cut down on costs, and improve patient outcomes by making resource management more flexible and adaptable [17].

7.4.10 Disease Simulation

Quantum simulation is a revolutionary way to model biological systems and disease paths that are very complex. These systems often have a lot of dimensions, interactions that do not follow a straight line, and quantum-level chemical effects that are hard for regular computers to correctly show. The built-in ability of quantum computing to directly simulate quantum events means that researchers can more accurately

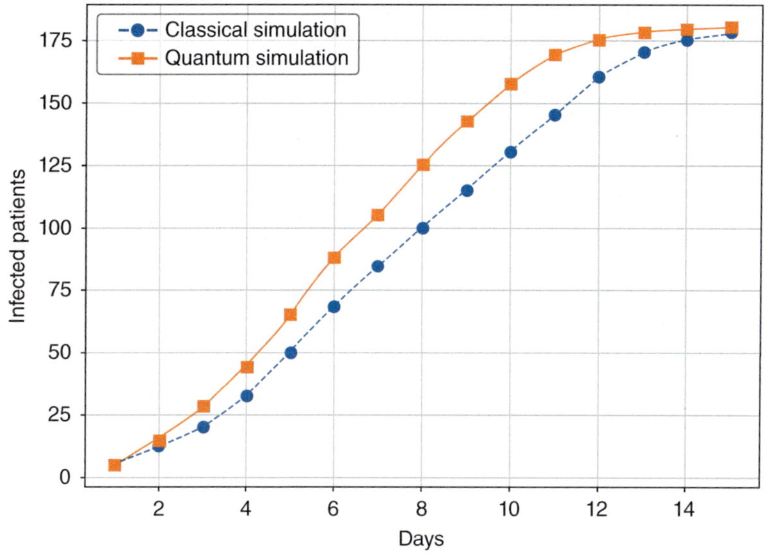

FIGURE 7.6 Disease spread simulation over time.

model complex processes, such as protein folding, enzyme catalysis, and molecular interactions, than with traditional methods. These studies help us learn more about how diseases progress, such as how misfolded proteins can lead to neurodegenerative diseases or how cancer cells can mess up signaling pathways. Quantum algorithms can detect small dynamic changes and entanglement effects in proteins that can lead to unstable states. This gives us a more complete picture of how living things work.

Furthermore, quantum-enhanced models make it easier to test drug–target interactions in the computer by modeling quantum-level binding events. This makes it possible to more accurately predict both treatment effectiveness and off-target effects. This feature helps make personalized treatments by taking into account differences in molecules and complex reactions in the body as a whole. Beyond the level of molecules, mixed quantum–classical frameworks may help optimize parameters in epidemic models. Figure 7.6 describes disease spread simulation over time.

This would allow for more detailed simulations of how infectious diseases spread and change when different types of interventions are used. Because of this, quantum simulation has the potential to make disease prediction models much better and speed up the process of turning molecular insights into clinical uses.

7.5 CHALLENGES AND LIMITATIONS OF QUANTUM COMPUTING IN HEALTHCARE

Even though quantum computing has the ability to completely change the healthcare field, there are a lot of big problems that are making it hard for it to become widely used. To get the most out of quantum computing in healthcare, all of these problems must be solved, including those that are scientific, practical, moral, and governmental. This part takes a thorough look at the main problems that are stopping quantum computing from being used in healthcare right now.

7.5.1 Technological Challenges

7.5.1.1 Hardware Limitations and Scalability

Quantum computer hardware is still in its early stages of development, and there are big limits on the quality, number, and coherence times of qubits. The quantum devices we have now are called NISQ systems. They only have a few hundred qubits, make a lot of mistakes, and do not stay coherent for long. Maintaining and expanding a lot of high-fidelity qubits is a huge technical challenge because

- **Decoherence**: Environmental interactions cause qubits to lose their quantum states rapidly, limiting computation lengths and complexity.
- **Qubit Connectivity and Crosstalk**: It's hard to keep many qubits entangled and ensure stable gate operations because of interference and limitations in the physical layout.
- **Rates of Error**: Quantum gates and qubit readings have a much higher rate of mistakes than regular computers, so they need complex ways to reduce them.
- **Different Types of Hardware**: There are many types of hardware platforms, such as superconducting qubits, trapped ions, and photonic qubits. Each has its own pros and cons, which makes standardization harder.

Because of this, the complexity of quantum algorithms that can be consistently run is limited, which in turn limits the range of useful healthcare applications.

7.5.1.2 Quantum Error Correction (QEC) and Fault Tolerance

Quantum error correction (QEC) is a key part of fault-tolerant quantum computing that makes computations secure even when hardware is not working right, or the data are not coherent. But the way QEC is currently set up, a single logical qubit has to be encoded into hundreds or thousands of physical qubits, which is too big for the gear we have now. The extra work that goes into running gates and using qubit resources:

- Drastically increases hardware complexity and operational demands.
- Extends computational time, potentially exceeding qubit coherence windows.

Until advances produce scalable fault-tolerant quantum computers, many healthcare-related quantum simulations and algorithms will remain theoretical or limited to simplified models.

7.5.2 Practical Implementation Challenges

7.5.2.1 Integration with Existing Healthcare Infrastructure

Incorporating quantum computing systems into existing healthcare workflows presents significant integration challenges. Healthcare environments rely heavily on established EHR systems, clinical decision support tools, and imaging platforms, which are designed around classical computing paradigms. Key issues include the following:

- **Data Interoperability**: Translating and mapping classical healthcare data formats (e.g., DICOM and HL7) into quantum-compatible representations requires sophisticated encoding methods.
- **Hybrid Computing Architectures**: Near-term quantum applications will likely operate as accelerators linked to classical systems, necessitating seamless communication layers and middleware.
- **Latency and Throughput**: At the moment, quantum devices work on timescales and access methods that might not be able to meet the needs of real-time clinical applications. For integration to work well, new software tools, standards, and close cooperation between quantum engineers and healthcare IT experts [14] will be needed.

7.5.2.2 Data Security and Privacy Concerns

Healthcare data are very private and is protected by strong privacy laws (such as HIPAA and GDPR), so it must be kept secret at all times. Using quantum computing brings up a lot of complex security issues:

- **Risks of Data Transmission**: Sending patient data to quantum computing services, especially cloud-based ones, creates security holes that need to be fixed with strong protection.
- **Implications for Cryptography**: Quantum computing poses a threat to standard cryptographic schemes, which could weaken current data security measures until new solutions that are not affected by quantum computing are fully implemented.
- **Quantum Cryptography**: Quantum key distribution (QKD) offers better security, but it is still in the testing phase and is hard to combine with healthcare systems.

Finding the right balance between quantum computing's benefits and strict privacy protections is one of the biggest problems with putting it into practice.

7.5.2.3 Regulatory and Compliance Challenges

Healthcare technologies are closely watched by regulators to make sure they are secure and effective for patients. Because quantum computing is so new, there are questions about the following:

- **Validation**: Demonstrating that quantum-augmented analytics or simulations produce clinically valid, reproducible results is non-trivial, requiring new testing frameworks.
- **Standardization**: Lack of established guidelines or standards for quantum healthcare applications complicates regulatory approval processes.
- **Liability and Accountability**: Determining responsibility in cases where quantum-based clinical decisions contribute to treatment outcomes poses ethical and legal questions.

Regulatory agencies will need to evolve policies and assessment methodologies tailored to quantum-enabled healthcare tools before widespread clinical adoption [12].

7.5.3 Human Capital and Knowledge Gaps

Quantum computing in healthcare requires knowledge from many fields, including quantum physics, computer science, biology, and clinical fields. There is a significant shortage of workers with a mixed subject understanding right now. Some specific problems are as follows:

- **Workforce Scarcity**: Few researchers and practitioners possess sufficient expertise in both quantum technologies and biomedical sciences to drive applied innovation.
- **Barriers in Education**: there are not many training programs that combine quantum computing with healthcare uses, which slows the growth of skilled talent pools.
- **The Difficulty of Working Together**: For crossover research to be useful, it needs teams from different fields to work together and communicate using different science languages and ways of thinking.

To close these gaps, we need to improve training programs, build joint study networks, and encourage relationships between businesses and universities.

7.5.4 Ethical and Societal Challenges

Besides technical and legal issues, using quantum computing in healthcare has big social issues that need to be dealt with right away:

- **Bias and Fairness**: Quantum algorithms that are trained on healthcare data that is biased run the risk of making treatment results even less equal or more unequal.
- **Transparency and Explainability**: Quantum algorithms can be difficult to understand because they are complex and based on probabilities, which can make it harder for patients to trust and accept them.
- **Access for Everyone**: Due to high prices and technology requirements, quantum-enhanced healthcare advances may only be used in places with lots of resources. This could worsen global health disparities.
- **Told Consent**: Patients need to be fully told about how quantum-assisted decision-making will affect their care. This will require new ways of talking to them.

To make sure that quantum healthcare technologies are developed and used responsibly, we need ethical frameworks and control models that are specifically made for them [13].

7.6 FUTURE PERSPECTIVES AND TRENDS

The next 10 years will see a lot of progress and maturity in the field of quantum computing, especially when it comes to healthcare. It is believed that as quantum technologies improve, they will interact more deeply with artificial intelligence (AI) and traditional computer models, building frameworks that use the best parts of both. This part discusses the expected changes in quantum technology, new algorithms, integrating structures, regulatory ecosystems, and game-changing medical uses that will shape the future.

7.6.1 Advancements in Quantum Hardware

Sustained progress in quantum hardware is core to unlocking practical quantum advantage in healthcare. Current NISQ devices, while valuable for algorithm testing and early experiments, are limited by qubit counts, noise levels, and coherence times. Future generations of quantum processors are expected to deliver:

- **Increased Qubit Numbers**: Scalable quantum chips with thousands to millions of qubits, enabling simulation and optimization of biomedical systems at unprecedented complexity.
- **Improved Qubit Fidelity and Stability**: Advances in materials science, error correction codes, and control electronics will reduce error rates and extend coherence times, allowing longer and more accurate computations.
- **Diverse Qubit Modalities**: Integration of multiple qubit architectures (superconducting, trapped ions, photonics, and topological qubits) within modular quantum networks could harness complementary advantages tailored for specific healthcare tasks.
- **Quantum Networking and Distributed Quantum Systems**: Development of quantum internet infrastructure may enable distributed computing and secure quantum data sharing between clinical centers, research labs, and cloud quantum services.

These hardware improvements will be foundational to transitioning quantum computing from experimental platforms to clinically relevant tools, expanding the scope of feasible healthcare applications.

7.6.2 Integration of Quantum Computing with AI and Classical Systems

Future quantum healthcare solutions are poised to emerge from synergistic hybrid architectures, combining quantum processors with classical high-performance computing systems and AI models. This integration will enable:

- **Quantum-Enhanced Machine Learning**: Augmenting classical AI algorithms with quantum subroutines that accelerate training, feature extraction, or dimensionality reduction in complex biomedical datasets, improving prediction accuracy, and discovery of novel biomarkers.
- **Hybrid Quantum–Classical Optimization**: Employing quantum algorithms such as QAOA and VQAs as accelerators within classical optimization loops to solve combinatorial problems, such as drug candidate screening or treatment scheduling, more efficiently.

- **Co-Processing Architectures**: Seamless data exchange and task distribution between quantum and classical processors to achieve the best balance of speed, precision, and robustness, especially for medically critical workflows requiring validated, explainable results.
- **Cloud-Based Quantum Services**: Expansion of quantum cloud platforms offering access to quantum processors and integrated AI toolkits for healthcare researchers and clinicians, democratizing technology adoption and collaboration.

The evolution of software ecosystems and middleware that facilitate these integrations will be instrumental in realizing practical quantum-accelerated healthcare applications [23, 24].

7.6.3 Anticipated Breakthroughs in Medical Applications

The convergence of improved hardware and hybrid architectures supports ambitious projections for quantum computing's impact on medicine, including:

- **Precision Drug Design**: Quantum simulation of larger, more complex molecules and biochemical interactions will enable more reliable identification of therapeutic candidates, reducing drug development timelines and failure rates.
- **Real-Time Genomic Analytics**: Rapid quantum-enabled processing of large-scale multi-omics data will facilitate on-demand, highly personalized treatment recommendations that incorporate dynamic patient-specific molecular signatures.
- **Enhanced Diagnostic Imaging**: Quantum-accelerated image reconstruction, noise reduction, and feature extraction could enable ultra-high-resolution imaging with faster turnaround, aiding in earlier detection of pathological conditions.
- **Adaptive Healthcare Operations**: Quantum-optimized resource allocation and logistics algorithms may dynamically adjust to changing patient loads, emergency scenarios, and supply chain disruptions, improving responsiveness and care quality.
- **Advanced Disease Modeling**: Hybrid quantum–classical simulations may elucidate complex disease pathways and interaction networks, informing novel therapeutic strategies and predictive epidemiology.

These breakthroughs depend on continuous cross-disciplinary efforts to translate quantum innovations into clinically actionable solutions. Table 7.2 depicts classical and quantum computing.

7.6.4 Evolution of Regulatory Frameworks and Ethical Considerations

The integration of quantum computing into healthcare demands adaptive regulatory and ethical oversight to ensure safety, efficacy, and equitable access.

TABLE 7.2
Classical and Quantum Computing

Aspect	Classical Computing	Quantum Computing
Computation basis	Bits (0 or 1)	Qubits (0, 1, or superposition of both)
Processing power	Limited by classical hardware	Exponentially higher for certain problems
Data encryption	Classical cryptography	Quantum cryptography (quantum key distribution) – more secure
Drug discovery	Slow, requires many simulations	Potentially faster molecular simulations and optimization
Genomic analysis	Complex data processing, limited speed	Can handle huge genomic datasets efficiently
Optimization problems	Often heuristic or approximate	Can find better solutions faster via quantum algorithms
Error correction	Mature and reliable	Still developing, quantum error correction is challenging
Application in imaging	Conventional image processing	Potential enhancement via quantum machine learning
Current practical use	Widely used, mature technologies	Experimental, research-stage mostly

- The Creation of Quantum Healthcare Standards: Regulatory bodies such as the FDA and EMA are likely to set up specific evaluation criteria and certification processes for diagnosis and treatment tools that use quantum technology.
- Hybrid Algorithm Transparency Guidelines: As hybrid quantum–classical models become more common, it will be important for clinical acceptance and trust that algorithms can be explained, audited, and biased less.
- Data Privacy and Quantum-Safe Security: To protect private healthcare data, new security standards that can withstand quantum threats must be put in place. Additionally, quantum cryptography technologies must be used to ensure secure communication within healthcare networks.
- Ethical Governance: As the technology is used, rules will change to deal with issues such as fair sharing of quantum healthcare benefits, getting full permission for quantum-assisted treatments, and keeping an eye on quantum-driven predictive analytics.

Technologists, doctors, ethicists, lawmakers, and patient support groups will be able to develop models that balance new ideas with patient rights and public trust if they work together.

7.6.5 Research Directions and Collaborative Initiatives

Open, creative, and joint study platforms will have a significant impact on the future of quantum computing in healthcare. Key places that need to keep getting attention are as listed in the following:

- Creating custom algorithms for biomedical issues: creating quantum algorithms that solve problems in molecular modeling, biological data analysis, and making clinical decisions.
- Developing the skills of experts and healthcare workers in areas such as quantum computing, data science, and biology through interdisciplinary education and workforce development.
- Public–Private Partnerships: Getting university researchers, businesses, government agencies, and healthcare providers to work together to share resources, data, and knowledge.
- Open Datasets and Standardized Benchmarking: Making benchmarks, simulations, and selected biological datasets to test quantum algorithms and hardware for healthcare uses in a way that is clear and consistent.
- Early clinical trials and pilot programs: using controlled, real-world studies to test how well quantum solutions work in the clinic and how useful they are to speed up the transfer paths.

These well-coordinated efforts will spur new ideas and speed up the safe introduction of quantum computing into the healthcare system.

7.7 CONCLUSION

This chapter addresses how basic ideas, such as superposition and entanglement, can make quantum computing completely change the way healthcare is done. These features make it possible to solve hard, high-dimensional problems that standard systems cannot handle. Some important uses are finding new drugs by running accurate molecular models, making medicine more personalized by analyzing data in a quantum way, getting better medical images, and making the processes of healthcare run more smoothly. Quantum models can also help us learn more about how diseases work and how to treat them. But there are still big problems to solve. Hardware limits, mistake repair, data protection, interaction with current systems, and legal uncertainty all make it harder to adopt right away. Expertise from different fields is also needed, as well as care for social issues such as fairness and equal access. In the future, it will be very important for quantum technology, mixed algorithms, and AI integration to get better, along with strong legal and moral frameworks. Working together across disciplines and continuing to spend will speed up progress. Overall, quantum computing is a new field that has the potential to change the way healthcare is provided by allowing more accurate diagnoses, faster drug creation, and more personalized treatments. This could lead to better patient care and health outcomes worldwide.

REFERENCES

1. Aspuru-Guzik, Alán, Anthony D. Dutoi, Peter J. Love, and Martin Head-Gordon. "Simulated quantum computation of molecular energies." *Science* 309, no. 5741 (2005): 1704–1707.
2. Biamonte, Jacob, Peter Wittek, Nicola Pancotti, Patrick Rebentrost, Nathan Wiebe, and Seth Lloyd. "Quantum machine learning." *Nature* 549, no. 7671 (2017): 195–202.

3. Cao, Yudong, Jonathan Romero, Jonathan P. Olson, Matthias Degroote, Peter D. Johnson, Mária Kieferová, Ian D. Kivlichan et al. "Quantum chemistry in the age of quantum computing." *Chemical Reviews* 119, no. 19 (2019): 10856–10915.
4. Dunjko, Vedran, and Hans J. Briegel. "Machine learning & artificial intelligence in the quantum domain: A review of recent progress." *Reports on Progress in Physics* 81, no. 7 (2018): 074001.
5. Havlíček, Vojtěch, Antonio D. Córcoles, Kristan Temme, Aram W. Harrow, Abhinav Kandala, Jerry M. Chow, and Jay M. Gambetta. "Supervised learning with quantum-enhanced feature spaces." *Nature* 567, no. 7747 (2019): 209–212.
6. Kassal, Ivan, James D. Whitfield, Alejandro Perdomo-Ortiz, Man-Hong Yung, and Alán Aspuru-Guzik. "Simulating chemistry using quantum computers." *Annual Review of Physical Chemistry* 62, no. 1 (2011): 185–207.
7. Montanaro, Ashley. "Quantum algorithms: an overview." *npj Quantum Information* 2, no. 1 (2016): 1–8.
8. Nielsen, Michael A., and Isaac L. Chuang. *Quantum Computation and Quantum Information*. Cambridge University Press, 2010.
9. Perdomo-Ortiz, Alejandro, Marcello Benedetti, John Realpe-Gómez, and Rupak Biswas. "Opportunities and challenges for quantum-assisted machine learning in near-term quantum computers." *Quantum Science and Technology* 3, no. 3 (2018): 030502.
10. Preskill, John. "Quantum computing in the NISQ era and beyond." *Quantum* 2 (2018): 79.
11. Schuld, Maria, Ilya Sinayskiy, and Francesco Petruccione. "An introduction to quantum machine learning." *Contemporary Physics* 56, no. 2 (2015): 172–185.
12. Shor, Peter W. "Polynomial-time algorithms for prime factorization and discrete logarithms on a quantum computer." *SIAM Review* 41, no. 2 (1999): 303–332.
13. Trott, M., A. T. Sornborger, and E. Barnes (2020). "Quantum algorithms for biomedical data analysis." In M. J. Field (Ed.), *Advances in Healthcare Technology and Computational Methods* (pp. 327–357). Elsevier.
14. Azencott, C-A. "Machine learning and genomics: precision medicine versus patient privacy." *Philosophical Transactions of the Royal Society A: Mathematical, Physical and Engineering Sciences* 376, no. 2128 (2018): 20170350.
15. Zhang, J., Y. Chen, and& G. Feng (). "Quantum computing applications for personalized medicine: Potentials and challenges." *Frontiers in Pharmacology*, 12(2021): 644812.
16. Raju, Nandhakumar, Fardin Quazi, and Prashant Kondle. "Quantum computing in healthcare-unlocking new frontiers in drug discovery and data management." *International Journal of Global Innovations and Solutions (IJGIS)* (2024). https://doi.org/10.21428/e90189c8.e5dab7bb
17. Desai, R.. "Application of quantum computing in healthcare billing - USA." *International Journal of Science and Research Archive* 4, no. 4 (2025): 49–59. https://doi.org/10.30574/ijsra.2025.14.1.0102
18. Prajapat, Sunil, Garima Thakur, Pankaj Kumar, Ashok Kumar Das, Sajjad Shaukat Jamal, and Willy Susilo. "Designing lattice-enabled group authentication scheme based on post-quantum computing in healthcare applications." *Computers and Electrical Engineering* 123 (2025): 110028.
19. Minu, M. S., P. Satapathy, I. Dwivedi, S. S. Subashka Ramesh, M. B. Sudhan, and G. Agalya. "Sentinal. AI on emergency call operator using artificial intelligence and blockchain." In *Optimizing Patient Outcomes Through Multi-Source Data Analysis in Healthcare* (pp. 319–338). IGI Global Scientific Publishing, 2025.
20. Kawle, K., and S. Dhavale. "Applications of quantum computing for business analytics in healthcare management." *Journal of Student Research.* (2023). https://doi.org/10.47611/jsrhs.v12i3.4832

21. Malviya, Rishabha, and Sonali Sundram. "Exploring potential of quantum computing in creating smart healthcare." *The Open Biology Journal* 9, no. 1 (2021): 56–57.
22. Jhessim, E., and V. Anku. "Quantum computing for cybersecurity in healthcare systems: A multi-modal approach." *International Journal of Science and Research Archive.* (2025). https://doi.org/10.30574/ijsra.2025.14.1.0127
23. Davids, Joseph, Niklas Lidströmer, and Hutan Ashrafian. "Artificial intelligence in medicine using quantum computing in the future of healthcare." In *Artificial Intelligence in Medicine* (pp. 423–446). Springer International Publishing, 2022.
24. Sundaram, Aishwarya. "Challenges and opportunities in quantum computing in healthcare." *Quantum Computing for Healthcare Data* (2025): 91–118. https://doi.org/10.1016/B978-0-443-29297-2.00010-1

8 Enhancing Deep Learning with Quantum Computing, Its Challenges, Opportunities, and Applications

I. Samuel Peter James, D. Magdalene Delighta Angeline, and T. Prabakaran

8.1 INTRODUCTION

The development of machines, particularly with deep learning in every sector, plays a major role in the period of artificial intelligence (AI). An enormous number of datasets is processed and analyzed with quantum computers far quickly than the traditional counterparts, for deep learning applications [1].

Deep learning has made significant steps in recent years, with tremendous development in fields such as natural language processing (NLP), image recognition, and autonomous vehicles. At its core, deep learning involves training Artificial Neural Networks on vast amounts of data, enabling these networks to learn and make decisions or predictions [2]. However, the effectiveness of deep learning is fundamentally tied to the quality and quantity of data it processes. As datasets become larger and more complex, the computational difficulties increase exponentially, frequently exceeding the capabilities of classical computers [3].

Traditional computing systems, even high-powered ones, struggle with the enormous datasets and the complex, multi-layered neural networks used in advanced deep learning models, facing challenges with processing speed, power consumption, and the ability to handle large-scale, parallel computations efficiently [4]. This computational restriction limits the speed and accuracy of training deep learning models, later affecting their performance and practical pertinency.

Moreover, as deep learning endeavors into more experienced fields, such as generative models and reinforcement learning, the need for more powerful computing

DOI: 10.1201/9781003587835-8

resources becomes even more noticeable. The ability to quickly process and analyze large datasets is vital for these models to learn effectively and develop [5]. This challenge emphasizes the requirement for a new computational approach with the growing demands of deep learning—an approach where quantum computing steps in as a game-changer [6].

On a corresponding line, quantum computing was once considered largely theoretical but has become a reality. The mixture of these two powerful disciplines has created an extraordinary path for innovation, eventually giving rise to quantum machine learning (QML) [3]. This novel concept potential to transform computational science, data analytics, and predictive modeling in various areas, from optimization to pattern recognition [7].

Quantum computing provides the necessary computational capability to speedup complex machine learning algorithms, providing a toolkit for the optimization of quantum circuits or the decoding of quantum states. Here, how QML—especially quantum deep learning and quantum large language models (QLLMs) redefines the future of machine learning is postulated.

8.2 QUANTUM FOR ENHANCED LEARNING

The quantum hardware available at present is referred to as Noisy Intermediate-Scale Quantum (NISQ) devices and is limited by scalability issues, noise, and decoherence, posing a great obstacle for implementing large-scale quantum deep learning models [4]. Additionally, there is still work to be done to develop quantum algorithms that perform well with their classical peers in practical situations [2].

The data representation is a great challenge, whereby the conversion of classical data into quantum states by quantum computers is an important task implemented with various techniques, such as tensor networks and amplitude encoding, to provide practical solutions are still in development [8].

Quantum algorithms are capable of handling problems related to optimization, search, and sampling, whereas quantum-enhanced machine learning algorithms achieve faster training times and handle larger, more complex datasets than their classical equivalent. The most important characteristics of quantum computing lie in feature selection and dimensionality reduction. In high-dimensional data spaces, quantum algorithms identify patterns and correlations that are not identified in classical methods [9].

Also, quantum neural network models, quantum neural networks (QNNs), use the properties of quantum mechanics for processing information in ways that classical neural networks cannot. QNNs are a model complex having non-linear relationships in data, with larger complexity leading to an innovation in understanding complex datasets used in genetics, brain research, climate modeling, etc. Quantum computers are still in the early stages of development, and practical, large-scale applications in deep learning are yet to be fully realized. To develop algorithms using the full concepts of quantum computing requires an understanding of quantum mechanics and machine learning that unlocks the new innovations in AI research and application [10].

8.3 CHALLENGES IN INTEGRATING QUANTUM COMPUTING WITH DEEP LEARNING

Figure 8.1 depicts the challenges in integrating quantum computing with deep learning are hardware limitations, algorithmic barriers, and resource requirements [11].

8.3.1 Hardware Limitations

- Inadequate qubit counts, vulnerability to noise, consistency, and scalability are the limitations in hardware [12].

8.3.2 Algorithmic Barriers

- Quantum platforms do not accept several deep learning algorithms. Also, hybrid quantum–classical models necessitate the whole incorporation.

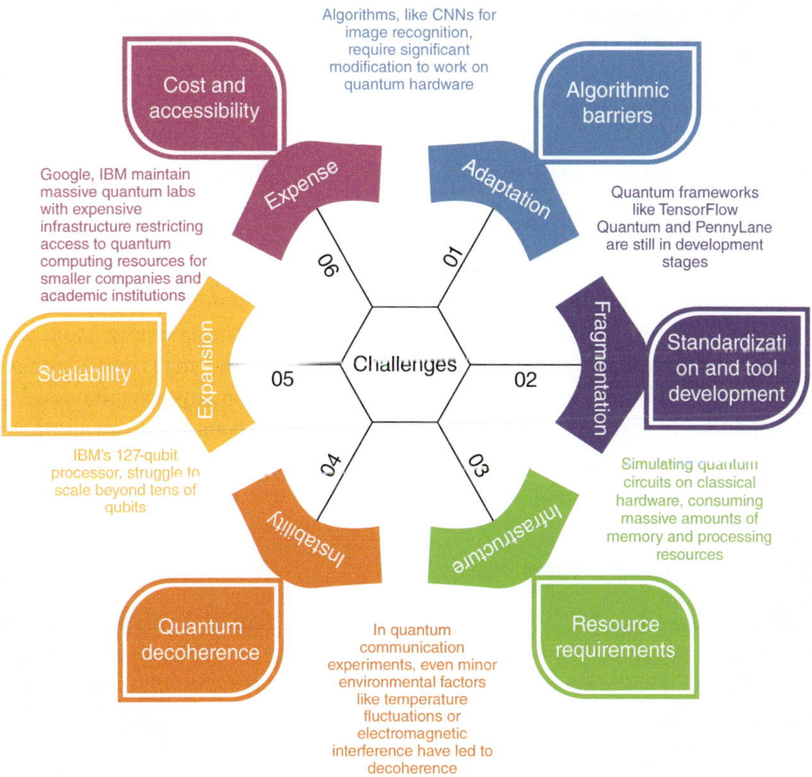

FIGURE 8.1 Challenges in integrating quantum computing with deep learning.

8.3.3 Resource Requirements

- During development, simulating quantum systems on classical computers requires high computational demands.

8.3.4 Scalability

Scalability remains a momentous challenge in quantum computing and deep learning integration as the current quantum hardware is limited by a comparatively small number of qubits, whereas the quantum algorithms have the potential to process a wide range of datasets with excessive speed. To scale these systems, researchers must maintain consistency over an extended length of time, reduce noise, and validate stability over intricate quantum circuits, all of which are crucial for maintaining accuracy and performance.

8.3.5 Error Correction

Quantum error correction is a crucial hurdle in merging quantum computing with deep learning. Quantum systems are highly susceptible to noise and decoherence, which can corrupt the delicate quantum states necessary for accurate computations. Implementing error correction schemes, such as surface codes and fault-tolerant protocols, requires significant computational resources and sophisticated algorithms. Developing efficient and scalable error correction methods is essential to ensure the reliability and feasibility of quantum-enhanced deep learning models.

8.3.6 Data Integration

Integrating quantum computing with deep learning requires addressing the challenge of converting classical data into a quantum-compatible form. The process of encoding classical data into quantum states often introduces inefficiencies and information loss. Efficient quantum data encoding and retrieval mechanisms must be developed to preserve the integrity of the input data while taking advantage of quantum computation's parallelism and speed. Additionally, maintaining seamless communication between classical and quantum layers in hybrid models is a growing research area.

8.3.7 Quantum–Classical Integration

Hybrid quantum–classical models need to combine the strengths of quantum speedups with the infrastructure of classical machine learning systems, which requires complex communication protocols and synchronization between classical and quantum components, resulting in reduced efficiency and increased latency.

8.3.8 Cost and Accessibility

Quantum computing hardware and infrastructure are more expensive and standoffish to many organizations and researchers due to the cost of maintaining specialized quantum processors, dedicated facilities, and cryogenic systems restricts prevalent innovation and experimentation. Also, expertise in quantum mechanics and quantum computing is less, requiring extremely specialized skills. It is essential to make quantum technology reachable, reducing costs is important for innovation and research across industries.

8.3.9 Measurement and Observation Challenges

In quantum computing, the measurement process is difficult as detecting quantum states ruins them, which destroys valuable quantum information. This poses a great challenge for deep learning algorithms to rely on maintaining quantum states to capture correlations and patterns over a period of time. The research is going on to measure quantum states without collapsing them.

8.3.10 Standardization and Tool Development

In QML, standardized tools and frameworks are not widely available, creating a difficult environment for developers and researchers to implement and test quantum algorithms. Therefore, it is essential to develop a programming language, simulation tools, and open-source libraries for collaborating with industry and academia.

8.3.11 Quantum Decoherence

In a quantum system, qubits exist in superpositions of states, providing the potential for huge computational speedups. However, quantum states are affected by temperature fluctuations, material imperfections, and electromagnetic interference. Decoherence disrupts quantum superpositions into classical states, erasing the quantum information crucial for processing and learning, negotiating the accuracy and reliability of quantum computations.

8.4 OPPORTUNITIES IN INTEGRATING QUANTUM COMPUTING WITH DEEP LEARNING

Quantum-enhanced neural networks are used in applications of drug discovery, natural language processing (NLP), and image recognition. For training classical models, Quantum Generative Adversarial Networks (QGANs) have the capability to generate high-quality synthetic data (Xue et al., 2024). QLLMs enable faster and efficient processing of huge amounts of text to transform AI applications such as conversational agents, real-time translation, and automated content creation (Wang & Liu, 2024).

The various opportunities that lie in integrating quantum computing are revolutionizing model training, developing quantum-specific models, and cross-industry transformations.

8.4.1 Revolutionizing Model Training

- Quantum computing allows faster merging of complex models, making deep learning manageable for real-time applications.

8.4.2 Development of Quantum-Specific Models

- Another opportunity is the creation of quantum-native neural network architectures such as QNNs.

8.4.3 Cross-Industry Transformations

- It is used in healthcare for preparing personalized medicine, in energy to enhance smart grids, optimize renewable energy systems, and in finance to detect fraud and enhance risk analysis.

8.5 APPLICATIONS OF QUANTUM COMPUTING WITH DEEP LEARNING

There are many applications where quantum computing plays a major role.

8.5.1 Drug Discovery and Personalized Medicine

Simulating chemical structures and comprehending relationships for drug discovery are difficult tasks for classical computers. International Business Machines (IBM) and Google are the two firms that use quantum-enhanced molecular simulations. Quantum AI is investigating quantum-enhanced molecular simulations that combine deep learning models and quantum computers to anticipate behavior, optimize medicinal compounds, and analyze protein folding.

Example: For instance, ProteinQure, a biotech startup, designs therapeutic peptides using machine learning and quantum-inspired algorithms, significantly advancing the drug discovery process.

8.5.1.1 Workflow for Quantum Drug Design

The workflow depicted in Figure 8.2 starts with data preprocessing that collects experimental and structural data to optimize accuracy for quantum computation. Experimental Structure Determination uses NMR spectroscopy, X-ray crystallography, and mass spectrometry as its tools for acquiring protein and peptide molecular structural data. Computational Geometry Refinement processes the obtained data to produce perfect molecular structure geometries. The present optimization process maintains precise measurements of bond lengths, accurate angles, and spatial position arrangements needed for subsequent quantum analysis. The workflow then enters the quantum computation phase after executing data preprocessing. The first operation in this phase uses initial state preparation to process molecular data into quantum states through qubit transformation. Through quantum representation, the system creates conditions that replicate atomic and molecular level interactions. Quantum algorithms execute in the second step through variational quantum eigensolver or quantum phase estimation (QPE). By simulating molecule-to-molecule interactions through their algorithms, these systems generate predictions about ground-state energy values and electron position profiles. Quantum simulations

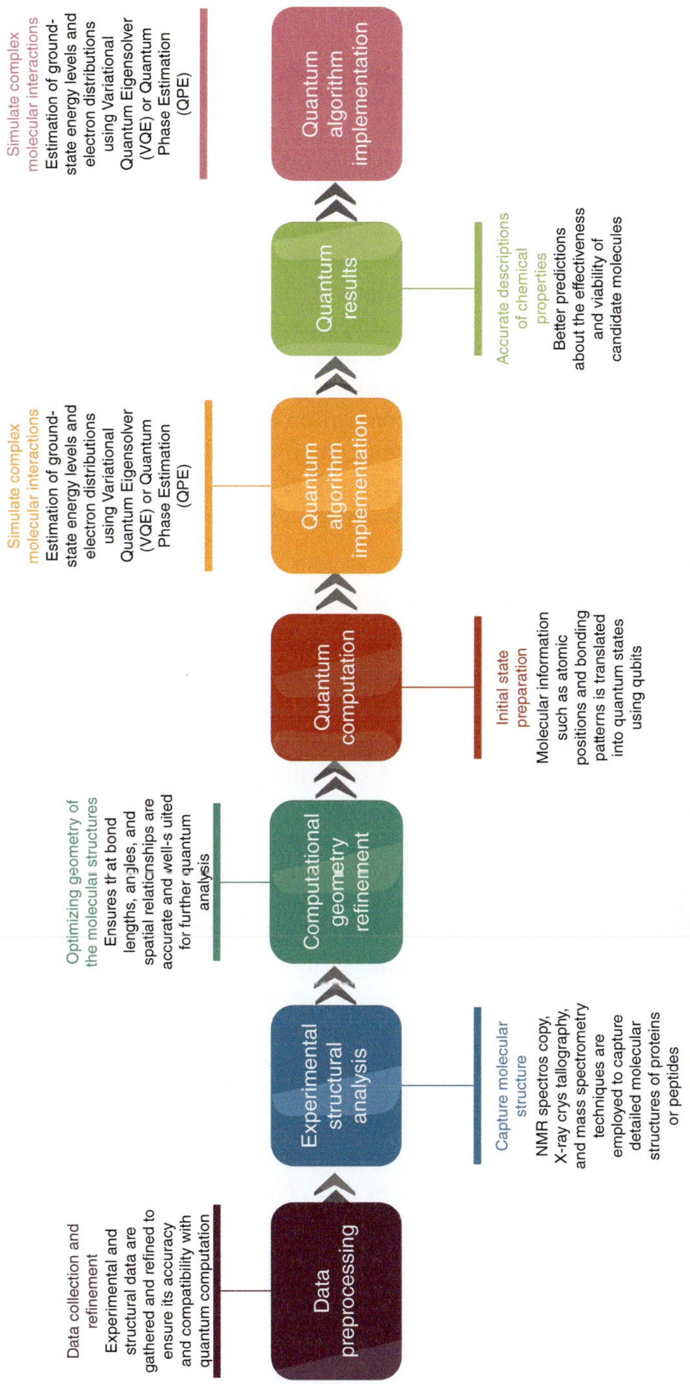

FIGURE 8.2 Workflow of quantum drug design.

provide an understanding of physical properties that remain beyond the reach of traditional computing because of their limited accuracy potential.

Figure 8.2 depicts the workflow of quantum drug design. Quantum algorithms produce accurate chemical depictions, which the drug development industry requires as foundational characteristics. Processing the chemical system requires binding affinity analysis of electronic interactions and molecular stability, followed by chemical reactivity testing. The analyzed properties help scientific teams determine how peptides and compounds react with target proteins, together with other molecules, thus evaluating their possible use as therapeutic agents. The method provides researchers with improved forecasting abilities regarding candidate molecules' performance during pharmaceutical development. The Experimental Validation and Iterative Optimization steps perform as termination mechanisms for this workflow. The validity of quantum-based scientific measurements becomes proven through laboratory experiments, which involve peptide production procedures and protein binding tests. The analysis performs a comparison between forecasted quantum data and experimental results to enable ongoing improvements to the quantum models. Drummed-up accuracy rates of discovery methodologies grow because predictions match genuine molecular bond reactions during this period.

8.5.2 Financial Portfolio Optimization

Financial institutions need to optimize investment portfolios through assessing many asset combinations under specified constraints in operations that require extensive computations. When quantum computing operates with deep reinforcement learning models, it enables accelerated financial dataset evaluation processes. The complex optimization problems become easier to solve through the Quantum Approximate Optimization Algorithm (QAOA). The financial institution Goldman Sachs uses active quantum algorithm research to optimize portfolio asset allocation alongside deep learning optimization of financial risk management operations.

8.5.2.1 Workflow of Financial Portfolio Optimization Using QAOA

The QAOA optimizes financial portfolio assets by determining the best possible risk–return balance that satisfies budget requirements and diversification needs, along with asset exposure guidelines. A workflow analysis for financial portfolio optimization with QAOA) starts with data acquisition and normalization. The first processing stage involves acquiring relevant historical financial data from stock databases and financial APIs through which stock prices, market indicators, and returns become available. After cleaning and preprocessing data, ensure all information is free from errors and missing values, as well as noisy data points. The derived financial indicators through statistical analysis include mean returns as well as volatility and asset correlations that help examine portfolio risk and return characteristics.

A financial portfolio storage optimization with QAOA enables investors to find a balance between risk and return through controlled allocation of funds. A workflow analysis for financial portfolio optimization with QAOA starts with data acquisition and normalization (Figure 8.3). The first processing stage involves acquiring relevant historical financial data from stock databases and financial APIs through which stock

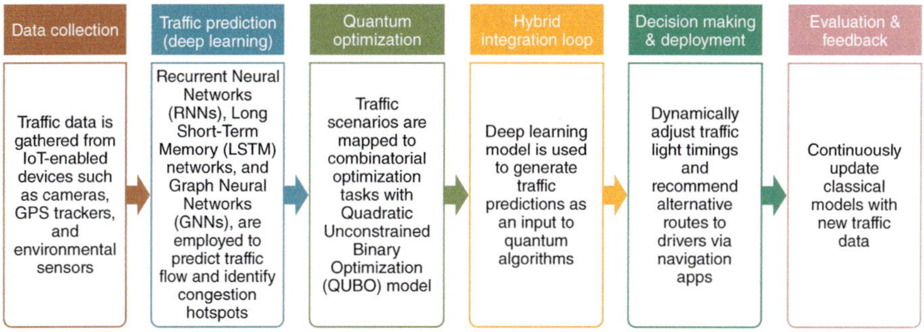

FIGURE 8.3 Workflow of traffic optimization in smart cities.

prices, market indicators, and returns become available. After cleaning and preprocessing data, ensure all information is free from errors and missing values, as well as noisy data points. The derived financial indicators through statistical analysis include mean returns as well as volatility and asset correlations that help examine portfolio risk and return characteristics.

8.5.3 Traffic Optimization and Smart Cities

Real-time optimization problems that appear in urban traffic management increase non-linearly when more vehicles combine with additional routes at each time interval. Deep learning models enable predictions of traffic patterns, and quantum computing provides real-time optimization functions for traffic flow.

> **Example**: Quantum computing helped Volkswagen improve Beijing taxi traffic routing. The system used classical deep learning techniques for traffic prediction together with quantum algorithms for instant determination of optimal path solutions.

8.5.3.1 Traffic Optimization in Smart Cities Using Hybrid Classical Deep Learning and Quantum Algorithms

The workflow shown in Figure 8.3 begins with extensive data collection. Data related to traffic comes from three sources: Internet of Things (IoT) devices, which include cameras, GPS trackers, environmental sensors, and historical traffic records. Before the analysis starts, the raw data requires preprocessing functions that clean it and convert it to structured formats from unstructured ones. Deep learning models, including recurrent neural networks (RNNs) and long short-term memory (LSTM) networks together with GNNs, operate through classical methods to predict traffic flow alongside detecting areas of congestion. The deployed models succeed in processing temporal and geographical dependencies to achieve exact future traffic predictions both in the near-term and over long periods. Figure 8.3 workflow of traffic optimization in smart cities

Quantum algorithms expand predictive capabilities by using them to tackle sophisticated optimization issues, including dynamic traffic route modifications and resource distribution problems. The Quadratic Unconstrained Binary Optimization (QUBO) model serves traffic scenarios by transforming them into combinatorial optimization tasks that QAOA solves. The quantum models function to optimize decisions related to signal timings, route allocations, and resource deployments by using their efficient computational abilities for better real-time management. The efficient operation depends on a combination of quantum processing and classical processing through a closed-loop system where classical deep learning models exchange inputs with quantum algorithms for receiving optimized outputs. Repeated feedback between systems allows for improved traffic strategy development through enhanced predictions. The optimized traffic solutions get implemented to control signals adaptively and to generate routing instructions that support infrastructure development plans. The system maintains effectiveness through dashboards that display traffic patterns and optimization results, but administrators' base performance reviews on key metrics, which include average travel time, congestion reduction, and CO_2 emission metrics. Real-time data consolidation allows the refinement of classical models and quantum systems to establish sustainable and smart urban traffic management solutions. The fusion of deep learning prediction models with quantum optimization capabilities results in a superior framework that optimizes traffic management systems in urban areas.

8.5.4 Climate Modeling and Weather Prediction

Manufacturers of climate models need to process huge datasets that contain numerous variables. The whole process of simulating weather patterns along with studying climate change exceeds the processing capabilities of conventional computing approaches. The analysis of climate data, combined with pattern recognition, becomes possible using deep learning models that use quantum computing enhancements to produce long-term forecasts. The ability to run parallel calculations through quantum parallelism leads to both faster computations and better accuracy levels.

Example: The startup Zapata Computing joins forces with other technology companies to merge quantum and classical computer systems for advanced disaster prediction systems and climate modeling.

8.5.4.1 Work Flow for Climate Modeling and Weather Prediction with Quantum-Enhanced Deep Learning Models

Quantum-enhanced deep learning models provide an advanced framework to enhance both climate modeling and weather prediction, according to Figure 8.4. Multiple data sources, including satellite imagery and both ground-based sensors and historical climate records, are used during the initial phase. The dataset receives information from real-time atmospheric measurements that come from weather stations and oceanographic measurement instruments. The data need preprocessing to cleanse and normalize information, after which it becomes ready for deep learning models.

The combination of classical deep learning engines, including Convolutional Neural Nets and LSTM networks, processes meteorological data to make predictions about weather fluctuations from both short-term and long-term scales. The models

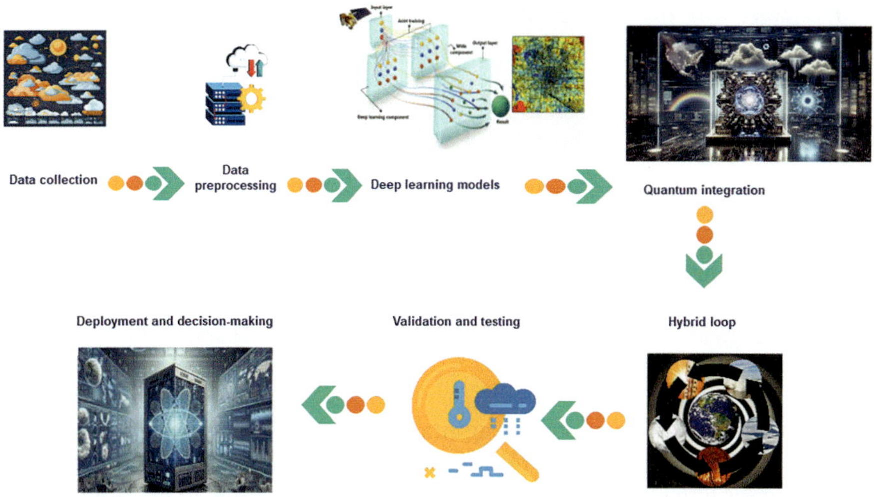

FIGURE 8.4 Advanced framework on Quantum-enhanced deep learning models.

analyze crucial features, including temperature modifications with precipitation patterns and atmospheric pressure measurements. The workflow integrates quantum computing features to boost the effectiveness and accuracy of these predictions. The deep learning optimization process achieves performance gains through quantum computing implementations, which handle tasks such as hyperparameter tuning and large-scale data processing. Two quantum algorithms, QVC and QAOA, function to resolve intricate subproblems, which enhances the speed and accuracy of computations. A quantum–classical hybrid system applies quantum output results to classical prediction models, which are repeatedly refined for developing better climate models as well as weather forecasting accuracy. The prediction validation process happens by using historical weather measurements, while simulation runs check the model's forecasting abilities regarding extreme weather conditions and long-term climate events. The Weather Prediction System deploys its final outputs directly into real-time weather observation systems, helping decision makers develop contractual measures to address climate risks. Continuous learning systems modify both classical and quantum models through updates, enhancing their operational performance over time. The combination of classical and quantum models improves accuracy while cutting down computational expenses, thus producing essential climate change solutions for governmental institutions and commercial sectors, as well as community-based management.

8.5.5 Fraud Detection in Banking and Cybersecurity

The detection of fraudulent activities within large financial transactions alongside cyber networks requires sophisticated pattern detection methods, together with anomaly detection capability. QML techniques analyze big data to maximize efficiency and discover patterns and anomalies that classical models would overlook.

Example: The financial institution, the Hongkong and Shanghai Banking Corporation (HSBC), uses quantum computing technologies and deep learning models to improve its transaction fraud detection velocity as part of enhanced fraud detection system development.

8.5.6 Healthcare Diagnostics and Imaging

Medical facility staff use numerous resources to process various medical images, including magnetic resonance imaging (MRI), computed tomography (CT) scans, and X-rays, while maintaining strict accuracy standards. The incorporation of quantum enhancement into deep learning models leads to faster diagnosis through better image analysis accuracy.

Example: The quantum computing firm 1QBit works with healthcare institutions to generate quantum-inspired algorithms that help medical picture analyses through faster diagnoses while reaching superior accuracy levels.

8.5.7 Optimization in Logistics and Supply Chain

Diverse supply chain systems demand real-time decision-making for route planning, together with inventory control and delivery planning. Quantum deep learning models unite predictive analytics with quantum optimization techniques, which optimize logistics operations.

Example: DHL tested quantum computing technology, which optimized its logistics network while cutting down operational expenses and delivery duration.

8.5.8 NLP for Sentiment Analysis

The analysis of sentiment within large, unorganized textual data needs deep learning models that demand intensive computational resources for training purposes. Modern NLP algorithms, which use quantum approaches, handle text processing with greater effectiveness, thus delivering superior outcomes in sentiment analysis alongside translation and chatbot responses.

Example: Academic experts study quantum transformers to upgrade GPT language models for real-time applications within customer support and social media monitoring.

8.5.9 Quantum-Assisted Materials Design

The production of innovative materials intended for aerospace and energy applications demands information about material atomic properties. Material simulation speeds up through the use of quantum computing techniques that work alongside deep learning model predictions to determine materials' properties.

Example: Microsoft Quantum leads its research into hybrid quantum–classical modeling for designing energy-efficient batteries and superconductors alongside other companies.

8.5.10 Space Exploration

Space mission trajectory optimization, together with astronomical data analysis, requires high computing power. Quantum computing systems enhanced by deep learning technology help process extensive telescope data to optimize mission planning tasks in space.

Example: NASA investigates the use of quantum-enhanced deep learning to expedite the process of detecting exoplanets through space imaging data examination.

8.6 IMPACT OF QUANTUM COMPUTING ON DEEP LEARNING

Quantum computing possesses revolutionary power for deep learning through its ability to solve computational problems while establishing novel data processing methods that achieve results beyond classical computing limits. The development of deep learning will undergo three major changes through quantum computing, according to the following points:

8.6.1 Exponential Speedup in Training

The optimization of model parameters through deep learning requires multiple iterations on extensive datasets for its calculation processes. Quantum computing offers:

- **Quantum Parallelism**: Quantum Parallelism uses qubits to run multiple calculations simultaneously, thus shortening training time periods.
- **Faster Linear Algebra**: Two quantum algorithms, named Quantum Singular Value Decomposition (QSVD) and Quantum Fourier Transform, work together to expedite deep learning calculations that depend on matrix operations.
- **Optimization Speedup**: Faster optimal solution achievement becomes possible through QAOA-based optimization while using quantum-enhanced methods that reduce the requirement for expensive iterative operations.

8.6.2 Enhanced Feature Extraction and Pattern Recognition

The capacity of deep learning models to detect patterns improves when datasets become complex, while the process of extracting valuable features from these datasets remains difficult. Quantum computing:

- **Expands Feature Spaces**: The usage of quantum kernels expands data feature spaces to quantum dimensionality for discovering patterns that standard approaches would fail to detect.

- **Improves Clustering and Classification**: Quantum algorithms increase the accuracy and efficiency of tasks where clustering and classification algorithms are used, as well as image recognition operations.
- **Boosts Neural Networks**: The QNNs use quantum states for data representation and processing, which results in improved learning performance.

8.6.3 Scalability for Large Models and Big Data

Modern deep learning models using GPT, along with large-scale transformers, depend on the processing capabilities of classical systems for their execution. Quantum computing offers:

- **Compact Data Representation**: Nearly limitless data sets become manageable for quantum systems that operate through qubits, which allow scalability.
- **Efficient Data Handling**: The processing speed of data through quantum-enhanced sampling methods enhances deep learning model workflows when dealing with large datasets.
- **Optimized Architectures**: Quantum computers possess the capability to scan and rate complex neural network architectures for selecting the most optimal designs.

8.6.4 New Frontiers in Generative Models

Generative models consisting of Generative Adversarial Networks (GANs) and Variational Autoencoders (VAEs) serve as foundational elements for deep learning improvements in art, together with design and science. Quantum computing effectively boosts such models through these functionalities:

- **Improving Sampling Efficiency**: Quantum systems utilize their capabilities to create better and more efficient samples from high-dimensional probability distributions.
- **Enhancing Creativity**: Quantum-enhanced GANs explore wider solution areas, which produce more creative results from diverse output possibilities.
- **Applications in Simulation**: Quantum-powered generative models run complex simulations to model molecular drug discovery relationships in chemistry as well as environmental climate pattern dynamics.

8.6.5 Solving Previously Intractable Problems

Deep learning performs better when matched with quantum computing for solving unattainable problems that exist outside classical computation.

- **Protein Folding and Drug Design**: Quantum simulations that use deep learning technology develop predictions about molecular interactions with unmatched accuracy for protein folding and drug development applications.
- **Financial Modeling**: Both portfolio optimization and risk assessment become more efficient through deep learning models, which quantum algorithms enhance.

- **Complex System Analysis**: Quantum deep learning enables effective analysis and prediction of chaotic system behaviors, including traffic patterns and energy distribution networks.

8.6.6 Reducing Computational Costs

A classical computing system needs substantial computational power for training deep learning models at a high expense of both money and energy usage. Quantum computing:

- **Reduces Energy Consumption**: Quantum systems run multiple calculations at once, which minimizes power usage throughout the entire system.
- **Shortens Time-to-Insight**: Real-time model operations shorten the time needed to generate insights, thus enabling more practical and cost-effective AI applications.

8.6.7 Revolutionizing Transfer Learning and Fine-Tuning

With quantum computing, transfer learning models achieve dependable modifications of pre-trained systems for new applications.

- **Quantum Transfer Learning**: Pre-trained models achieve better industry scalability by using quantum-enhanced methods, which adapt models to work across various datasets.
- **Real-Time Adjustments**: New data reception enables quantum systems to adjust their models in real time, which builds model adaptability.

8.6.8 Breaking the Barrier of Classical Limits

Deep learning models operate within the limitations of von Neumann architecture since memory operates independently from processing, yet these operations physically remain isolated. Quantum systems overcome this by:

- **Quantum Coherence**: Quantum Coherence brings data processing together with memory functions, so data moves through traditional limits.
- **Superposition and Entanglement**: The combination of superposition and entanglement techniques creates special data encoding and processing mechanisms that expand AI capabilities.

8.6.9 Driving Innovation in Artificial General Intelligence (AGI)

AI strives to establish computer systems that match human reasoning abilities, along with learning capabilities (AGI). Quantum computing applies these capabilities through the following method:

- **Exploring Novel Learning Algorithms**: Quantum AI develops more efficient learning algorithms through its novel approach to algorithm creation.

- **Handling Complex Knowledge Graphs**: Quantum-enhanced systems use their capabilities to handle complex connected information networks and perform reasoning functions across them.
- **Enabling Continuous Learning**: Continuous learning becomes possible through quantum computing as it provides fundamental capabilities needed for AGI.

8.7 QUANTUM-ENHANCED AI: FUTURE POSSIBILITIES

Quantum computing, when deeply integrated with deep learning technology, will generate tremendous effects throughout future operations. Quantum-enhanced AI accelerates drug discovery together with materials science by improving molecular structure modeling, which leads to shortened new drug and material development times. Quantum computing, when integrated with finance and logistics operations, enables the enhancement of system efficiency, which produces better supply chain performance and safer risk management capabilities. The development of artificial general intelligence represents an intriguing opportunity at the border of current possibilities. The theoretical concept AGI describes computational systems that mimic human brain functions by learning through understanding to find solutions to any difficulty. The strong computational power of quantum devices has emerged as an essential component needed to create artificial general intelligence.

Quantum-enhanced AI processes data at rates beyond modern possibilities and learns from immense quantities of information, which culminates in groundbreaking intellectual achievements unknown to humankind. Quantum computing frameworks for AI applications create a substantial environmental impact that should be taken seriously. Traditional data centers consume massive amounts of power, resulting in substantial carbon dioxide emissions during operation. Quantum computers demonstrate superior energy efficiency compared to classical systems, so they should decrease environmental impacts from running large-scale data operations and AI training processes.

8.8 CONCLUSION

The combination of deep learning with quantum computing represents an absolute breakthrough, which enables access to scientific breakthroughs considered unrealizable just a few years ago. Our access to a technological revolution now requires dual investments that combine both research and development, together with educational measures for future scientists and engineers. Scientists expect the full advent of quantum-enhanced deep learning to appear eventually, but its vast opportunities are already visible today. The merging of these technologies will produce extensive effects that could lead to the advancement of Artificial General Intelligence. The advancement into the quantum age requires balanced execution united with decisive attention to ethical matters and social effects. The upcoming era of AI developed through quantum computing will create both great surprises and mysteries we need to explore as a worldwide collective.

REFERENCES

1. Xue, C., Z.-Y. Chen, X.-N. Zhuang, Y.-J. Wang, T.-P. Sun, J.-C. Wang, … & G.-P. Guo (2024). End-to-end quantum vision transformer: Towards practical quantum speedup in large-scale models. *arXiv preprint arXiv:2402.18940*. https://doi.org/10.48550/arXiv.2402.18940
2. Zaman, K., A. Marchisio, M. A. Hanif, & M. Shafique (2023). A survey on quantum machine learning: Current trends, challenges, opportunities, and the road ahead. *arXiv preprint arXiv:2310.10315*. https://doi.org/10.48550/arXiv.2310.10315
3. Wang, Y., & J. Liu (2024). A comprehensive review of quantum machine learning: From NISQ to fault tolerance. *arXiv preprint arXiv:2401.11351*. https://doi.org/10.48550/arXiv.2401.11351
4. Li, J., Z. Wang, Z. Hu, P. Date, A. Li, & W. Jiang (2023). A novel spatial-temporal variational quantum circuit to enable deep learning on NISQ devices. *arXiv preprint arXiv:2307.09771*. https://doi.org/10.48550/arXiv.2307.09771
5. Patel, R. (2023). Application of tensor neural networks to pricing Bermudan swaptions. *arXiv preprint arXiv:2304.09345*. https://doi.org/10.48550/arXiv.2304.09345
6. Symons, Benjamin CB, David Galvin, Emre Sahin, Vassil Alexandrov, & Stefano Mensa. "A practitioner's guide to quantum algorithms for optimisation problems." *Journal of Physics A: Mathematical and Theoretical* 56, no. 45 (2023): 453001.
7. Tacchino, Francesco, Alessandro Chiesa, Stefano Carretta, & Dario Gerace. "Quantum computers as universal quantum simulators: State-of-the-art and perspectives." *Advanced Quantum Technologies* 3, no. 3 (2020): 1900052.
8. Orús, R. "Topological transitions from multipartite entanglement with tensor networks: A procedure for sharper and faster characterization." *Physical Review Letters* 113, no. 25 (2014): 257202. https://doi.org/10.1103/PhysRevLett.113.257202
9. Mehmood, Shahid. "Quantum computing: The intersection of physics and advanced mathematics." *Frontiers in Applied Physics and Mathematics* 1, no. 1 (2024): 17–41.
10. Mughal, Muhammad Usman. "Omniverse: A quantum AI-powered multidimensional robotic system." https://www.researchgate.net/profile/Muhammad-Usman-Mughal-2/publication/392326385_Omniverse_A_Quantum_AI-Powered_Multidimensional_Robotic_System/links/683dbe3bc33afe388ac99986/Omniverse-A-Quantum-AI-Powered-Multidimensional-Robotic-System.pdf
11. Hosseini, Eghbal, Kayhan Zrar Ghafoor, Ali Emrouznejad, Ali Safaa Sadiq, & Danda B. Rawat. "Novel metaheuristic based on multiverse theory for optimization problems in emerging systems." *Applied Intelligence* 51, no. 6 (2021): 3275–3292.
12. Sarvari, Samira, Nor Fazlida Mohd Sani, Zurina Mohd Hanapi, & Mohd Taufik Abdullah. "An efficient quantum multiverse optimization algorithm for solving optimization problems." *International Journal of Advances in Applied Sciences* 9, no. 1 (2020): 27–33.

9 Design and Optimization of Quantum Arithmetic Circuits for Next-Generation Quantum Systems

Yogeswari Palanisamy, Kathirvelu Murugan, G.B. Mohankumar, D. Ganeshkumar, K. Poornima, and S. Amsaveni

9.1 INTRODUCTION

9.1.1 What Is Q-computing?

The theory of quantum mechanics (QM), a part of fundamental physics, describes the behavior of energy and matter at the minimum scales, is the basis for the innovative computing method known as quantum computing (Q-computing). Q-computing depends on Q-bits (qubits), which can exist in several conditions at the same time; in contrast, classical computing (C-computing) utilizes bits that can only be 0 or 1 [1, 12, 14]. Along with other Q phenomena, such as entanglement and interference, the capacity to represent numerous possibilities simultaneously allows Q computers to tackle some kinds of problems far more quickly and effectively than a classical computer.

9.1.2 C-computing vs. Q-computing: A Key Comparison

The bit is the basic unit of data in conventional computing. There are two possible states for a classical bit: 0 and 1. All computational tasks performed on a classical computer, whatever they may be, be it calculation, data sorting, or encryption, are in terms of a sequence of binary values processed through classical logic gates (AND, OR, NOT, etc.). Q-computing, however, works with qubits, making it possible to occur in a superposition of both 1 and 0 at the same time. As a result, the computational capability for certain kinds of problems can be exponentially increased by using a Q computer that can manage several outcomes simultaneously.

DOI: 10.1201/9781003587835-9

TABLE 9.1
C-computing vs. Q-computing

Feature	C-computing	Q-computing
Bit	It can be either 0 or 1	It can be both 0 and 1 simultaneously (superposition).
Operation	Performed sequentially (one at a time)	Can be performed in parallel on multiple states due to superposition, with entanglement linking qubits in a way that allows faster problem-solving.
Scalability	Linear scaling with additional bits	Exponential scaling with qubits
error handling	Low error rates with deterministic outcomes	Requires advanced error correction techniques
Applications	Limited to polynomial-time problems	Efficient for factoring, optimization, and simulation
Speed	Slower – more time to complete the same task as Q computers.	Faster – Offers exponential speedup and quadratic speedup.
Reversibility	Most classical gates, such as the AND gate, lose information during their operation, making it irreversible. For example, if you know the output of an AND gate is 0, you cannot deduce the two input values that produced it.	All Q gates are **reversible** by nature. This means you can always "undo" the process of a Q gate to retrieve the original state of the qubits.

Q-computing can also benefit from other peculiarities, such as entanglement and Q interference, which classical computers cannot easily mimic. Some of the defining characteristics of C-computing vs. Q-computing are listed in Table 9.1. According to Moore's Law, which states that transistors on a chip will double in size every 2 years, C-computing has been driven for decades by exponential increases in processing power. However, as transistors approach the atomic scale, classical scaling faces physical limitations, where the rate of progress decelerates. Q-computing breaks the Moore's Law horizon by using qubits and Q phenomena such as superposition and entanglement [4, 5, 6, 14]. Unlike classical systems that scale linearly, Q computers can exponentially scale with the addition of qubits, which means that problems previously intractable by computation can be solved.

9.1.3 History and Evolution of Q-computing

When physicists and computer scientists realized that quantum mechanics (QM) might be used for computation, their theoretical work became the foundation for the area of Q-computing:

- **1927**: Niels Bohr and Werner Heisenberg introduced QM.
- **1935**: Podolsky, Rosen, and Einstein put forth the Einstein-Podolsky-Rosen (EPR) dilemma, foundational to quantum entanglement (Q entanglement).

TABLE 9.9
Overview of Q Gates: Symbols, Matrices, and Circuit Representations

Q gate type	No of Qubits	Operator Symbol	Matrix representation	Circuit Representation
Hadamard gate	1	H	$\frac{1}{\sqrt{2}}\begin{bmatrix} 1 & 1 \\ 1 & -1 \end{bmatrix}$	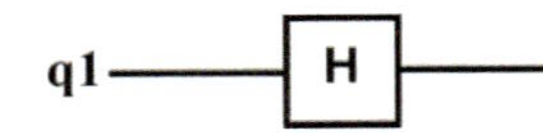
Pauli X or NOT, bit flip	1	X, NOT or σ_x	$\begin{bmatrix} 0 & 1 \\ 1 & 0 \end{bmatrix}$	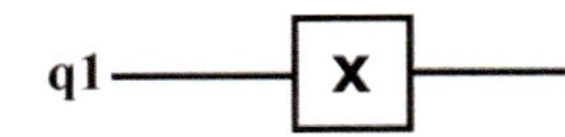
Pauli Y	1	Y, σ_y	$\begin{bmatrix} 0 & -i \\ i & 0 \end{bmatrix}$	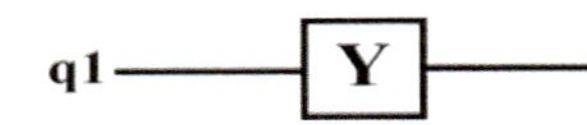
Pauli Z	1	Z, σ_z	$\begin{bmatrix} 1 & 0 \\ 0 & -1 \end{bmatrix}$	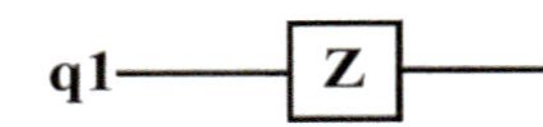
Controlled- NOT Gate	2	CNOT	$\begin{bmatrix} 1 & 0 & 0 & 0 \\ 0 & 1 & 0 & 0 \\ 0 & 0 & 0 & 1 \\ 0 & 0 & 1 & 0 \end{bmatrix}$	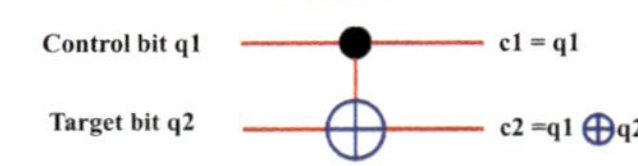
SWAP	2	SWAP	$\begin{bmatrix} 1 & 0 & 0 & 0 \\ 0 & 0 & 1 & 0 \\ 0 & 1 & 0 & 0 \\ 0 & 0 & 0 & 1 \end{bmatrix}$	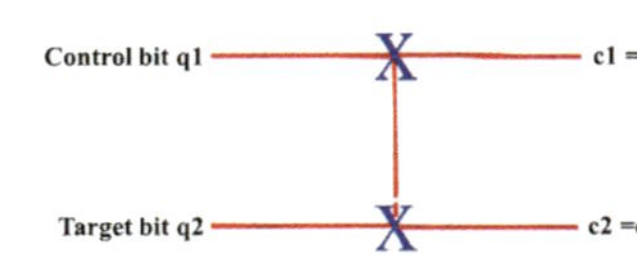
Toffoli Gate	3	CCNOT Or C^2NOT	$\begin{bmatrix} 1 & 0 & 0 & 0 & 0 & 0 & 0 & 0 \\ 0 & 1 & 0 & 0 & 0 & 0 & 0 & 0 \\ 0 & 0 & 1 & 0 & 0 & 0 & 0 & 0 \\ 0 & 0 & 0 & 1 & 0 & 0 & 0 & 0 \\ 0 & 0 & 0 & 0 & 1 & 0 & 0 & 0 \\ 0 & 0 & 0 & 0 & 0 & 1 & 0 & 0 \\ 0 & 0 & 0 & 0 & 0 & 0 & 0 & 1 \\ 0 & 0 & 0 & 0 & 0 & 0 & 1 & 0 \end{bmatrix}$	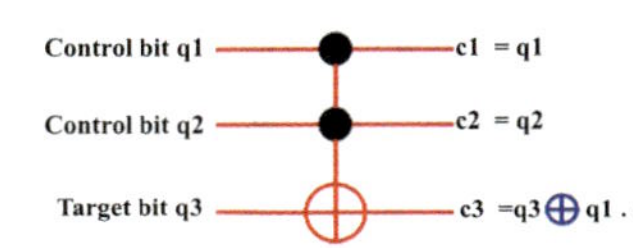

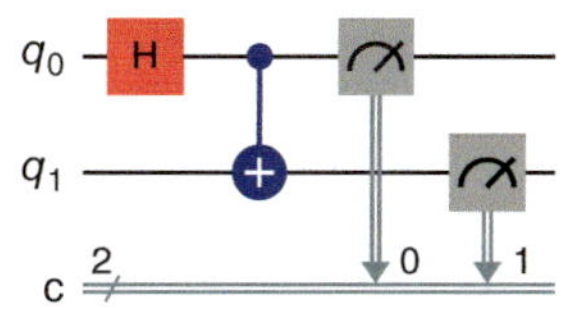

FIGURE 9.5 Bell state circuit.

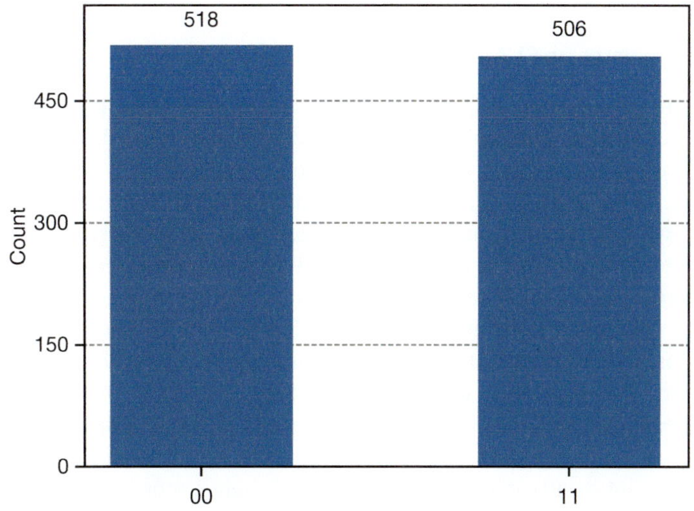

FIGURE 9.6 State vector representation.

9.2.2.1 Steps to Create a Bell State $|\Phi^+\rangle$

To generate a Bell state:

1. Put a Hadamard gate on qubit q_0. $H|0\rangle = \frac{1}{\sqrt{2}}(|0\rangle+|1\rangle)$.
2. Use a CNOT gate to entangle the qubit q_0 with the qubit q_1. This entangles the qubits: $CNOT(\frac{1}{\sqrt{2}}(|0\rangle+|1\rangle)\otimes|0\rangle)$.
3. Resulting State $|\Phi^+\rangle$: $\frac{1}{\sqrt{2}}(|00\rangle+|11\rangle)$

General Bell States have four Bell states:

1. $|\Phi^+\rangle = (|00\rangle + |11\rangle)/\sqrt{2}$
2. $|\Phi^-\rangle = (|00\rangle - |11\rangle)/\sqrt{2}$
3. $|\Psi^+\rangle = (|01\rangle + |10\rangle)/\sqrt{2}$
4. $|\Psi^-\rangle = (|01\rangle - |10\rangle)/\sqrt{2}$

The choice of gates can be modified to generate different Bell states:

- To reverse the phase, add a Z gate to one of the qubits.
- To flip the qubit states, add an X gate.

9.3 Q ARITHMETIC CIRCUITS BASICS

Q arithmetic circuits form the heart of most Q algorithms and operations. The circuits perform such basic arithmetic tasks as addition, subtraction, multiplication, and division within the Q context. Q arithmetic circuits form the crux of numerous Q algorithms. Most of the Q algorithms depend on such circuits where significant computational power is acquired as compared to their classical algorithm counterparts. Such algorithms include Shor's and Grover's algorithms.

9.3.1 Principles of Q Arithmetic Circuits

Q arithmetic circuits exploit QM—the theory that explains how particles behave at the Q scale. Q-circuits use qubits, which can exist simultaneously in various states because of the superposition principle, as opposed to classical systems that use bits (0s and 1s). At the heart of Q arithmetic circuits is Q parallelism and entanglement, which allows Q-circuits to process information that, in some situations, enables Q-circuits to process information significantly quicker compared to classical systems in certain cases. This enables Q-circuits to process exponentially more data in parallel. Moreover, entanglement is crucial. The state of one particle (such as its spin, position, or polarization) is directly related to the state of an alternative particle, even if the particles are separated by huge distances. This correlation permits Q-circuits to implement simultaneous actions across multiple qubits, greatly increasing computational efficiency. Combining these Q principles gives Q arithmetic circuits inherently distinct—and potentially much more efficient—than their classical [15] counterparts.

For example, in Q adder, two qubits might be entangled so that measuring the value of one qubit instantly reveals the value of another qubit. This is particularly important in many arithmetic operations in which there is a need to jointly manipulate two or more qubits, such as the sum and carry outputs in binary addition.

Entanglement also underlies Q algorithms such as Q teleportation and Q key distribution (QKD), where the state of one qubit is transferred or shared between parties without direct physical transmission.

9.3.2 Q Arithmetic Operations

Mathematical operations on qubits are essential to Q arithmetic circuits. The important arithmetic operations in Q-computing are:

- **Addition**: Addition is the basic Q arithmetic operation, which is attainable using Q half-adders and full-adders. Q half and full adders use Q gates to compute the sum as well as the carry from two qubits.
- **Subtraction**: Q subtraction can be obtained using Q adders with an inverted carry. Usually, in classical two's complement subtraction, the algorithm is followed by adding the one's complement of the number to be subtracted.
- **Multiplication**: Q multiplication is complex; however, it can also be performed using circuits implementing addition circuits multiple times, as in classical multiplication, where repeated addition is used.

- **Division**: Q division is a topic that is currently still under research, although generally, Q multiplication and subtraction can be used in a cycle with the help of Q gates to simulate the division process.

9.3.3 Classification of Q Adders

A fundamental element of Q arithmetic circuits is Q adders. In Q-circuits, there exist two primary types of adders: half-adders and full-adders.

9.3.3.1 Q Half-Adder

A Q half-adder is the most basic form of a Q adder. It accepts two input qubits and generates two outputs: the sum and the carry. A half-adder is used in binary addition, and Q gates can be used to apply its design to Q-computing [3, 7].

9.3.3.1.1 Key Components

- CNOT Gate: The CNOT gate is used to calculate the sum of two qubits. The CNOT gate essentially computes the XOR action on two qubits, which is the classical sum for a half-adder.
- CCNOT Gate: It is used to compute carry in the half-adder. In addition, the carry in case of binary addition occurs if both the input qubits are $|1\rangle$. Figure 9.7 [8] represents the Q half-adder circuit. Figure 9.8 [8] depicts the state vector representation for the circuit shown in Figure 9.7.

9.3.3.1.2 Q Measurement

1. **Classical Registers**: We assign 3 classical bits to store measurement results from the 3 qubits.
2. **Measurement Mapping**:

q [0] = c [0] (A)
q [1] = c [1] (Sum: A⊕B)
q [2] = c [2] (Carry: A·B)

3. **Execution**: The circuit is executed 1,024 times (shots), and the measurement frequencies are recorded.
4. **Result Interpretation**: The output {000': 1024} means all the shots resulted in $|000\rangle$.

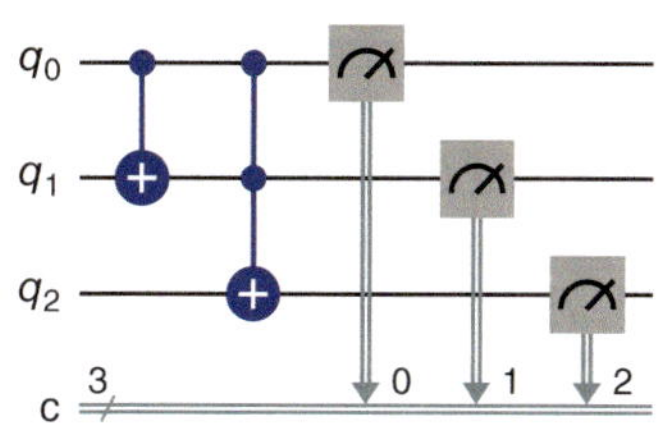

Figure 9.7 Q half-adder circuit.

9.4.1.1 Design and Operation of QRCAs

In QRCA, the addition of two multi-bit numbers is done as follows:

- **Input**: Two qubit registers are fed into the Q adders representing the binary numbers to be added.
- **Gate Operations**: Each Q bit is passed through a series of Toffoli and CNOT gates in each full-adder unit. The sum is the output of each quantum bit, and the carry output is forwarded to the next adder unit.
- **Carry Propagation**: The carry produced by the first adder is carried over to the next one. Every bit is dependent on the carry-out of the preceding stage, which results in a delay.
- **Example**: For the addition of a 3-bit number, where A = 101 and B = 110. The sum is 1011, and the final carry is 1. The propagation of carry will happen one after another from the next adder, thus making the computation slow.

9.4.1.2 Advantages of QRCA

- **Simplicity**: QRCAs have fewer Q gates to implement, hence simpler to design.
- **Lower gate complexity**: It only uses Toffoli and CNOT, which are easier to execute with current Q hardware.

9.4.1.3 Disadvantages of QRCA

- **Propagation Delay**: Since the carry needs to ripple through each bit, the delay is linearly proportional to the number of bits, making it less scalable.
- **Scalability**: It suffers from an exponentially increasing time complexity with the number of qubit, and hence it becomes unfeasible for large computations.

9.4.2 Q Carry-Look-Ahead Adders (QCLAs)

QCLAs refer to the method to overcome the major deficiency of QRCAs, as carry bits are calculated in parallel instead of sequentially. This reduces delay significantly and enhances performance, mainly for large-scale addition. QCLAs' design is much more complex but faster in operation, making it well-suited for Q applications that have a need for fast processing.

9.4.2.1 Design Principles of QCLAs

- **Carry-Look-Ahead Calculation in Parallel**: Rather than carrying the carry through to the next stage, QCLAs calculates all the carry bits simultaneously through a pair of carry generation and carry propagation functions.
- **Carries Generation**: At every stage, this generation step computes whether there will be a carry at that particular stage, depending on the input bits as well as the carry in.
- **Carry Propagation**: This process ensures that carry propagates in parallel throughout the adder, thus no ripple effect.

- **Sum Calculation**: At every stage, the sum is calculated using the carry bits and the input bits.
- Mathematical Representation

For a 3-bit adder with inputs A, B, and Carry_in:

- **Carry Generation**: Gi = Ai·Bi (carry generation bit for each stage)
- **Carry Propagation**: Pi = Ai + Bi (carry propagation bit for each stage)
- **Final Carry-out**: Carry_out = G2 + P2·G1 + P2·P1·G0

9.4.2.2 Example

For a 3-bit addition A = 101, B = 110, and Carry_in = 0, the carry generation and propagation steps occur in parallel for all bits. The final sum and carry-out are much faster than in a ripple-carry adder.

9.4.2.3 Advantages of QCLAs

- **Speed**: Due to the parallelization of carry computation, QCLAs significantly reduce the time complexity of addition. This makes it more scalable than QRCAs.
- **Efficient for Large Bit-widths**: The more the number of bits, the more apparent the performance gain of QCLAs.
- **Lower Gate Depth**: Parallel processing requires fewer gate layers than QRCA, making it more efficient in terms of hardware resources.

9.4.2.4 Drawbacks of QCLAs

- **Gate Complexity**: The parallel carry computation requires extra gates, especially Toffoli gates, which can increase the overall gate complexity.
- **Implementation Complexity**: QCLAs are more complex in terms of implementation due to more Q gates and a much more complicated design.

9.4.3 Optimizations in Adder Design

To take the performance of Q adders to the next level, especially for larger-scale computations [11], many optimizations can be implemented as follows:

9.4.3.1 Optimization Strategies

- **Gate Minimization**: Q-circuits should have fewer gates for their efficiency to improve. Methods such as gate fusion or the decomposition of large gates into smaller ones can help reduce the number of overall gates.
- **Qubit Recycling**: In large Q-circuits, some qubits may be used for multiple stages of computation. This means that their usage is reduced, and the resources can be more efficiently utilized.
- **Error Correction**: Because Q systems are noisy, using error-correcting codes will enhance the quality of Q adders. Optimized Q adders can be used in large Q algorithms such as Q simulations, the generation of cryptographic keys, and big machine learning algorithms where fast arithmetic operations are required.

However, progress is being made in developing stronger qubits and error correction techniques, while quantum algorithms are being refined for practical applications. Industry leaders such as IBM, Google, and Microsoft, along with academic institutions and start-ups, are all contributing to advancing Q-computing technology.

9.6.1.1 Qubit Instability

Qubits are very prone to errors because of their fragile nature. Q-bit instability arises from the fact that it is difficult to maintain a qubits' Q state for a long time. This phenomenon is called decoherence, wherein qubits lose their Q characteristics as a result of interactions with their surroundings, including cosmic rays, electromagnetic radiation, and thermal fluctuations.

- **Decoherence Time**: For the majority of physical implementations, the coherence time—the period that maintains its Q state—is currently on the order of microseconds. This is an important limitation for large-scale Q computations, as often operations on Q-circuits require that qubits maintain their state over extended periods.
- **Environmental Noise**: Qubits are sensitive to noise, which is prone to causing mistakes in Q operations. Such mistakes are fundamentally different from the classical bit mistakes, as they may lead to the collapse of the Q superposition or unwanted entanglements.

9.6.1.2 High Error Rates

Q gates are prone to errors that arise from imperfections in gate operations. The imperfections arise from the non-ideal properties of qubits and Q gates themselves. In Q systems, the error rate is still much higher than in classical systems.

- **Gate Fidelity**: Gate fidelity refers to how accurately a Q gate will perform its intended operation. Higher fidelity is critical for getting the right result from the Q-circuits. But now, gate fidelities are still very low, such that the Q operations frequently tend to result in errors.
- **Q Noise**: Q operations are often noisy, which is a result of the interaction between qubits and the environment. This noise can significantly affect the outcome of Q computations, leading to incorrect results.

9.6.1.3 Scalability Issues

Scalability denotes the potential of a Q computer to sustain its performance and reliability with increased numbers of qubits. Q systems are intrinsically fragile and prone to error, so increasing the number of qubits poses quite a few challenging issues.

- **Error Propagation**: With increasing qubits in a Q-circuit, the potential error increases exponentially. This is perhaps the biggest problem when the system size needs to grow. As the quantity of qubits rises, small errors in individual qubits get propagated and amplified across the entire system, and error-free computation becomes a complex task.

- **Q-circuit Depth**: As the size of quantum circuits increases, both the gate count and circuit depth grow. The greater the circuit depth, the more error-prone it becomes, and current error correction methods struggle to efficiently handle this complexity.

9.6.2 Research in QEC

QEC is a thrust area of research undertaken to overcome the issues brought about by qubit instability and high error rates. QEC schemes are specifically intended to identify and rectify the mistakes that arise in Q calculation so that results for Q algorithms are reliable.

9.6.2.1 QEC Codes

The application of QEC codes is among the most effective techniques for reducing mistakes in Q-circuits. These codes function by encoding Q information in a manner that enables QEC and detection [13].

- **Shor's Code**: This is the oldest of the QEC codes that are widely recognized, with Shor's code encoding one qubit of information on nine physical qubits. This code rectifies for both phase-flip and bit-flip errors.
- **Surface Codes**: These codes are a variety of QEC codes, in particular well-suited for current Q hardware. In essence, they are predicated on the notion of encoding data in a two-dimensional grid of qubits, thereby having neighboring qubits providing this redundancy to detect and eventually correct errors.
- **Steane Code**: This code is a generalization of Shor's code and is capable of correcting errors in both the phase-flip and bit-flip channels. It uses seven qubits to encode one logical qubit.

9.6.2.2 Error-Tolerant Q Computation

Fault tolerance in Q-computing refers to the capability to perform Q computations even when mistakes occur. Researchers are developing error-tolerant methods where errors can be corrected during computation without interrupting the overall operation [16].

- **Logic Qubits**: Such encoding of multiple physical qubits ensures that the majority of errors within the involved single qubits are detectable. This would make computation at the Q level rather unaffected by such types of errors.
- **Robust Gates**: These provide ways of implementing Q computation using gates, minimizing how noisy conditions might impact computations. This is absolutely pivotal to making large-scale, reliable Q-circuits.

9.6.3 Scalability and Hardware Innovations

As Q-Computing systems scale up, new hardware innovations are needed to overcome the challenges of scalability, qubits instability, and high error rates [16].

9.6.3.1 Qubit Technologies

Several technologies are being explored to create more stable, scalable qubits. These include:

- **Superconducting Qubits**: Superconducting qubits are at the moment the most commonly applied qubit. These qubits are manufactured through superconducting circuits, which display Q properties. Companies such as IBM and Google apply superconducting qubits in developing their Q computers. In contrast, the major drawback with superconducting qubits is the diminishment of environmental noise and coherence times.
- **Trapped Ions**: Trapped ion qubits are another very promising qubit technology in which ions are manipulated and trapped using electromagnetic fields. The coherence times of these systems are comparatively long and have high gate fidelities, but the scalability of trapped ions remains a challenge due to the complexity of ion manipulation and the need for large vacuum chambers.
- **Topological Qubits**: This technology promises very robust error-resilient Q-Computing since topological qubits are less susceptible to local noise. Microsoft is exploring this technology, although practical implementation is years off.

9.6.3.2 Q Software and Algorithms

With hardware developments, researchers are also developing Q algorithms that can compute efficiently with fewer qubits. Some of the algorithms designed to solve optimization problems are QAOA and VQE, which can work with fewer qubits [11, 17].

By developing hybrid Q-classical systems, scientists expect to be able to use Q speedups without requiring large-scale Q computers. Q algorithms that are fault tolerant and efficient with small numbers of qubits will provide an immediate advantage in many industries.

9.6.4 Future Directions of Q Arithmetic Circuits

Q arithmetic circuits will continue to evolve as we tackle the challenges outlined in this section. Some future research directions include:

- **Hybrid Systems Combining Q and Classical Computations**: The benefits of Q-circuits will be made possible by combining Q-computing and C-computing with much less demanding scalability in the Q hardware, that is, it also somewhat addresses some of the challenges associated with current Q hardware.
- **Q Machine Learning**: Hybrid circuits involving Q arithmetic circuits together with machine learning algorithms may represent some breakthroughs in AI optimization and data analysis.
- **Q Cryptography Evolution**: It will be possible to apply a QKD system as hardware matures, where arithmetic circuits for Q computation guarantee high-security, tamper-proof communication.

9.7 CONCLUSION

Q Arithmetic Circuits are critical blocks of the Q-computing platform. They form the underlying constructs of efficient computation within the Q world, thus doing tasks that are otherwise unable for their classical counterparts to execute even within reasonable time scales. This chapter delved into the theoretical and practical matters of these circuits and, accordingly, their application in Q cryptography, machine learning, image processing, and the related areas. However, it is just a starting point. Q arithmetic circuits can revolutionize whole industries to make problems previously unmanageable with classical computers solve impossible problems. We are currently in the nexus of Q-computing's full potential; both promises and challenges must be understood. Q arithmetic circuits form a core part of the Q-computing revolution. They will provide faster, more efficient computation leveraging the unique qualities of QM: superposition, entanglement, and interference. The circuits will continue to get more reliable and scalable as we improve our qubits, Q gates, and methods of error correction.

9.8 FUTURE OF Q-COMPUTING

The imminent emergence of Q-computing is bright. Q-computing holds the potential for resolving issues that traditional computers are unable to handle. In fields, such as drug discovery, machine learning, optimization, and cryptography, solutions can be found with Q computers. As the Q hardware improves and the effectiveness of error correction increases, we can expect to see Q computers solving real-world problems that were once considered intractable. The transformative abilities of Q-Computing are being achieved; still, they can potentially reform the industry sectors and deliver new scientific discoveries. This new generation of Q systems will not only be capable of solving some of those previously thought unsolvable problems but will also create possibilities to surpass current frontiers of computation.

REFERENCES

1. "Q-computing." Wikipedia. Accessed December 25, 2024. https://en.wikipedia.org/wiki/Q_computing.
2. "Q-computing." Wikipedia. Accessed December 25, 2024. https://en.wikipedia.org/wiki/Q_logic_gate
3. Rohini, H., and S. Rajashekar. "Design of reversible logic based basic combinational circuits." *Communications on Applied Electronics* 5, no. 9 (2016): 38–43.
4. Arute, Frank, Kunal Arya, Ryan Babbush, Dave Bacon, Joseph C. Bardin, Rami Barends, Rupak Biswas et al. "Quantum supremacy using a programmable superconducting processor." *Nature* 574, no. 7779 (2019): 505–510.
5. Hey, Tony. "Q-computing: an introduction." *Computing & Control Engineering Journal* 10, no. 3 (1999): 105–112.
6. Kaye, Phillip, Raymond Laflamme, and Michele Mosca. *An Introduction to Q-computing*. OUP Oxford, 2006.
7. Haq Shaik, Enaul, and Nakkeeran Rangaswamy. "Implementation of Q gates based logic circuits using IBM Qiskit." In *2020 5th International Conference on Computing, Communication and Security (ICCCS)*, pp. 1–6. IEEE, 2020.

8. Qiskit Documentation. Accessed December 25, 2024. https://qiskit.org/documentation
9. Colab Research Notebooks. Accessed December 25, 2024. https://colab.research.google.com
10. Nielsen, Michael A., and Isaac L. Chuang. *Q Computation and Q Information*. Cambridge University Press, 2010.
11. Preskill, J. (1998). Q-Computing in the NISQ era and beyond. *Q*, *2*, 79.
12. Rieffel, E., and W. Polak (2011). *Q-computing: A Gentle Introduction*. MIT Press.
13. Barenco, Adriano, Charles H. Bennett, Richard Cleve, David P. DiVincenzo, Norman Margolus, Peter Shor, Tycho Sleator, John A. Smolin, and Harald Weinfurter. For Q computation." *Physical Review A* 52, no. 5 (1995): 3457.
14. M. AbuGhanem and H. Eleuch, "NISQ computers: a path to quantum supremacy," *in IEEE Access*, 12 (2024): 102941–102961, doi: 10.1109/ACCESS.2024.3432330
15. Yanofsky, Noson S., and Mirco A. Mannucci. *Q-Computing for Computer Scientists*. Cambridge: Cambridge University Press, 2008.
16. "Future of Q-computing." AI multiple. Accessed December 25, 2024. https://research.aimultiple.com/future-of-Q-computing
17. "Introduction to Q-computing." Q inspire. Accessed December 25, 2024. https://www.Q-inspire.com/kbase/introduction-to-Q-computing

10 Quantum Key Distribution

Visualizing the Foundations of Future-Proof Secure Communication

R. Naveenkumar, N. M. Sivamangai, C. M. Lingesh, G. Saranya, G. Indhumathi, and N. Vini Antony Grace

10.1 INTRODUCTION

At the intersection of quantum physics and information science, quantum information and cryptography are areas that are changing rapidly. They look into basic questions about how information can be stored, handled, and kept safe using quantum physics rather than traditional theories. This part tells you everything you need to know about these areas by explaining basic quantum ideas and what they mean for cryptography [1, 2].

10.1.1 Fundamental Concepts of Quantum Information

In contrast to conventional information, which is often denoted by bits that assume a value of either 0 or 1, quantum data is conveyed using qubits. It is a two-level quantum system capable of being in the classical states $|0\rangle$ and $|1\rangle$, as well as in a superposition of both states concurrently. A qubit state may be precisely represented as

$$|\psi\rangle = \alpha|0\rangle + \beta|1\rangle \tag{10.1}$$

The complex coefficients α and β must adhere to the normalization requirement $|\alpha|^2 + |\beta|^2 = 1$. Superposition enables qubits to probabilistically encode greater amounts of information than conventional bits, enabling powerful computational and communication protocols [3–5].

Another key quantum phenomenon is entanglement, a unique correlation that arises between a minimum of two qubits whereby the state of each qubit cannot be separately characterized from the others. When qubits are entangled, measurements

DOI: 10.1201/9781003587835-10

conducted on one qubit instantaneously influence the results of measurements on the other, irrespective of their spatial distance. This non-classical connection is crucial in quantum data theory and facilitates protocols that are unattainable within classical frameworks.

10.1.2 Quantum Mechanics as the Foundation of Quantum Information

Quantum information rests upon the fundamentals of quantum mechanics:

- **Superposition**: As noted, qubits can be in multiple states at once, allowing complex information encoding.
- **Measurement Postulate**: Measuring a qubit collapses its state from a superposition to one of the basis states probabilistically, inherently introducing uncertainty and randomness.
- **No-Cloning Theorem**: Creating a perfect replica of an undetermined quantum state is unfeasible, a feature that differentiates quantum from classical data and underpins quantum cryptographic security.
- **Entanglement**: Enables strong correlations and non-local effects that can be leveraged to enhance communication security and computation.

These concepts, when combined, enable innovative methods of information processing that surpass traditional capabilities.

10.1.3 The Motivation for Quantum Cryptography

Contemporary encryption fundamentally depends on computational hardness assumptions – the premise that certain mathematical problems are difficult for conventional computers to resolve within an acceptable timeframe. For instance, prevalent methods such as Rivest–Shamir–Adleman (RSA) and elliptic curve cryptography (ECC) rely on the challenge of factoring huge integers or calculating discrete logarithms.

Nonetheless, the emergence of quantum computing presents a fundamental threat to this paradigm [6]. Quantum algorithms, particularly Shor's algorithm, may effectively resolve these issues. Posing a risk to several traditional cryptography schemes once scalable quantum computers are realized. This potential weakness drives the creation of cryptographic techniques that are intrinsically safe against quantum assaults, resulting in the advent of quantum cryptography [7, 8]. Moreover, traditional key distribution systems depend on trusted third parties or intricate mathematical assumptions, which are susceptible to compromise. The aspiration for demonstrable security based on physical principles instead of unverified computational assumptions motivates the use of quantum mechanics in cryptography systems.

10.2 QUANTUM KEY DISTRIBUTION (QKD): AN INNOVATIVE FRAMEWORK FOR SECURE COMMUNICATION

A novel paradigm for secure QKD is one of the most developed and promising applications of quantum cryptography. In contrast to conventional key exchange methods, QKD allows two distant parties to produce a shared cryptographic key, with security assured by the principles of quantum mechanics.

The core idea behind QKD harnesses two quantum principles:

- **Measurement Disturbance**: Any effort by a hacker to capture quantum information always disrupts the quantum states, revealing their presence.
- **No-Cloning Theorem**: Prevents attackers from copying unknown quantum states without detection.

Through carefully designed protocols, such as the pioneering BB84 protocol, legitimate users can generate a key and verify its secrecy by checking for anomalies caused by spying. Upon detection of eavesdropping, the compromised key is eliminated to maintain secrecy. Figure 10.1 depicts QKD.

QKD systems often include the exchange of qubit sequences contained in attributes such as photon polarization or phase, followed by traditional communication to rectify faults and augment privacy. This combination of quantum-state transmission and classical post-processing safeguards the shared key against attackers with unbounded computing capabilities [9].

10.2.1 Summary of Key Challenges Addressed by Quantum Cryptography

The shift from classical to quantum cryptography seeks to address essential challenges:

- **Computational Vulnerabilities**: Classical cryptographic systems risk obsolescence due to powerful quantum algorithms.
- **Assumption-Free Security**: Quantum cryptography offers security established on physical principles rather than conjectures about adversaries' computational limits.
- **Eavesdropping Detection**: Quantum mechanics inherently exposes attempts to intercept communications, which classical systems cannot guarantee.

These benefits provide the basis for a new epoch of information security that is resilient to forthcoming technical advancements.

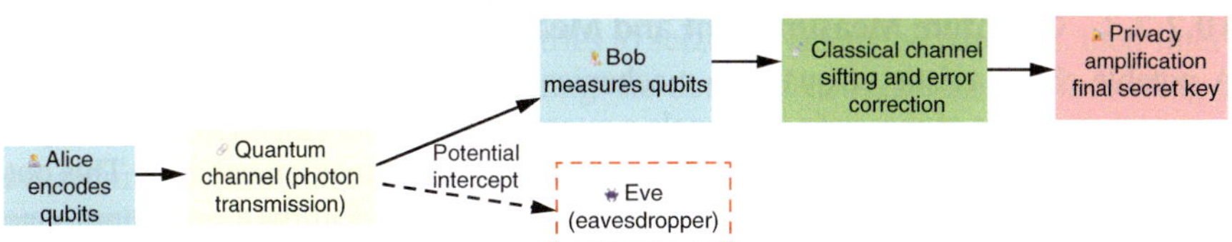

FIGURE 10.1 Quantum key distribution (QKD).

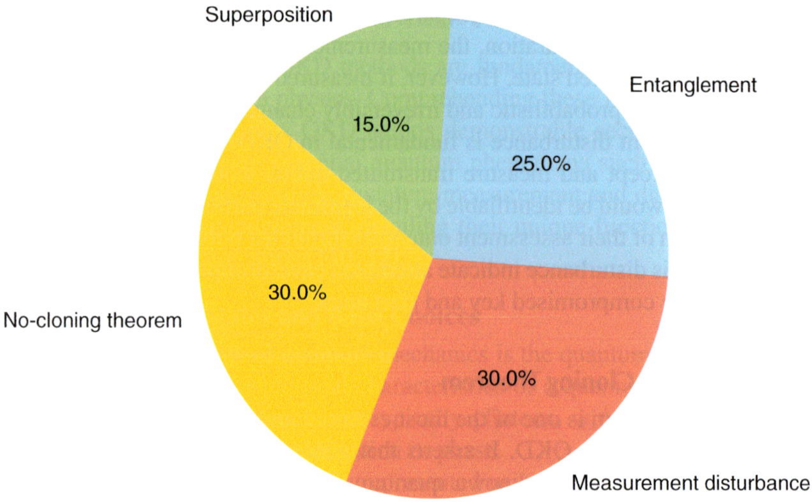

FIGURE 10.2 Security contributions in quantum key distribution (QKD).

10.2.3 Linking Quantum Principles to Cryptographic Security

The integration of these concepts provides a resilient foundation for secure communication.

- **Superposition and Basis Choice**: Encoding bits in non-orthogonal bases ensures that potential measurements by an adversary introduce unavoidable uncertainty.
- **Measurement Disturbance**: Any measurement by an eavesdropper irreversibly alters the quantum states, causing detectable errors.
- **No-Cloning Theorem**: Prevents covert duplication of qubits, stopping unnoticeable interception.
- **Entanglement**: Provides intrinsic correlations that serve both to distribute cryptographic keys and verify their untampered origin.

These quantum mechanical properties combine to ensure that any effort at eavesdropping always leaves traces that can be detected by authorized entities. This is a profound departure from classical cryptographic methods, where security mostly relies on computational intractability rather than physical laws.

10.3 QKD: OUTLOOK AND PROTOCOLS

QKD is an innovative cryptographic method that allows two people, often referred to as Alice and Bob, to generate a shared, confidential cryptographic key, the security of which is assured by the basic principles of quantum physics. In contrast to traditional key distribution techniques that depend on computational assumptions (i.e., problems being hard to solve for current computers), QKD provides security based on physical principles, offering a pathway toward information-theoretically safety communication.

The primary objective of QKD is not to send secret messages directly, but to create a mutual secret key that can then be used with classical symmetric encryption algorithms (such as Advanced Encryption Standard [AES]) to encrypt and decrypt sensitive data transmitted over any communication channel (classical or quantum) [18].

The safety of QKD stems from several key quantum properties discussed previously, notably the measurement postulate (any measurement of a quantum state generally disturbs it), the no-cloning theorem (an unknown quantum state cannot be perfectly copied), and entanglement (strong correlations between distant particles). Any attempt by an eavesdropper (conventionally Eve) to intercept the quantum transmission will inevitably leave a detectable trace, alerting Alice and Bob to the presence of an adversary and allowing them to discard the potentially compromised key.

10.3.1 General QKD Workflow

While specific QKD protocols differ in their implementation details (e.g., how quantum states are prepared or if entanglement is used), the general process for establishing a secret key typically involves a series of steps, employing both a quantum channel (for transmitting quantum states) and a classical channel (for communicating information publicly).

1. **Quantum Transmission**: Alice generates a series of quantum states, such as photons, and transmits them to Bob via a quantum channel, which may include optical fibers or free-space links. The information represented in these quantum states relates to possible bits of the final key.
2. **Quantum Measurement**: Bob obtains the quantum states and conducts measurements utilizing randomly selected measurement bases. In quantum mechanics, Bob's selection of a basis is essential, particularly in protocols that involve non-orthogonal states.
3. **Classical Communication (Sifting)**: Following Bob's measurement of all received quantum states, Alice and Bob utilize the classical channel to publicly discuss their selected encoding and measurement bases, excluding the measurement outcomes. The instances in which Bob's measurement basis aligned with Alice's encoding basis are identified. The results associated with the mismatched bases are eliminated, resulting in a raw key sequence that is shared between Alice and Bob. The process is referred to as Basis Sifting.

   Error estimation and correction are essential due to channel noise, imperfect devices, and potential eavesdropping, which may result in errors in the raw keys possessed by Alice and Bob. They publicly compare a randomly selected subset of their raw key bits to estimate the error rate. When the error rate surpasses a specified threshold, it is inferred that eavesdropping or excessive noise is occurring, leading to the termination of the key generation process. When the error rate is deemed acceptable, classical error correction (EC) protocols are employed to identify and rectify discrepancies in the key sequences while maintaining the confidentiality of the complete key. Errors are publicly disclosed; however, the process guarantees that Eve remains unaware of the corrected key bits.

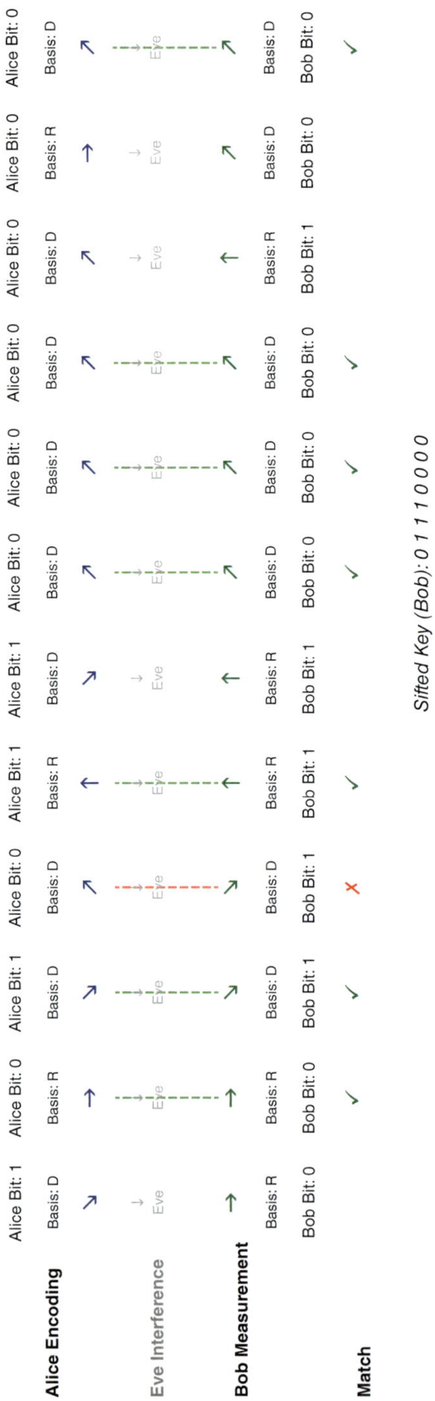

FIGURE 10.4 BB84 quantum key distribution visualization.

- **Key Generation**: Following the measurement of all particles, Alice and Bob publicly disclose the basis utilized for each measurement, while withholding the results. In pairs with matching bases, the measurement outcomes will exhibit perfect anti-correlation (or correlation), contingent upon the specific entangled state and basis selection. These outcomes constitute their fundamental key.
- **Security Feature**: The security of E91 is based on testing the correlations between their measurement outcomes for the cases where they chose different bases. These correlations should ideally violate a Bell inequality (e.g., Clauser–Horne–Shimony–Holt [CHSH] inequality) if the particles were truly entangled and no eavesdropping occurred. If Eve interacts with the entangled particles, she disrupts the entanglement, weakening the non-local correlations and potentially preventing the violation of the Bell inequality or increasing the error rate in the cases where bases match. By checking for the expected Bell inequality violation and rate of error in the matching basis measurements, both can verify the presence (or absence) of an eavesdropper.

10.3.2.3 B92 (Bennett 1992)

A simplified version of BB84, the B92 protocol uses only two non-orthogonal quantum states, such as $|0\rangle$ and $|+\rangle$. The safety of B92 relies on those measurements in non-orthogonal bases that yield only probabilistic information. Importantly, a failed measurement (i.e., no detection) often reveals more about the transmitted state than a successful one. This probabilistic behavior, combined with the no-cloning theorem, guarantees that any attempt at eavesdropping will result in observable disturbances.

10.3.2.4 Decoy State QKD

This is a practical enhancement used with prepare-and measure protocols such as BB84. Real-world single-photon sources are often weak laser pulses that sometimes contain more than one photon. An eavesdropper may exploit these multi-photon pulses through a photon number splitting (PNS) assault. Where they peel off some photons from a pulse and let the others pass undetected. Decoy states involve Alice sending "decoy" pulses prepared in different intensities or states alongside the "signal" pulses. By monitoring the observed error rate and yield (percentage of received pulses) for both can identify signal and decoy states. The PNS attacks and estimates the information Eve could have gained [22].

Table 10.1 describes types of QKD protocols and Figure 10.5 depicts a comparison of QKD protocols.

TABLE 10.1
Types of QKD Protocols

Feature/Protocol	BB84 (1984)	E91 (1991)	B92 (1992)	Decoy-State BB84
Quantum Resource	Single photons in 4 states of polarization	Entangled-photon- pairs	2 States of non-orthogonal	Single photons + decoy pulses
Security Basis	No-cloning + measurement disturbance	Bell inequality violation (entanglement)	No-cloning + state indistinguishability	Photon number statistics + BB84
Eavesdropper Detection	Basis mismatch errors	Entanglement degradation	Detection failure patterns	Statistical detection of PNS attacks
Implementation Type	Prepare and measure	Entanglement	Prepare & Measure	Prepare and measure (enhanced)
Advantages	Simple; widely implemented	High security via entanglement	Minimal states required	Secure with imperfect photon sources
Limitations	Vulnerable to PNS without a decoy	Complex to generate entangled pairs	Higher error rates	Added complexity in state management

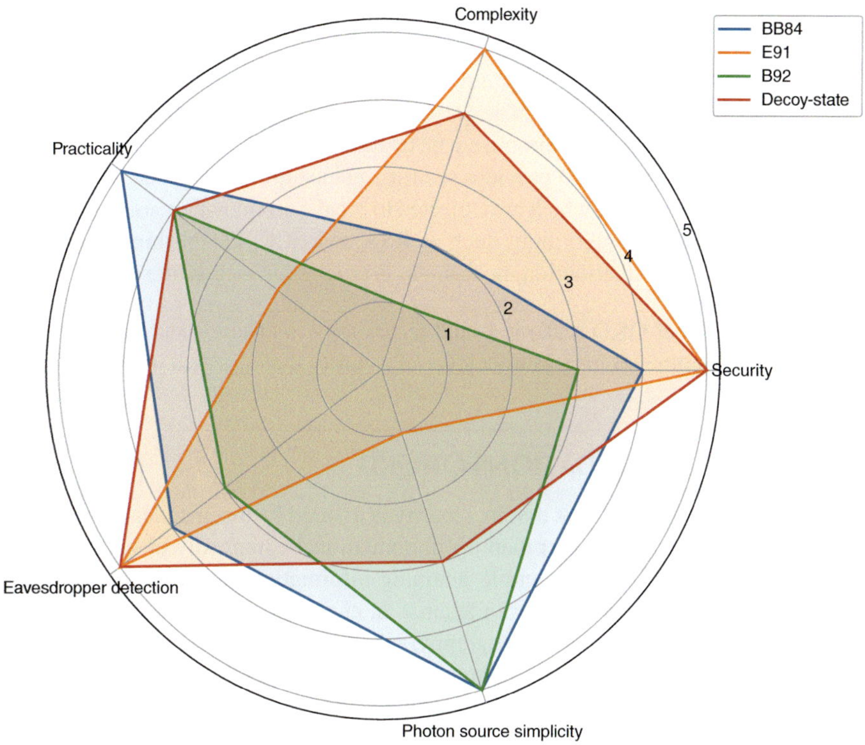

FIGURE 10.5 Comparison of QKD protocols.

10.4 ADVANTAGES OF QKD OVER CLASSICAL KEY DISTRIBUTION METHODS

QKD offers significant advantages compared to traditional methods for establishing shared secrets:

- **Unconditional Security (Information-Theoretic Security)**: The security of QKD, when implemented correctly under ideal conditions, depends on the fundamental laws of quantum mechanics, rather than on the assumed computational difficulty of mathematical problems. This means its security is theoretically guaranteed against adversaries with unlimited computational power, including future quantum computers. Classical methods, reliant on computational hardness, are vulnerable to algorithms that could significantly address the issues [23].
- **Eavesdropping Detection**: A cornerstone of QKD is the inherent detectability of eavesdropping. Any effort to intercept or measure quantum states results in disturbances that can be detected by the authorized parties. Traditional key exchange protocols, including Diffie–Hellman, lack this characteristic; an adversary may execute a man-in-the-middle attack undetected.

- **Forward Secrecy (Implied)**: While not universally true for all QKD implementations against all attacks, the principle of using a fresh, genuinely random key derived from quantum measurements for each communication session naturally lends itself to forward secrecy, meaning the compromise of one key does not compromise past or future keys.
- **Future-Proofing**: QKD provides security against the threat posed by future quantum computers, which are expected to break current widely used public-key cryptography algorithms such as RSA and ECC. Establishing a quantum-secure key distribution mechanism is crucial for long-term security.

These benefits of QKD make it a vital technology to ensure secure communications in the quantum era, providing a level of security that classical methods cannot achieve.

10.5 SAFETY FOUNDATIONS OF QKD

The core advantage of QKD is that its security is assured by the unchangeable principles of quantum physics, rather than the computational complexity of mathematical problems. This establishes a route to attaining information-theoretic security, indicating that the security persists even against an enemy with unbounded computing capabilities. Unlike classical cryptography, where security relies on the adversary being unable to perform certain computations efficiently, QKD security relies on the inherent physical properties of quantum systems, specifically how information is encoded, transmitted, and measured [24]. Figure 10.6 illustrates security features addressed by the QKD protocol.

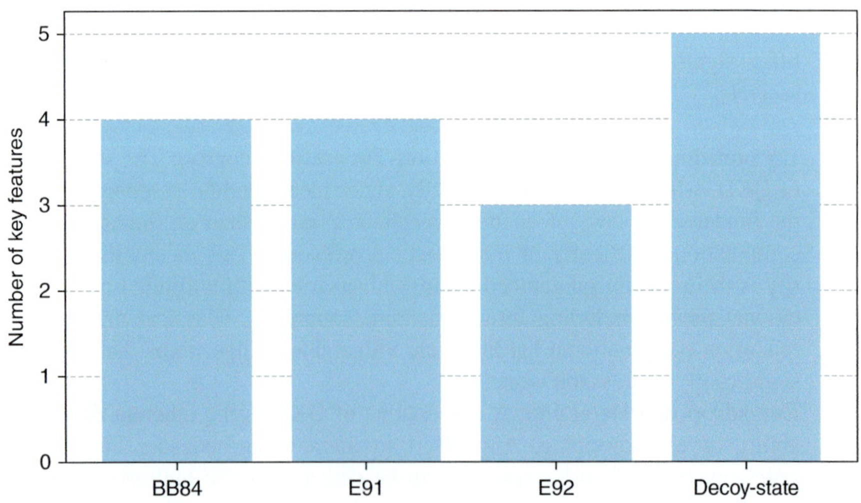

FIGURE 10.6 Security features addressed by the QKD protocol.

The fundamental principle that ensures the security of QKD is that any effort to measure or replicate an unknown quantum state will necessarily alter it. The disturbance is observable to legitimate users Alice and Bob, enabling them to recognize the presence of an eavesdropper (Eve) and eliminate any potentially compromised key material. This detection mechanism is a radical departure from classical key exchange protocols, where an attacker can often intercept communications passively without leaving a trace.

10.5.1 Quantum Mechanical Guarantees Against Eavesdropping

The security of QKD protocols, particularly prepare and measure methods such as BB84 and entanglement-oriented methods such as E91, stems directly from the principles discussed earlier:

- **Measurement Disturbance**: According to the measurement postulate of quantum mechanics, measuring a quantum state generally alters its state. Suppose Alice sends a qubit in a specific basis state (e.g., a photon polarized horizontally) and Bob measures it in that same basis; he obtains the expected outcome without disturbing the state. However, if Eve intercepts the photon and measures it in a basis different from the one Alice used (which she must guess, as Alice's basis choice is random and unknown to Eve), her measurement will likely collapse the state into one of the basis states she chose. When she then resends a photon in that new state to Bob, and Bob measures it in the correct basis (matching Alice's original basis), he may obtain an incorrect outcome with a certain probability.
- These incorrect outcomes manifest as errors in the raw key shared by Alice and Bob. The laws of quantum mechanics dictate that for non-orthogonal states, such a measurement attempt by Eve will introduce a minimum amount of disturbance that can be detected by Alice and Bob if they monitor their channel's error rate.
- **No-Cloning Theorem**: This theorem prevents Eve from simply making a perfect copy of the transmitted quantum states and measuring the copy at her leisure while forwarding the original (or a copy) to Bob. Since quantum states utilized in QKD protocols are typically unknown to Eve, she cannot create perfect replicas. Any attempt to approximate a clone will inevitably introduce errors or disturbance into the state that is forwarded to Bob, again leading to detectable discrepancies. This contrasts sharply with classical information, which can be copied perfectly and undetectably.
- **Entanglement Correlations (for E91-type protocols)**: In entanglement-based QKD, security is verified by testing the quantum correlations between Alice's and Bob's measurement outcomes on their respective entangled particles. If Eve interacts with the entangled particles in transit, she will disrupt the entanglement. This disruption will weaken the correlations between Alice's and Bob's measurements, particularly when they choose non-compatible bases for some subset of their measurements. By checking

for expected strong correlations (e.g., by testing for a violation of a Bell inequality such as the CHSH inequality) and comparing them with the expected value without eavesdropping, Alice and Bob could identify Eve's availability [17].

These quantum mechanical properties ensure that any attempt by Eve to gain information about the transmitted qubits necessarily affects them, leaving a measurable footprint. Alice and Bob exploit this fundamental principle by checking for the presence of such footprints.

10.5.2 Detecting Eavesdropping Through Error Rates

In a perfect QKD system free from noise and eavesdropping, Alice and Bob's raw keys (after sifting) would be identical. However, real-world systems experience noise from various sources (e.g., detector dark counts, imperfect state preparation, channel loss leading to re-emissions). Crucially, eavesdropping also introduces errors.

During the classical post-processing phase, Alice and Bob publicly compare a random subset of their sifted key bits. This enables the estimation of the QBER. It represents the ratio of erroneous bits in their raw keys. A high QBER suggests either significant channel noise or, more importantly, potential eavesdropping. If the estimated QBER exceeds a predetermined threshold (which depends on the specific protocol and desired security level), Alice and Bob conclude that the channel is compromised (either by Eve or excessive noise) and abort the key generation process, discarding the entire raw key. If QBER is less than the threshold, it proceeds with the assumption that any eavesdropping was limited enough to be counteracted by the subsequent post-processing steps. The maximum tolerable QBER is a critical parameter derived from security proofs, often around 11% for standard BB84 with ideal single-photon sources. Figure 10.7 depicts QBER vs distance in quantum communication.

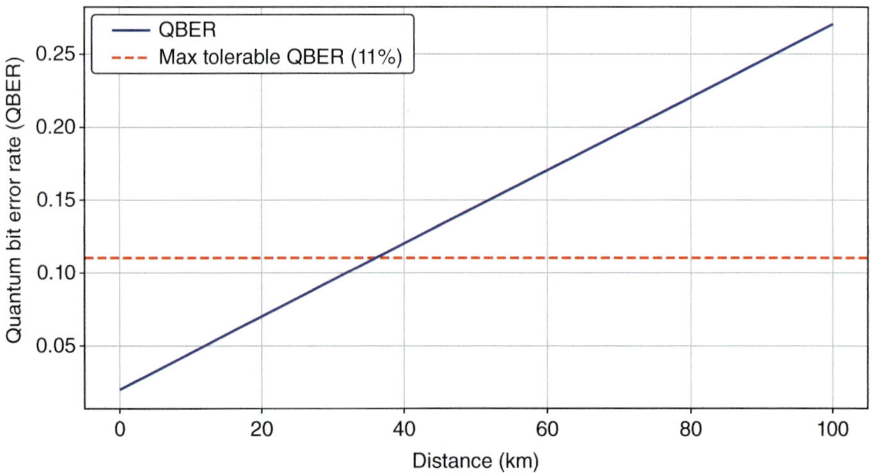

FIGURE 10.7 QBER vs distance in quantum communication.

10.5.3 Traditional Post Processing Involves Two Critical Components: Error Correction and Privacy Amplification

Even when the QBER is below the detection threshold, the raw key likely contains errors due to noise and may also exhibit residual information leakage to Eve. Two essential classical post-processing steps are used to address these issues: Information Reconciliation and Privacy Amplification [14].

10.5.3.1 Information Reconciliation (EC)

The goal of Information Reconciliation is for Alice and Bob to agree on an identical secret key. This is achieved by correcting the errors detected during the error estimation phase. Alice and Bob use classical EC protocols over the public channel. These protocols allow Bob (or Alice) to inform the other party about the locations and types of errors in their raw key without revealing the actual values of the bits. Common techniques include the Cascade protocol or Low-Density Parity-Check (LDPC) codes. During this process, some public information about the key bits is inevitably exchanged. Eve, listening to the classical channel, can gain partial information about the raw key from this exchange. The amount of information leaked depends on the EC protocol used and the key length. A successful EC phase results in Alice and Bob sharing an identical key, but Eve may hold some correlational information about this key [16].

10.5.3.2 Privacy Amplification

Following Information Reconciliation, Alice and Bob possess an identical key. Nonetheless, Eve may retain residual information, either from intercepted messages during EC or through potential side channels. Privacy Amplification is a method employed to derive a shorter, highly secure key from a longer, error-corrected key. Alice and Bob reach a public agreement on a hash function selected at random from a publicly recognized family of hash functions. The hash function is subsequently applied to the identical, error-corrected key. The result is a condensed string, which serves as the final secret key. The length of the final key is determined by the estimated information that Eve may possess, which is typically inferred from the quantum bit error rate (QBER) and the volume of public information exchanged. A significant finding in privacy amplification theory indicates that if Eve's knowledge of the original key is limited by a specific entropy measure, an appropriately selected hash function can diminish her knowledge of the final key to an arbitrarily small amount. Let the final key length be defined as

$$\ell = \mathrm{n} - \mathrm{leak\,EC} - 2\log 2\left(1/\epsilon\,\mathrm{sec}\right), \tag{10.7}$$

where

- n is the length of the reconciled key,
- leak EC is the amount of information leaked during error correction,
- ϵ sec is the security parameter, a small value representing the desired maximum probability that Eve knows anything about the final key.

This process ensures that Eve's information is negligible, making the final key secure for cryptographic use.

10.6 ATTACK STRATEGIES AND COUNTERMEASURES

While QKD offers unconditional security in principle, real-world implementations face vulnerabilities from practical imperfections and sophisticated attack strategies.

10.6.1 Quantum Attack Strategies

10.6.1.1 Intercept Resend Assault

Eve intercepts photons transmitted by Alice, conducts measurements (selecting a basis), and subsequently generates new photons informed by her measurement outcomes to send to Bob. As discussed, this attack is detected by the resulting increase in the QBER measured by Alice and Bob, provided ideal single-photon sources and identifiers are used, and the QBER threshold is set appropriately [9].

10.6.1.2 PNS Attack

This attack exploits the use of weak laser pulses instead of true single-photon sources in many practical QKD systems. Weak pulses occasionally contain more than one photon. Eve can intercept these multi-photon pulses, split them, keep one photon, and send the others to Bob. She can store her collected photons in a quantum memory (even a classical memory might suffice if she can measure later when Alice announces bases) and measure them only after Alice announces the bases. This attack is undetectable unless countered. The primary countermeasure involves the implementation of decoy states. Alice transmits pulses with differing strengths (varied average photon counts, including vacuum states or low-intensity "decoy" states).

By monitoring the observed yield and error rate for various intensity pulses, Alice and Bob could identify the availability of PNS attacks and estimate the maximum information Eve could have gained, which informs the length of the final secret key after privacy amplification.

10.6.1.3 Trojan–Horse Attack

Eve sends a bright pulse of light into Alice's or Bob's device. Reflections from internal components might carry information back to Eve about the device's state or settings. Countermeasures involve placing isolators and filters at the device input ports to block incoming light or detect outgoing light caused by such intrusions [20].

10.6.2 Classical and Implementation Attack Strategies

Even though the quantum part of QKD offers unconditional security, the classical post-processing requires a secure classical channel.

10.6.2.1 Man-in-the-Middle (MITM) Assault on the Traditional Channel

While QKD ensures the secrecy of the key derived from quantum transmissions, Alice and Bob communicate publicly over a classical channel during sifting, EC, and privacy amplification. An attacker could intercept and alter this classical communication. For example, Eve could impersonate Alice to Bob and Bob to Alice, establishing two separate QKD sessions with each of them and relaying information.

To prevent this, the classical channel used for public communication must be authenticated. This typically requires a pre-shared secret key or public-key infrastructure, although bootstrapping trust with QKD itself is an area of research.

The authentication itself does not need to be quantum-secure, but it must be robust enough to prevent impersonation and message manipulation.

10.6.2.2 Side-Channel Attacks

These attacks exploit physical leakage from the QKD system implementation, such as timing information, power consumption, or unintended light emissions from components (e.g., detectors). These attacks target the specific devices used rather than the fundamental protocol. Much research and engineering effort goes into building 'provably secure' devices that eliminate or mitigate such side channels. Examples include attacks that exploit detector blinding or efficiency mismatches in the receiver's detectors. In summary, the security of QKD against sophisticated adversaries is a complex interplay between the fundamental quantum mechanical guarantees, the robustness of the post processing algorithms (Information Reconciliation and Privacy), and the careful design and implementation of the quantum hardware to prevent side-channel exploits and mitigate vulnerabilities arising from non-ideal components (such as the need for decoy states to counteract PNS attacks). Although unconditional security is established for theoretical protocols using perfect components, the pursuit of 'device-independent' or 'measurement-device-independent' QKD remains a vigorous research domain focused on reducing security dependence on assumptions on the internal processes of devices.

10.7 TECHNOLOGICAL IMPLEMENTATIONS AND CHALLENGES OF QKD

The implementation of QKD systems has progressed markedly in recent decades, transitioning from laboratory demonstrations to pilot initiatives and commercial offerings. Notwithstanding its robust theoretical basis, the implementation of QKD in actual settings involves an interaction among sensitive hardware components, quantum channels, and conventional post-processing units. This section analyses the present status of QKD technology, its fundamental components, and the primary obstacles encountered in practical applications [22].

10.7.1 Core Hardware Components of QKD Systems

A conventional QKD configuration has certain essential hardware components that provide secure quantum communication between two distant parties, often designated as Alice and Bob. The components comprise:

- **Photon Sources**: The quantum states used in QKD are often encoded on individual photons or Weak Coherent Pulses (WCP). High-quality photon sources are crucial for the reliable generation of quantum states with precisely specified features. Various methodologies exist for photon sources:
  - True Single-Photon Sources: Devices include quantum dots, color centers in diamond, or heralded sources that may generate photons individually with excellent purity.
  - However, these sources often require cryogenic cooling and intricate optical setups, limiting their current commercial viability.

10.9.1.2 Financial Sector

The financial industry relies heavily on secure data transmission for transactions, customer information, and interbank communications. Confidentiality and integrity are paramount. QKD can be deployed to secure high-value links between banks, financial data centers, and stock exchanges, where the security of exchanged keys is critical, and the volume of data is high. Protecting sensitive financial data from being compromised years into the future is a significant driver for exploring quantum-safe solutions, such as QKD.

10.9.1.3 Critical Infrastructure and Data Protection

Operators of essential infrastructure, including electrical grids, water systems, and telecommunications networks, face increasing cyber threats. Securing the command-and-control links and sensor data is vital.

QKD can provide tamper-evident security for these links. Furthermore, data centers holding vast amounts of sensitive personal, corporate, or governmental data require robust protection for data in transit between sites, and potentially for key management related to data at rest. QKD offers a method to secure the keys used to encrypt this valuable data, providing long-term protection.

10.9.1.4 General Secure Communications

Beyond high-security niches, QKD is also applicable to general enterprise communication where enhanced security is desired, such as securing virtual private networks (VPNs) between corporate offices, protecting sensitive research data, or establishing secure links for healthcare information exchange. While cost and infrastructure currently limit widespread adoption, ongoing technological advancements are making QKD more accessible for broader enterprise applications.

10.9.1.5 Integration with Classical Networks

QKD systems are designed to work alongside existing classical communication infrastructure. QKD generates a secret key, but the actual data transmission typically occurs over standard classical networks, encrypted using the quantum-generated key. Integration is achieved by co-propagating quantum signals (carrying the key information) and classical data signals on the same fiber using techniques such as WDM, where quantum and classical signals are transmitted at different wavelengths. This allows organizations to leverage their existing fiber optic networks for both purposes, reducing the need for separate infrastructure. Hybrid networks combining QKD links with classical encryption provide layers of security.

10.9.2 Role in the Emerging Quantum Internet

The notion of a “Quantum Internet” proposes a worldwide network using quantum technology. Quantum information itself can be transmitted and processed across distances. This network would enable applications far beyond QKD, including distributed quantum computing and enhanced sensing. QKD is often seen as a foundational building block or the first application layer for such a network. Quantum communication technologies developed for QKD, such as quantum repeaters (though still under development) and entangled photon distribution, are essential components of a future Quantum Internet, facilitating secure key distribution between any two points in the network.

10.9.3 Future Prospects and Challenges

While QKD provides strong theoretical security, its journey toward widespread, practical deployment faces several technological and economic challenges. The future prospects involve overcoming these hurdles and leveraging synergies with other quantum technologies.

10.9.3.1 Scalability

A major challenge for QKD is scaling beyond point-to-point links over limited distances. Fiber attenuation significantly restricts the direct QKD range.

Current networks typically rely on trusted nodes to extend reach, but these nodes introduce security vulnerabilities (as they must be trusted not to leak the key).

Future scalability heavily depends on the development of the following:

- **Quantum Repeaters**: Devices capable of extending quantum communication distances by mitigating photon loss without measuring and destroying the quantum state. They rely on quantum memory and entanglement swapping and are essential for a global quantum network, but remain complex experimental systems.
- **Quantum Networks**: Developing network architectures, protocols, and management systems to route quantum keys and potentially quantum information efficiently across multiple users and nodes.
- **Satellite-Based QKD**: Offers a path to cover very large distances and connect locations without fiber links, potentially forming a global backbone for quantum-secure communication [17].

10.9.3.2 Commercial Deployment

QKD technology is transitioning from research labs to commercial products, but cost, complexity, and integration challenges persist. Wide-scale commercial deployment requires:

- **Cost Reduction**: Making QKD systems more affordable compared to classical solutions.
- **Miniaturization and Integration**: Developing smaller, integrated photonics-based QKD methods that are simpler to set up and keep up.
- **User-Friendliness**: Simplifying operation and management for IT professionals without deep quantum expertise.
- **Standardization**: Establishing industry standards for QKD protocols, hardware interfaces, and security testing to ensure interoperability and trust.

As these aspects improve, QKD is expected to move from niche high-security markets toward broader adoption in critical infrastructure and enterprise networks.

10.9.3.3 Interplay with Quantum Computing Developments

The creation of quantum computers that can withstand errors is the primary driver for quantum-safe cryptography. While QKD addresses the key distribution problem, it does not solve the vulnerability of classical encryption (such as AES) or digital signatures (such as RSA/ECC) to quantum algorithms (specifically Grover's and Shor's algorithms, respectively).

A complete quantum-safe cryptographic posture requires a combination of:

- **QKD**: For distributing secret keys whose security relies on quantum physics, providing quantum-proof key exchange.
- **Post-Quantum Cryptography (PQC)**: Novel classical cryptography methods engineered to withstand assaults from both conventional and quantum computers. PQC is needed for asymmetric functions such as digital signatures and public-key encryption, which QKD does not directly provide.

QKD and PQC are complementary. PQC can handle the digital signatures needed to authenticate QKD classical communication. QKD provides a key distribution method immune to quantum algorithms, whereas PQC depends on the calculation hardness assumption concerning certain mathematical issues. The future will likely see hybrid approaches combining QKD and PQC for layered security [24].

10.9.3.4 Potential Evolution of Quantum-Safe Cryptographic Standards

The threat of quantum computing is driving significant activity in cryptographic standardization bodies globally.

- **Post-Quantum Cryptography Standardization**: National Institute of Standards and Technology (NIST) in the United States is leading a multi-round process to standardize quantum-resistant public-key algorithms for digital signatures, key exchange, and encryption. This is crucial for the broad migration away from vulnerable classical schemes.
- **QKD Standards**: Organizations such as European Telecommunications Standards Institute (ETSI) are developing standards for QKD system components, protocols, and security certification. These standards are essential for the interoperability and reliable deployment of QKD technology.

The co-evolution of PQC and QKD standards reflects the understanding that a multi-faceted approach is necessary to secure information against future quantum threats. Future standards will likely address the integration of QKD and PQC into hybrid safety features.

10.10 CONCLUSION

QKD provides an innovative method for secure communication by leveraging underlying quantum principles rather than depending on computational complexity. Visualizing key concepts through charts such as the bar chart comparing QKD protocols, the line chart showing how QBER increases with distance, and the pie chart illustrating the contributions of quantum principles helps clarify the strengths, limitations, and foundational elements of QKD. These insights demonstrate how protocols such as BB84 and E91 balance simplicity, robustness, and security, while emphasizing the critical roles of the no-cloning theorem, measurement disturbance, entanglement, and superposition. Collectively, these visual tools highlight QKD's potential to provide future-proof, physics-based security in an era of advancing quantum threats.

REFERENCES

1. Nath, A., Maity, S., Banerjee, S., and Roy, R. (2024). Quantum Key Distribution (QKD) for symmetric key transfer. *International Journal of Scientific Research in Computer Science, Engineering and Information Technology*. https://doi.org/10.32628/cseit24103105
2. Djordjevic, Ivan B. "Quantum Key Distribution (QKD) Fundamentals." In *Physical-Layer Security, Quantum Key Distribution, and Post-Quantum Cryptography*, pp. 305–362. Cham: Springer Nature Switzerland, 2025.
3. Ranganathan, Swetha, Shanmitha Karthikeyan, Chandrashekhar Pomu Chavan, and P.T. Shanthala "Integrating Quantum Key Distribution (QKD) with Post-Quantum Cryptography (PQC): Combining BB84 Protocol with Lattice-Based Cryptographic Techniques." In *2024 IEEE 4th International Conference on ICT in Business Industry & Government (ICTBIG)*, pp. 1–9. IEEE, 2024.
4. Nguyen, Tu N., Dung H.P. Nguyen, Manh V. Nguyen, Thinh V. Le, Bing-Hong Liu, and Thang N. Dinh. "Maximizing Key Distribution Capability: An Application in Quantum Cryptography." In *2023 IEEE International Conference on Quantum Computing and Engineering (QCE)*, vol. 1, pp. 1187–1197. IEEE, 2023.
5. Anilkumar, Chunduru, Swathi Lenka, N.E.S.V. Neelima, and V.E. Sathishkumar "A secure method of communication through bb84 protocol in quantum key distribution." *Scalable Computing: Practice and Experience* 25, no. 1 (2024): 21–33.
6. Bennett, Charles H., and Gilles Brassard. "Quantum cryptography: Public key distribution and coin tossing." *Theoretical Computer Science* 560 (2014): 7–11.
7. Shor, P.W., and J. Preskill. Simple proof of security of the BB84 quantum key distribution protocol. *Physical Review Letters*, 85, no. 2 (2000), 441–444. https://doi.org/10.1103/PhysRevLett.85.441
8. Srividya, B.V., and S. Sasi (2021). An emphasis on quantum cryptography and quantum key distribution. *Cryptography - Recent Advances and Future Developments*. https://doi.org/10.5772/INTECHOPEN.95383
9. Malwade, Sulakshana, Shilpa Choudhary, Santosh H. Lavate, Parikshit N. Mahalle, Samir N. Ajani, and Vinit Khetani. "Enhancing Data Security in Transmission Through Quantum Key Distribution in Cryptography." In *2025 International Conference on Emerging Smart Computing and Informatics (ESCI)*, pp. 1–6. IEEE, 2025.
10. Djordjevic, Ivan B. "Physical-layer security, quantum key distribution, and post-quantum cryptography." *Entropy* 24, no. 7 (2022): 935. https://doi.org/10.3390/e24070935
11. Rusca, Davide, and Nicolas Gisin. "Quantum cryptography: An overview of quantum key distribution." *arXiv preprint arXiv:2411.04044* (2024). https://doi.org/10.48550/arXiv.2411.04044
12. Chander, Bhanu. "Quantum Cryptography Key Distribution: Quantum Computing." In *Research Anthology on Advancements in Quantum Technology*, pp. 325–344. IGI Global, 2021.

13. Padamvathi, V., B. Vishnu Vardhan, and A.V.N. Krishna. "Quantum Cryptography and Quantum Key Distribution Protocols: A Survey." In *2016 IEEE 6th international conference on advanced computing (IACC)*, pp. 556–562. IEEE, 2016. https://doi.org/10.1109/IACC.2016.109
14. Mehic, M., M. Niemiec, S. Rass, J. Ma, M. Peev, A. Aguado, V. Martín, S. Schauer, A. Poppe, C. Pacher, and M. Voznák. "Quantum key distribution." *ACM Computing Surveys (CSUR)*, 53 (2020), 1–41. https://doi.org/10.1145/3402192
15. Begimbayeva, Yenlik, Temirlan Zhaxalykov, Amir Akhtanov, Ruslan Pashkevich, and Mukaddas Arshidinova. "Centerless Quantum Key Distribution Protocol based on Superposition." In *2024 20th International Asian School-Seminar on Optimization Problems of Complex Systems (OPCS)*, pp. 7–11. IEEE, 2024. https://doi.org/10.1109/OPCS63516.2024.10720385
16. Malhotra, V., S. Yadav, and Vishal (2024). Quantum cryptography: Advancements, challenges, and applications in modern communication. *International Journal of Advanced Research in Science, Communication and Technology*. https://doi.org/10.48175/ijarsct-17591
17. Krishna, Marrapu Hari, Alekhya Juttiga, Meesala Shobharani, D. Deepa, Chunduru Anilkumar, and Ashok Sarabu. "Exploring Quantum Key Distribution for Secure Communication: A Comprehensive Survey." In *2023 International Conference on Energy, Materials and Communication Engineering (ICEMCE)*, pp. 1–5. IEEE, 2023. https://doi.org/10.1109/ICEMCE57940.2023.10434018
18. Bennett, Charles H., François Bessette, Gilles Brassard, Louis Salvail, and John Smolin. "Experimental quantum cryptography." *Journal of Cryptology* 5, no. 1 (1992): 3–28. https://doi.org/10.1007/BF00191318
19. Giroti, Ishika, and Meenakshi Malhotra. "Quantum Cryptography: A Pathway to Secure Communication." In *2022 6th International Conference on Computation System and Information Technology for Sustainable Solutions (CSITSS)*, pp. 1–6. IEEE, 2022. https://doi.org/10.1109/CSITSS57437.2022.10026388
20. Sharma, Meenakshi, and Sonia Thind. "A Quantum Key Distribution Technique Using Quantum Cryptography." In *Research Anthology on Blockchain Technology in Business, Healthcare, Education, and Government*, pp. 263–271. IGI Global Scientific Publishing, 2021.
21. Kour, Jasleen, Saboor Koul, and Prince Zahid. "A survey on quantum key distribution protocols." *International Journal of Computer Applications (IJCA)* 7, no. 3 (2017). https://doi.org/10.5121/IJCSA.2017.7302
22. Lella, Eufemia, and Giovanni Schmid. "On the security of quantum key distribution networks." *Cryptography* 7, no. 4 (2023): 53. https://doi.org/10.2139/ssrn.4348222
23. Win, Myat Su, and Thet Thet Khin. "Analysis of quantum key distribution protocols." In *2023 IEEE Conference on Computer Applications (ICCA)*, pp. 357–362. IEEE, 2023. https://doi.org/10.1109/ICCA51723.2023.10181682
24. Subramani, Shalini, M. Selvi, A. Kannan, and Santhosh Kumar Svn. "Review of security methods based on classical cryptography and quantum cryptography." *Cybernetics and Systems* 56, no. 3 (2025): 302–320. https://doi.org/10.1080/01969722.2023.2166261

11 Challenges and Opportunities of Quantum Computing in Medical Imaging

Pratibha C. Kaladeep Yalagi, C. Nandagopal, M. Vallikannu, K. Vijayalakshmi, C. Mariyammal, and R. Jeevitha

11.1 INTRODUCTION

The intersection of medical and computing technologies has long produced revolutionary breakthroughs, such as automated diagnosis and telemedicine, as well as genome sequencing and personalized treatment [1]. In recent years, the emergence of quantum computing (QC) has brought a new frontier with the potential to transform and accelerate many critical healthcare processes, particularly in medical imaging, drug discovery, and clinical decision support [2]. While traditional computational machines have come a long way, they are increasingly being tested for managing intricate, high-dimensional information characteristic of modern health systems [3]. QC, by its potential to leverage the principles of superposition, entanglement, and quantum parallelism, offers a completely new paradigm that is poised to transcend such limitations and leverage unprecedented computational power [4]. Medical imaging is probably the most computationally demanding sector of medicine, including technologies such as magnetic resonance imaging (MRI), computed tomography (CT), positron emission tomography (PET), ultrasound, and digital pathology [5]. These modalities generate vast quantities of high-resolution, multi-dimensional data that require sophisticated approaches to interpretation, classification, and segmentation [6]. In this regard, quantum machine learning (QML), which is a combination of machine learning (ML) and QC, has been a future solution for boosting the speed, accuracy, and robustness of medical image analysis [7]. QML models, such as quantum neural networks (QNNs), quantum kernel methods, and quantum-inspired convolutional networks, have demonstrated potential advantages in learning from noisy or sparse data, feature representation, and model generalization [8].

DOI: 10.1201/9781003587835-11

Apart from imaging, QC is also more and more explored for the potential to simulate atomic-level molecular interactions that are beneficial for drug design and protein folding [9]. Traditional methods of molecular docking and dynamic simulation are computationally intensive and scale poorly as molecules become more complicated [10]. QC algorithms such as Gaussian Boson Sampling and quantum annealing offer new avenues for the simulation of biomolecular behavior more succinctly [11]. These skills are of significant utility within pharmaceutical discovery, wherein speed and accuracy are so important for the production of new drugs [12]. Another critical field where QC is picking up pace is secure medical data exchange and privacy-preserving computation [13]. With the emergence of medical Internet of Things (IoT) devices and wireless body sensor networks, ensuring patient data security is a matter of urgency [14]. Quantum cryptographic methods, such as BB84 and post-quantum cryptography algorithms, are being investigated to protect sensitive health information from classical and quantum-based cyber-attacks [15].

Although its potential is vast, QC in the healthcare sector remains in its infancy [16]. Numerous impediments prevent its universal application: low qubit fidelity, high error rates, the requirement for cryogenic conditions, unscalable quantum hardware, and insufficiently trained professionals with expertise in healthcare and quantum technology alike [17]. Additionally, regulatory environments for the clinical testing of quantum-based technologies are still under development, adding another degree of complexity to the system [18]. However, the field is rapidly changing. Research institutions, tech firms, and healthcare organizations are making significant investments in investigating quantum advantage, the quantum algorithm point at which it definitely surpasses classical counterparts—in actual clinical environments [19]. Various studies between 2020 and 2024 indicate how hybrid quantum–classical models are being developed for medical imaging applications, disease classification, and biomedical data analysis. Furthermore, theoretical surveys and experimental verifications are paving the way for scalable and noise-resilient quantum models, particularly during the Noisy Intermediate-Scale Quantum (NISQ) period [20].

This review of literature consolidates the emerging body of work that integrates QC with healthcare, highlighting applications to medical imaging, diagnostics, security, and clinical support systems. Through a review of chief contributions, implementation strategies, and comparisons against classical models, this chapter seeks to present an integrative understanding of the state of the art, limitations, and directions for the future of QC in healthcare. Literature review of various contributions shown in Table 11.1.

TABLE 11.1
Literature Review of Various Contributions

Author(s)	Year	Title/Focus	Application Area	Key Contribution
Flother et al. (IBM) [1]	2023	Exploring quantum computing use cases for healthcare	General healthcare	Identified use cases in genomics, drug discovery, and imaging, suggesting early adoption pathways.
Sadki and Bakkali [2]	2015	Toward negotiable privacy policies in mobile healthcare	Data privacy	Proposed adaptive privacy policies for mobile healthcare systems.
Zinner et al. [3]	2021	Toward the institutionalization of quantum computing in pharmaceutical research	Pharmaceutical research	Analyzed quantum integration in pharmaceutical research and development (R&D) workflows.
Banchi et al. [4]	2020	Molecular docking with Gaussian boson sampling	Drug discovery	Demonstrated quantum photonics-based molecular docking for drug screening.
Li et al. [5]	2018	Quantum annealing versus classical machine learning applied to a simplified computational biology problem	Computational biology	Compared quantum annealing and classical ML models on biological data.
Gyongyosi and Imre [6]	2019	Survey on quantum computing technology	General quantum technology	Provided a complete overview of QC systems, architectures, and healthcare applications.
Fernández-Caramés [7]	2019	From pre-quantum to post-quantum IoT security: a survey on quantum-resistant cryptosystems for the internet of things	IoT Security in Healthcare	Reviewed post-quantum cryptography solutions for securing medical IoT.
Arunachalam and de Wolf [8]	2017	Survey of quantum learning theory	QML	Introduced theoretical foundations of QML applicable to medical datasets.
Li et al. [9]	2020	Quantum optimization and quantum learning: a survey	QML and optimization	Discussed quantum algorithms for learning and optimization in healthcare.
Bharti et al. [10]	2020	Machine learning meets quantum foundations: a brief survey	QML	Bridged theoretical quantum principles with applied ML in medical domains.

(Continued)

TABLE 11.1 (Continued)

Author(s)	Year	Title/Focus	Application Area	Key Contribution
Kumar et al. [11]	2021	Heart failure detection using quantum-enhanced machine learning and traditional machine learning techniques for Internet of artificially intelligent medical things	Medical imaging and diagnosis	Used quantum-enhanced ML for early detection of heart failure using imaging.
Olgiati et al. [12]	2021	A quantum-enhanced precision medicine application to support data-driven clinical decisions for the personalized treatment of advanced knee osteoarthritis: the Development and Preliminary validation of precisionKNEE_QNN	Clinical Decision Support	Developed a QNN model for osteoarthritis staging and personalized intervention.
Gupta et al. [13]	2022	Quantum computing led innovation for achieving a more sustainable COVID-19 healthcare industry	Pandemic Response	Highlighted QC applications for managing coronavirus disease 2019 (COVID-19) diagnostics and logistics.
Ur Rasool et al. [14]	2023	Quantum computing for healthcare data: a review	General healthcare	Reviewed various healthcare applications of QC, including imaging, diagnostics, and biosimulation.
Abbott [15]	2021	Quantum computers to explore precision oncology	Oncology	Focused on using QC to improve personalization in cancer treatment.
Outeiral et al. [16]	2021	The prospects of quantum computing in computational molecular biology	Molecular biology	Explored QC capabilities in protein structure prediction and simulation.
Aswiga R V et al. [17]	2024	Leveraging quantum kernel support vector machine for breast cancer diagnosis from digital breast tomosynthesis images	Medical imaging	Applied a quantum kernel support vector machine (SVM) to improve breast cancer classification from tomosynthesis images.
Geng Zhang and Hong Lai [18]	2024	QTN-MLP: quantum tensor network-enhanced MLP for medical image classification	Medical imaging	Proposed Quantum Tensor Network (QTN)-based Multi-Layer Perceptrons (MLP) architecture for improved diagnostic accuracy.
Usha Desai et al. [19]	2024	Comparison of machine learning and quantum machine learning for breast cancer detection	Medical imaging	Performed comparative analysis of classical ML and QML in breast cancer detection.

Esraa Hassan et al. [20]	2024	A quantum convolutional network and ResNet (50)-based classification architecture for the MNIST medical dataset	Medical imaging	Built a hybrid quantum–classical model for high-accuracy medical image classification.
Sofana Reka et al. [21]	2024	Exploring quantum machine learning for enhanced skin lesion classification: a comparative study of implementation methods	Dermatology imaging	Compared different quantum models for classifying skin lesions.
Ria Khatoniar et al. [22]	2024	Quantum convolutional neural network for medical image classification: a hybrid model	Medical imaging	Designed a hybrid quantum convolutional neural network (QCNN) for efficient medical image classification.
Sergio Altares-Lopez et al. [23]	2024	AutoQML: automatic generation and training of robust quantum-inspired classifiers by using genetic algorithms on grayscale images	Medical imaging	Automated robust QML model generation for grayscale diagnostic images.
Sambit Mallick et al. [24]	2024	A novel approach to breast cancer histopathological image classification using cross-colour space feature fusion and quantum–classical stack ensemble method	Pathology imaging	Fused features across color spaces using a hybrid quantum–classical ensemble method.
Modupe Odusami et al. [25]	2024	Alzheimer's disease stage recognition from MRI and PET imaging data using Pareto-optimal quantum dynamic optimization	Neurological imaging	Used Pareto-optimal quantum dynamic optimization for Alzheimer's staging.
Anton Simen et al. [26]	2024	Digital–analog quantum convolutional neural networks for image classification	Medical imaging	Implemented analog-digital quantum convolutional neural networks (CNNs) for faster and scalable medical image classification.
Gunti Swathi et al. [27]	2024	QuCNet: quantum-inspired convolutional neural networks for optimized thyroid nodule classification	Endocrinology imaging	Built QUCNet for optimized thyroid nodule diagnosis in ultrasound imaging.

11.3.5 Integration of Different Imaging Modalities

Integration of information from various imaging modalities (such as PET and MRI) provides a more comprehensive understanding of a patient's status. Quantum technology would be able to manage the integration better than traditional approaches. The different kinds of opportunities are shown in Table 11.3.

11.4 IMPLEMENTATION CHALLENGES

11.4.1 Hardware Maturity

Modern quantum devices continue to have several limitations—limited qubit count, limited lifetimes of quantum states (coherence), and high error rates. These conditions render modern systems unworkable for dealing with the size and complexity of real-world medical data. Application in medical imaging is described in Table 11.4.

TABLE 11.3
Kinds of Opportunities

S. No.	Opportunity	Description
1	Faster image processing	QC can significantly speed up image reconstruction processes.
2	Improved image reconstruction	Enhances the quality of images from low-quality or noisy data.
3	Enhanced pattern recognition	Detects subtle anomalies using QML.
4	Real-time analysis	Enables instant diagnosis and quicker decision-making.
5	Integration with AI/ML	Strengthens AI-based diagnostics through quantum-enhanced learning models.
6	Non-invasive imaging advancements	Potential for more accurate and less invasive imaging techniques.
7	Multimodal image fusion	Efficient integration of data from different imaging modalities (MRI, PET, and CT).

TABLE 11.4
Applications in Medical Imaging

Imaging Tool	Potential Quantum Enhancement
MRI	Fast image reconstruction, denoising using quantum field theory (QFT), and QPCA.
CT Scans	Rapid inverse problem solving for tomographic reconstructions.
Ultrasound	Quantum-enhanced noise filtering and segmentation.
PET	Improved signal-to-noise ratio using quantum filters.
X-Ray	Quantum algorithms for better contrast resolution and tissue classification.

11.4.2 Immature Algorithms

In contrast to classical computing, which possesses an abundance of proven algorithms for image processing, QC has immature, scalable algorithms specific to medical imaging. A great deal of work remains in the domain of simulation or theory.

11.4.3 Challenges in Clinical Integration

Hospitals have strict protocols and are based on traditional computing hardware. Introduction of quantum systems would mean large upgrades and would also need to adhere to the standards of medical data processing.

11.4.4 Security and Privacy Threats

Imaging data of patients is highly sensitive. Utilization of cloud-based quantum platforms could bring risks unless strong quantum encryption standards are created and made uniform. Various use cases and its description is shown in Table 11.5.

TABLE 11.5
Various Use Cases and Their Description

S. No	Use Case	Description
1	Fast image reconstruction	Uses quantum algorithms such as QFT to rapidly reconstruct images from raw MRI/CT data, enabling real-time diagnostic imaging.
2	Enhanced image segmentation	QML improves segmentation of tissues (e.g., tumors and organs) with higher precision than classical approaches.
3	Noise reduction and denoising	Quantum filtering techniques help reduce artifacts and noise, improving image quality, especially in low-dose scans.
4	High-dimensional data processing	Efficiently handles large, multi-modal imaging datasets (e.g., 3D/4D scans) that are computationally intensive for classical systems.
5	Accelerated feature extraction (radiomics)	Speeds up the extraction of quantitative image features (shape, texture, etc.), which are crucial for cancer diagnosis and treatment response analysis.
6	Secure image transmission	Quantum cryptography (QKD) ensures secure sharing of medical images in telemedicine and cloud-based imaging environments.
7	Drug-imaging interaction simulation	Simulates how drugs interact with tissues seen in images, aiding in targeted therapy and theranostics.
8	Quantum image compression	Compresses high-resolution images using quantum methods, allowing efficient storage and fast transmission in medical databases.

11.4.5 Interdisciplinary Skill Gaps

The intersection of medical imaging, quantum physics, and computer science is recent. Few experts know both medical imaging and QC, which hinders development and utilization.

11.5 APPLICATIONS OF QC IN MEDICAL IMAGING

11.5.1 Tumor Detection

Quantum models that have learned from large numbers of MRI or CT scans might enhance precision in identifying tumors, minimize diagnostic mistakes, and enable early interventions. QC growth in medical imaging is shown in Figure 11.2.

11.5.2 Brain Scan Analysis

Quantum computations would be able to handle brain images (e.g., DTI or fMRI) more efficiently, which would aid in the detection and tracking of neurological diseases such as Alzheimer's, epilepsy, or multiple sclerosis.

11.5.3 Enhancing Heart Imaging

Heart scan analysis using quantum would aid physicians in more timely and precise detection of abnormalities such as faulty valves or artery obstructions.

11.5.4 Disease Outcome Prediction

QML could enable physicians to forecast disease development or response to treatment from imaging characteristics, to inform individualized care plans.

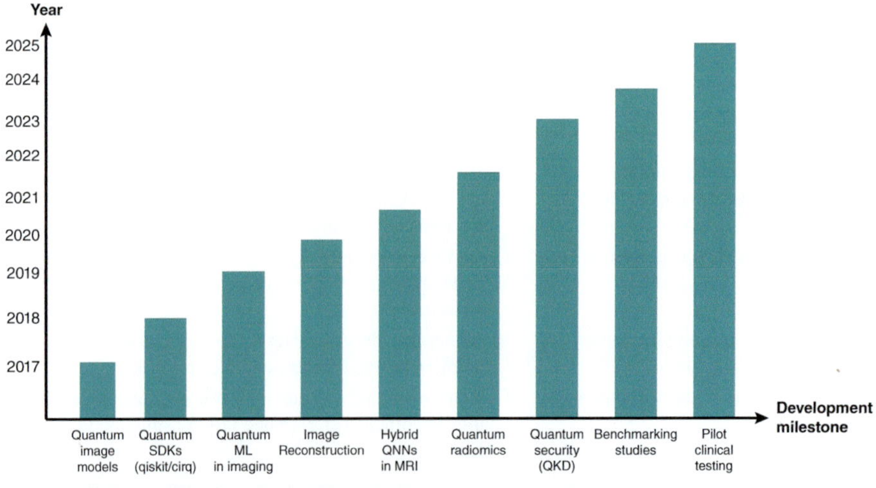

FIGURE 11.2 Growth of quantum computing (QC) in medical imaging.

11.5.5 Image Merging and Matching

Quantum computers can enhance image registration, by combining scans from multiple sources (such as CT and PET) to provide a more integrated perspective, which is vital for precise diagnosis and treatment planning.

11.6 CONCLUSION

QC promises to be truly amazing in medical imaging, with new means of managing the rising volume and variety of image data. The potential is tremendous, ranging from accelerating reconstructions to facilitating more precise diagnoses. That being said, actual implementation remains constrained by technological and practical issues. Going forward, significant advances will rely on ongoing research, more robust cross-field collaboration, and targeted training for practitioners. As quantum technology advances and becomes more widely available, it may become a key component of future healthcare, revolutionizing the way we diagnose and treat illness.

REFERENCES

1. Flöther, Frederik, J. Murphy, J. Murtha, and D. Sow. "Exploring quantum computing use cases for healthcare." IBM Institute for Business Value (2022). https://www.ibm.com/thought-leadership/institute-business-value/en-us/report/quantum-healthcare
2. Sadki, Souad, and Hanan El Bakkali. "Towards negotiable privacy policies in mobile healthcare." In *Fifth International Conference on the Innovative Computing Technology (INTECH 2015)*, pp. 94–99. IEEE, 2015, doi: 10.1109/INTECH.2015.7173478
3. Zinner, Maximillian, Florian Dahlhausen, Philip Boehme, Jan Ehlers, Linn Bieske, and Leonard Fehring. "Toward the institutionalization of quantum computing in pharmaceutical research." *Drug Discovery Today* 27, no. 2 (2022): 378–383.
4. Banchi, Leonardo, Mark Fingerhuth, Tomas Babej, Christopher Ing, and Juan Miguel Arrazola. "Molecular docking with Gaussian boson sampling." *Science Advances* 6, no. 23 (2020): eaax1950.
5. Li, Richard Y., Rosa Di Felice, Remo Rohs, and Daniel A. Lidar. "Quantum annealing versus classical machine learning applied to a simplified computational biology problem." *NPJ Quantum Information* 4, no. 1 (2018): 14.
6. Gyongyosi, Laszlo, and Sandor Imre. "A survey on quantum computing technology." *Computer Science Review* 31 (2019): 51–71.
7. Fernández-Caramés, Tiago M. "From pre-quantum to post-quantum IoT security: A survey on quantum-resistant cryptosystems for the Internet of Things." *IEEE Internet of Things Journal* 7, no. 7 (2019): 6457–6480.
8. Arunachalam, Srinivasan, and Ronald De Wolf. "Guest column: A survey of quantum learning theory." *ACM Sigact News* 48, no. 2 (2017): 41–67.
9. Li, Yangyang, Mengzhuo Tian, Guangyuan Liu, Cheng Peng, and Licheng Jiao. "Quantum optimization and quantum learning: A survey." *Ieee Access* 8 (2020): 23568–23593.
10. Bharti, Kishor, Tobias Haug, Vlatko Vedral, and Leong-Chuan Kwek. "Machine learning meets quantum foundations: A brief survey." *AVS Quantum Science* 2, no. 3 (2020): 1–12.

12 Quantum Computing and Industry Transformation

V. Preetha, K. K. Archana, R. Abinaya, S. A. Amala Nirmal Doss, and M. K. Sundaram

12.1 INTRODUCTION

With transistor sizes equal to atomic size, the age of classical computing—which was basically powered by Moore's law—is progressively slowing down. Moore's rule, which states that transistor density 2 times roughly doubles every 2 years, has propelled exponential performance increase for 50 years [1]. However, as semiconductor equipment get closer to their physical limits, issues include heat dissipation, quantum tunneling, and lithographic restrictions, which are making it harder and more expensive to maintain this rate of advancement. The plateau in classical efficiency is being tackled through other computer paradigms, and quantum computing (QC) has come as an intriguing alternative.

Using the topics of quantum mechanics, specifically superposition, entanglement, and quantum interference, QC manipulates data in fundamentally novel ways. As more qubits are added, computing power may increase exponentially because a quantum bit, or qubit, can be available in several states all at once. A qubit may represent both 0 and 1, but a classical bit can only represent one. This enables QC systems to process concurrent operations that are not possible for classical machines.

Recent improvements in quantum hardware have resulted in experimental devices crossing the 100-qubit threshold. Although these noisy intermediate-scale quantum (NISQ) systems are not yet capable of full fault tolerance, they are enough for demonstrating early quantum advantage in select domains. Pilot studies in portfolio optimization and molecular simulation have shown promising results [2]. For example, quantum variational algorithms have been successfully tested for solving combinatorial problems and quantum chemistry calculations.

Due to both private sector findings and public sector research initiatives, global investment in quantum technology has also improved dramatically. Industries are actively finding quantum-as-a-service (QaaS) models to create these equipment available through cloud platforms, and major economies are currently including national quantum agendas. Even though it might take years for full-scale commercial implementation, the rate of advancement in quantum algorithms and hardware gives a major shift in the industrial landscape.

 DOI: 10.1201/9781003587835-12

This content seeks to provide readers with a thorough grasp of QC, covering everything from its foundational ideas to its possible uses. It begins with the basics of QC, moves over the present status of quantum processors and algorithmic advancements, and explores how QC affects sectors in addition to finance, materials, pharmaceuticals, and logistics. A 2035 roadmap is given, outlining the anticipated emergence dates and locations of quantum advantage.

12.2 QUANTUM-COMPUTING FOUNDATIONS

By using the characteristics of quantum mechanics—superposition, entanglement, and interference—to encode and manipulate data, QC fundamentally behaves differently from classical computing. Being their seeming incongruity, these ideas serve as the mathematical and physical basics for the quantum computational paradigm. Starting from the qubit representation to the circuit-level implementation, this section discusses the fundamental building blocks of QC. It ends with major quantum algorithms that demonstrate the computational supremacy of quantum computers in particular areas [3].

12.2.1 Qubits and Quantum States

The quantum bit, also known as the qubit, which is a generalization of the classical binary bit and is at the heart of quantum processing. Superposition is a quantum characteristic that allows a qubit to reside in both states simultaneously. Because of this, it is essentially distinct and significantly more potent for specific computations.

A qubit's state characterizes its current condition. Complex values, known as amplitudes, influence the qubit's state, which is a combination of both 0 and 1.

The chance that the qubit will give either 0 or 1 when measured is determined by these amplitudes. The qubit state may be mathematically expressed and controlled through quantum operations because it exists in an abstract area called a Hilbert space.

The logic of the advantage of quantum—the capacity of quantum computers to give better performance than their classical counterparts for particular tasks—is based on this exponential scaling of representational power [4–5].

12.2.2 Entanglement and Interference

Entanglement is a concept that is specific to quantum mechanics, which means that no matter how distant apart two qubits are in space, their states cannot be given separately. Non-classical correlations that defy Bell inequalities and give QC speedups are made possible by the inability of an entangled state to be broken down into a tensor product of individual qubit states.

Another important characteristic is quantum interference, which allows probability amplitudes from several computing routes to interfere either constructively or destructively. Interference is used by well-designed quantum circuits to suppress wrong results and magnify correct ones. The design of quantum algorithms and error-reduction techniques heavily relies on this interaction between entanglement and interference.

12.2.3 Quantum Gates and Circuits

Quantum gates are unitary transformations that act on qubits to facilitate quantum computation. Quantum gates maintain the norm of the quantum state vector and are reversible, in contrast to classical logic gates. Any unitary transformation can be approximated to arbitrary precision using a universal set of quantum gates, including the Hadamard (H), phase (S), T, and Controlled-NOT (CNOT) gates.

12.2.4 Key Algorithms

Many different algorithms have been developed from QC, and they exhibit significant improvements over the most well-known classical alternatives [6–8]:

- The Gordon's Search Algorithm: This quantum technique, which was first given by Lov Grover in 1996, offers a quadratic speedup for black-box optimization issues or exploring unsorted databases.
- Variational Quantum Eigensolver (VQE): This hybrid quantum–classical technique manipulates the molecular Hamiltonian's ground state energy. As it uses short-depth circuits and classical optimization of parameters, it is especially well-suited to NISQ devices.

12.3 HARDWARE LANDSCAPE

Hardware for QC is developing rapidly, with several physical implementations vying for coherence, fault tolerance, and extensibility. Every platform has pros and cons, and current research examines the trade-offs between scalability, error rates, qubit connection, and control accuracy. Superconducting qubits, trapped-ion systems, and photonic quantum computers are among the most advanced architectures available today.

12.3.1 Superconducting Qubits: Transmon Architecture

The most advanced quantum hardware platforms are superconducting circuits, especially transmon qubits. Leading companies in this field include Google and International Business Machines (IBM). By using Josephson junctions to generate non-linear oscillators, these devices allow two discrete energy states to function as the $|0\rangle$ and $|1\rangle$ states of the qubit.

With 127 transmon qubits and single-qubit gate fidelities of over 99% and two-qubit gate fidelities of about 97%, IBM's Eagle processor was first released in 2021. In its 2019 "quantum supremacy" demonstration, Google's 53-qubit Sycamore processor completed a task in 200 s that would have taken a supercomputer 10,000 years.

Transmon qubits have the following main benefits:

- High gate speeds (~10–100 ns).
- Cryogenic control electronics integration.
- Using silicon foundries to establish fabrication techniques.

But they also have to deal with:

- Coherence times are comparatively short (~100 μs).
- Limited connectivity (in two-dimensional [2D] grids, nearest-neighbor is usually used).
- In multi-qubit processes, cross-talk.

12.3.2 Trapped-Ion Quantum Systems

Companies such as IonQ, Honeywell Quantum Solutions, and Quantinuum are pursuing trapped-ion quantum computers, which use atomic ions (such as Yb^+ and Ca^+) trapped in electromagnetic traps. The internal energy levels of the ions define the qubit states, which are then controlled by laser pulses.

These equipment have high-accuracy quantum gates and prominently high coherence times, which are regularly expressed in seconds or even minutes. All-to-all connectivity, which makes it easier to process quantum circuits by making direct interaction between any qubit, is another significant strength.

Among the noteworthy achievements are the following:

- IonQ's 32-qubit system with gate fidelities of approximately 99.9%.
- Error correction methods on tiny ion chains are demonstrated, and photonic interconnects are used to create scalable modular structures.

The following are the drawbacks:

- Slower gate speeds (~ μs–ms).
- Complex optical control.
- Sensitivity to external noise and vibrations.

12.3.3 Photonic Quantum Systems

Photons, which are quantum particles of light, are used as qubits in photonic QC. These qubits are usually encoded using a time-bin, polarization, or route. These platforms have the following advantages:

- Room-temperature functioning
- Innate resistance to decoherence

Adherence to the current telecommunications infrastructure.

Gaussian Boson Sampling (GBS) and time-multiplexed photonic devices are recent developments. Leading companies in this field include PsiQuantum, which uses silicon photonics to target large-scale fault-tolerant QC, and Xanadu, which uses continuous-variable photonics.

A photonic processor called Jiuzhang was utilized by researchers at the University of Science and Technology of China (USTC) in 2020 to complete a Gaussian Boson Sampling work that was ineffectively emulated by traditional supercomputers.

12.4 CLASSICAL WORKFLOW

Hybrid workflows refer to computing models where quantum and classical processes run in tandem, exchanging information iteratively. This is necessary because of the following:

- Current quantum hardware (NISQ) is limited in qubit count and error tolerance.
- Many real-world problems involve both quantum-amenable components and tasks that remain more efficiently solved.

The QC workflow is shown in Figure 12.1.

A typical hybrid loop may look like the following:

1. Initialize parameters.
2. Prepare a quantum circuit with those parameters.
3. Execute the quantum circuit on QPU.
4. Return measurements to the classical processor.
5. Optimize parameters using classical algorithms [9, 10].
6. Repeat until convergence.

12.4.1 Frameworks Enabling Hybrid Models

The following are the tools and frameworks for hybrid computing workflows:

- PennyLane (by Xanadu): It integrates QC with machine learning (ML) libraries such as TensorFlow and PyTorch.
- Qiskit Runtime (IBM): It provides hybrid primitives, such as Sampler and Estimator, for fast quantum–classical loops.
- Cirq and TensorFlow Quantum (Google): A combination of quantum circuit simulation with ML frameworks.
- Amazon Braket: Enables hybrid algorithms across different quantum hardware platforms.

12.4.2 Popular Hybrid Algorithms

Hybrid quantum–classical algorithms are designed to work within the constraints of NISQ hardware. Examples include the following:

- VQE: This estimates the ground state energy of molecules, with the quantum processor handling expectation value estimation.
- Quantum Approximate Optimization Algorithm (QAOA): This is used for solving combinatorial optimization problems, for example, MaxCut, scheduling.
- Hybrid Neural Networks: This combines quantum circuits with classical neural network layers for potential breakthroughs in AI [11–12].

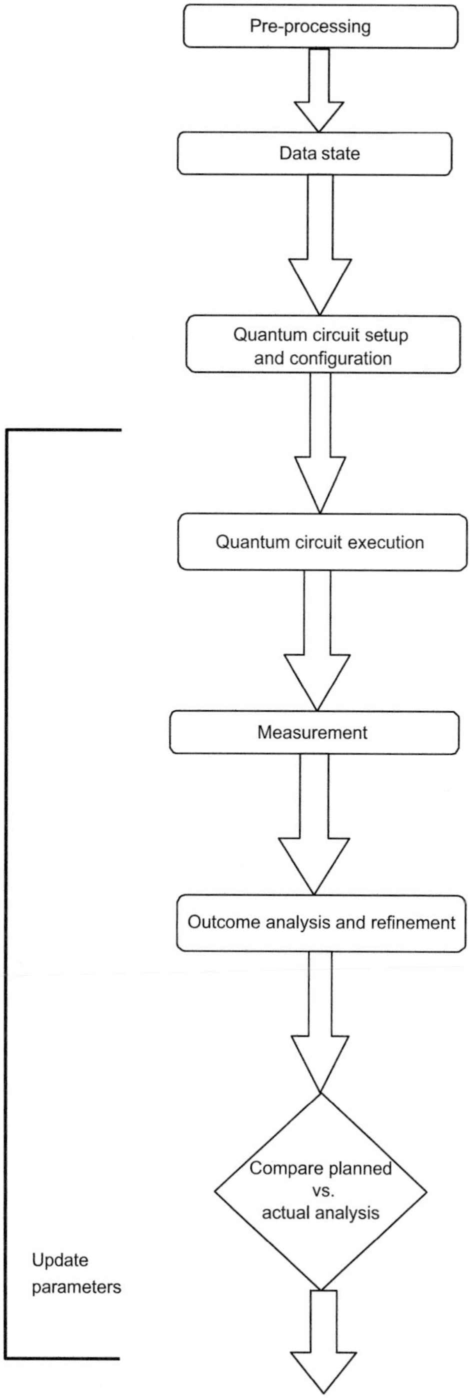

FIGURE 12.1 Quantum computing workflow.

12.4.3 Industry Applications of Hybrid Workflows

- Pharmaceuticals: VQE and related methods for simulating molecular structures and reaction dynamics.
- Finance: Portfolio optimization using QAOA-based approaches.
- Supply Chain and Logistics: Hybrid solvers for route optimization and resource allocation.
- Materials Science: Discovering new materials with quantum simulation guided by classical data.
- AI: Training hybrid quantum–classical models for pattern recognition and anomaly detection.

12.4.4 Benefits and Limitations

Benefits

- Makes QC useful with limited hardware.
- Promote mature classical infrastructure.
- Identifies specific problem domains through quantum advantage.

Limitations

- Communication latency between quantum and classical layers.
- Need for problem reformulation to fit hybrid models.
- Dependent on classical pre-processing and post-processing.

12.5 SECTOR-SPECIFIC TRANSFORMATION

QC is not a one-size-fits-all technology; its transformative potential varies across industries based on computational needs, data complexity, and existing infrastructure [13–15]. Below is an overview of how QC is redesigning

12.5.1 Healthcare and Pharmaceuticals

- Drug Discovery and Molecular Simulation: Quantum computers can simulate complex molecules more accurately, accelerating drug discovery (e.g., protein folding and interaction modeling).
- Personalized Medicine: Featured data processing and optimization could enable tailored treatments based on individual genetic profiles.
- Clinical Trial Optimization: Quantum feature-enabled ML may enhance patient cohort selection and trial optimization.

12.5.2 Finance and Banking

- Portfolio Optimization: Quantum algorithms such as Quantum Approximate Optimization Algorithm (QAOA) can solve complex problems rapidly than their classical counterparts.

- Risk Analysis: Enhanced modeling of complex financial systems using quantum Monte Carlo methods.
- Fraud Detection and Cryptography: Featured capabilities in pattern recognition and the upcoming need for post-quantum cryptography.

12.5.3 Logistics and Supply Chain

- Route Optimization: Provide a solution for the "traveling salesman problem" in real-time route planning.
- Inventory Management: Enhanced forecasting and optimization using quantum ML.
- Global Supply Chain Resilience: Simulation and stress-testing complex networks to predict disruptions.

12.5.4 Energy and Environment

- Grid Optimization: Quantum computers can provide optimized energy distribution and storage in smart grids.
- Material Discovery: Invent new catalysts for sustainable energy (e.g., hydrogen production, and CO_2 capture).
- Climate Modeling: High simulation of climate systems and energy consumption models.

12.5.5 Manufacturing and Automotive

- Design Optimization: QC aids in lightweight material design, aerodynamic simulation, and component testing.
- Production Scheduling: Solving problems related to job-shop scheduling and allocation of resources.
- Autonomous Vehicles: Optimized decision-making and pathfinding using quantum AI.

12.5.6 Cybersecurity

- Post-Quantum Cryptography: As quantum computers pose threats to current encryption systems (e.g., Rivest–Shamir–Adlema [RSA] and Elliptic Curve Cryptography [ECC]), industries are investing in quantum-resistant algorithms.
- Secure Communication: Quantum key distribution (QKD) offers unbreakable encryption, already being tested in sectors such as defense and banking.

12.5.7 Telecommunications and Networking

- Network Optimization: Quantum algorithms improve bandwidth allocation, congestion control, and signal routing.
- Quantum Internet: Development of secure communication channels using quantum entanglement and QKD.

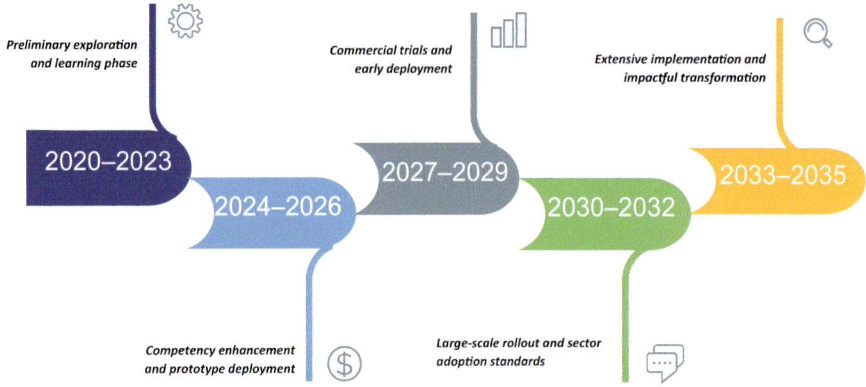

FIGURE 12.2 Quantum computing adoption roadmap.

12.5.8 Aerospace and Defense

- Navigation and Simulation: Quantum algorithms for optimization, satellite constellation management, and defense simulation.
- Materials Science: Development of ultra-strong, lightweight materials for aircraft and spacecraft.

12.6 ADOPTION ROADMAP

QC adoption road-map shown in Figure 12.2.

12.7 CHALLENGES AND ETHICAL CONSIDERATIONS

QC, which uses quantum mechanics to perform tasks that are far beyond the capabilities of ordinary computers, represents a paradigm leap in processing capability and architecture. Finance, healthcare, logistics, AI, and cybersecurity are among the industries expected to experience significant disruptions [16–18].

However, this developing technology brings with it a new bunch of problems and ethical concerns that must be carefully considered.

This section looks at seven significant problems in QC development and deployment, followed by a discussion of the ethical implications for industry and society.

12.7.1 Seven Key Challenges in QC

12.7.1.1 Hardware Scalability and Stability

Quantum computers depend on qubits, which are inherently fragile and require ultra-low temperatures and isolation from interference from outside. Developing scalable hardware able to host a high number of dependable qubits remains one of the most challenging technical problems. Maintaining coherence and avoiding interference are crucial to creating solid operations [19–21].

12.7.1.2 Error Correction and Quantum Decoherence

Compared to conventional bits, qubits are more susceptible to noise, loss of coherence, and operational errors. Since hundreds of physical qubits are often used to represent a single logical qubit, quantum error correction is both required and very resource-intensive. This significantly hinders the development of efficient, fault-tolerant quantum computers [22].

12.7.1.3 Software and Algorithmic Limitations

Programming has been performed significantly differently for quantum computers. The overwhelming majority of current algorithms are not directly translatable because they are made for classical systems. Given the exponential speedup potential demonstrated using quantum algorithms such as Shor's and Grover's, there are still a few algorithms that can be applied to actual industrial applications.

12.7.1.4 Talent and Workforce Shortage

Professionals with expertise in quantum physics, quantum engineering, and quantum software development are in great shortage. Widespread education and training are hampered by the field's interdisciplinary nature, which crosses physics, computer science, and electrical engineering. The introduction of structured programs in quantum technology by universities is just getting started.

12.7.1.5 Integration with Classical Systems

In hybrid systems, it is noted that quantum computers would enhance rather than replace conventional computers. Frameworks for effective division of labor and communication between quantum and classical devices continue to be developed.

12.7.1.6 Cost and Accessibility

Quantum systems require substantial funding for operation, maintenance, and infrastructure. The fact that only big businesses and government-funded research institutions can currently pay these expenses raises questions about equitable access to this revolutionary technology. It is expected that quantum computers would complement classical computers in hybrid systems rather than replace them. We are still in the early stages of creating frameworks to allow effective task division and communication between quantum and classical devices.

12.7.1.7 Standardization and Policy Frameworks

As QC matures, the lack of universally accepted standards, benchmarks, and regulatory frameworks becomes a problem. Interoperability among platforms, intellectual property rights, and ethical oversight requires coherent global governance.

12.7.2 Ethical Considerations in Quantum Industry Transformation

As QC continues to arise, it is imperative to examine its ethical dimensions. The change is that the power of this technology leads far beyond technical difficulties, and it raises fundamental queries about privacy, equity, and human agency.

12.7.2.1 Digital Inequality and Quantum Supremacy

Nations and corporations that achieve early mastery of quantum technologies may get disproportionate benefits in economics, cybersecurity, and geopolitical influence. This can exacerbate old digital divides and reinforce global inequities.

12.7.2.2 Cryptographic Disruption and Privacy Risks

It is theoretically possible for quantum computers to crack common cryptography schemes such as RSA and ECC. The confidentiality of financial transactions, digital communications, and national security systems has all been at risk. Innovation and privacy protection must be balanced.

12.7.2.3 Accountability in Quantum-AI Systems

AI with QC can work together to create autonomous systems capable of making complex decisions. There is an imperative ethical need to ensure accountability, explainability, and openness in such systems.

12.7.2.4 Militarization and Cyber Warfare

Quantum technologies may play a major role in surveillance, espionage, or cyberattacks. The ethical benefit of such an ability should be governed by international treaties and aimed at preventing misuse in conflict scenarios.

12.7.2.5 Environmental Impact

Operating quantum computers—especially those that depend on superconducting qubits—needs high cooling and energy consumption. Sustainable and environmentally conscious prototypes should be prioritized as QC scales up.

12.7.2.6 Employment Displacement

Quantum-accelerated optimization and automation may render a few job roles obsolete, especially in sectors logistics, manufacturing, and finance. This raises ethical questions about workforce reskilling and social safety nets.

12.7.2.7 Moral Dilemmas in Application Areas

QC can accelerate drug discovery, genetic research, and climate modeling. However, it could enable ethically contentious fields such as gene editing, surveillance enhancements, or autonomous weaponry. It says clear boundaries and ethical review mechanisms are crucial.

12.8 FUTURE OUTLOOK (2025–2035)

As we are into the decade ahead, QC is expected to change from research labs and specialized demonstrations to broader industrial and commercial applications. While the 2010s and the 2020s have been primarily exploratory, the time between 2025 and 2035 is poised to see maturation, integration, and impact on key sectors. This section gives a forecast of how QC may give the shape of the industrial landscape in the coming years, focusing on technological advances, adoption trends, and emerging ethical considerations.

12.8.1 Acceleration of Quantum Advantage in Specific Domains

By 2030, quantum systems are likely to attain practical advancement in solving problems faster than classical systems—especially in areas such as the following:

- Molecular modeling and drug discovery
- Financial modeling
- Logistics and supply chain optimization
- Materials science

12.8.2 Rise of Hybrid Quantum–Classical Systems

In 2035, hybrid quantum–classical systems become more popular, even universal fault-tolerant quantum computers may not be widely accessible. By fusing quantum processors into traditional computing infrastructure, these architectures enable companies to:

- Apply quantum modules to solve sub-problems.
- Integrate cloud-based workflows with QC; initiate shared memory and scheduling to carry out co-processing operations.
- Prominent cloud service companies are already providing early access to these systems, opening the door for wider availability.

12.8.3 Standardization and Ecosystem Development

The next decade will likely see the improvement of the following:

- International standards for quantum hardware, algorithms, and interoperability.
- Open-source platforms for quantum development (e.g., Qiskit, Cirq, and PennyLane).
- Academic–industry consortia driving collaborative research and commercialization.

This ecosystem development is critical to building trust, reducing entry barriers, and ensuring compatibility across vendors and systems.

12.8.4 Expansion of the Quantum Workforce

A focus on human capital development in the following:

- University-level QC degrees and micro-credentials.
- Industry partnerships for hands-on quantum training.
- Interdisciplinary curriculum merging quantum science in engineering, AI, and ethics.

By 2030, quantum literacy is expected to become a core skill for researchers and developers in computing-intensive fields.

12.8.5 Democratization and Cloud-Based Access

QC is expecting to follow the trajectory of AI and HPC from on-premise systems to cloud-delivered services. By 2035, the following are foreseen:

- Mid-sized companies and startups may access quantum capabilities via QaaS.
- Pay-per-use pricing design will encourage experimentation and innovation in tech.
- Global access can improve, albeit unevenly across regions.

This democratization helps close the technological gap between large tech companies and smaller players.

12.8.6 Emergence of Quantum Cybersecurity Standards

As quantum decryption capabilities are real, industries may change to post-quantum cryptography (PQC). Key developments will include the following:

- Government mandates to adopt PQC algorithms in the defense and financial sectors.
- Industry-wide migration plans from vulnerable protocols to quantum-safe standards.
- Growth of QKD in telecom and national security.

The cybersecurity landscape will evolve significantly under quantum threat and opportunity.

12.8.7 Ethical Frameworks and Global Governance

Ethical challenges will intensify as applications broaden. The period from 2025 to 2035 must see the following:

The setting up of international ethics councils for the use of quantum devices.

- The enforcement of rules governing dual-use technologies, particularly in the contexts of surveillance and the military.
- Encouraging fair access to avoid only a handful of countries or companies monopolizing technology.

Theoretical discussion of quantum ethics will give way to legislative and regulatory action.

12.8.8 Industrial Transformation across Key Sectors

The cumulative effect of technological advances and ecosystem maturity will lead to a quantum-led transformation, as listed in Table 12.2.

TABLE 12.2
Quantum Computing (QC) Sector

Sector	Quantum Impact by 2035
Pharmaceuticals	Rapid drug development and clinical trial simulation
Banking and finance	Advanced risk modeling and fraud detection
Energy	Smart grid optimization and battery material discovery
Aerospace	Simulation of fluid dynamics and aerodynamics
Telecom	Secure communication via quantum encryption
Manufacturing	Process optimization and predictive maintenance

12.9 CONCLUSION

QC is moving at a fast pace from theory into real-world problems, with its potential for change in fields including healthcare, banking, logistics, and power. QC is rapidly transforming from theory to practical issues. The technology has several ethical and technical hurdles, even though it has the potential to resolve complicated problems. To design it responsibly, it may be necessary to detail concerns such as scalability, data protection, and equal access. In this guarantee that QC provides society as a whole, collaborative, moral, and inclusive design can be necessary as we go ahead.

REFERENCES

1. T. N. Theis and H.-S. P. Wong, "The End of Moore's Law: A New Beginning for Information Technology," *Computing in Science & Engineering*, vol. 19, no. 2, pp. 41–50, 2017. https://doi.org/10.1109/MCSE.2017.29
2. M. A. Nielsen and I. L. Chuang, *Quantum Computation and Quantum Information*, 10th Anniversary Edition. Cambridge: Cambridge University Press, 2010.
3. Ginés Carrascal, Paula Hernamperez, Guillermo Botella, and Alberto del Barrio, "Backtesting Quantum-Computing Algorithms for Portfolio Optimization," *IEEE Transactions on Quantum Engineering*, vol. 5, pp. 1–20, 2023.
4. A. Peruzzo et al., "A Variational Eigenvalue Solver on a Quantum Processor," *Nature Communications*, vol. 5, no. 4213, pp. 1–7, 2014. https://doi.org/10.1038/ncomms5213
5. M. A. Nielsen and I. L. Chuang, "Quantum Computation and Quantum Information," *American Journal of Physics*, vol. 70, no. 5, pp. 558–559, May 2002. https://doi.org/10.1119/1.1463744
6. R. Horodecki, P. Horodecki, M. Horodecki, and K. Horodecki, "Quantum Entanglement," *Reviews of Modern Physics*, vol. 81, no. 2, pp. 865–942, Jun. 2009. https://doi.org/10.1103/RevModPhys.81.865
7. F. Arute *et al.*, "Quantum Supremacy Using a Programmable Superconducting Processor," *Nature*, vol. 574, no. 7779, pp. 505–510, Oct. 2019. https://doi.org/10.1038/s41586-019-1666-5
8. L. K. Grover, "A Fast Quantum Mechanical Algorithm for Database Search," In *Proceedings of the 28th Annual ACM Symposium on Theory of Computing (STOC)*, pp. 212–219, 1996. https://doi.org/10.1145/237814.237866

9. J. R. McClean, J. Romero, R. Babbush, and A. Aspuru-Guzik, "The Theory of Variational Hybrid Quantum-classical Algorithms," *New Journal of Physics*, vol. 18, no. 2, p. 023023, Feb. 2016. https://doi.org/10.1088/1367-2630/18/2/023023
10. H.-S. Zhong, H. Wang, Y.-H. Deng, et al.. "Quantum Computational Advantage Using Photons," *Science*, vol. 370,no. 6523, pp. 1460–1463, 2020. https://doi.org/10.1126/science.abe8770
11. K. Wright, K.M. Beck, S. Debnath, et al. "Benchmarking an 11-qubit Quantum Computer," *Nature Communications*, vol. 10,no. 1, p. 5464, 2019. https://doi.org/10.1038/s41467-019-13534-2
12. Raghavendra Srinivas, S. C. Burd, H. M. Knaack, R. T. Sutherland, Alex Kwiatkowski, Scott Glancy, Emanuel Knill et al. "High-fidelity Laser-free Universal Control of Trapped Ion Qubits." *Nature*, vol. 597, no. 7875, pp. 209–213, 2021.
13. J.M. Arrazola, V. Bergholm, K. Brádler, et al.. "Quantum Circuits with Many Photons on A Programmable Nanophotonic Chip," *Nature*, vol. 591, no. 7848, pp. 54–60, 2021.
14. Oscar CO Dahlsten, Roberto Oliveira, and Martin B. Plenio. "The Emergence of Typical Entanglement in Two-party Random Processes." *Journal of Physics A: Mathematical and Theoretical*, vol. 40, no. 28, p. 8081, 2007.
15. R. Drechsler and R. Wille, "Towards a System Design Flow for Quantum Circuits," *IEEE Transactions on Computer-Aided Design of Integrated Circuits and Systems*, vol. 25, no. 12, pp. 2957–2972, 2020.
16. Austin Gilliam, Marco Pistoia, and Constantin Gonciulea. "Optimizing Quantum Search Using a Generalized Version of Grover's Algorithm." *arXiv preprint arXiv:2005.06468*, 2020.
17. A. Peruzzo et al., "A Variational Eigenvalue Solver on a Quantum Processor," *IEEE Transactions on Quantum Engineering*, vol. 2, pp. 1–12, 2021.
18. Sanyam Singhal, Vandit Srivastava, P. Rohith, Prateek Jain, and Debanjan Bhowmik. "Performance Comparison for Quantum Approximate Optimization Algorithm (QAOA) across Noiseless Simulation, Experimentally Benchmarked Noisy Simulation, and Experimental Hardware Platforms." In *2024 8th IEEE Electron Devices Technology & Manufacturing Conference (EDTM)*, pp. 1–3. IEEE, 2024.
19. S. Sempere-Llagostera, R. B. Patel, I. A. Walmsley, and W. S. Kolthammer. "Experimentally Finding Dense Subgraphs Using a Time-bin Encoded Gaussian Boson Sampling Device." *Physical Review X*, vol. 12, no. 3, p. 031045, 2022.
20. L. Wang, S. K. Kowk, and W. H. Ip. "Design of an Improved Quantum-inspired Evolutionary Algorithm for a Transportation Problem in Logistics Systems." *Journal of Intelligent Manufacturing*, vol. 23, no. 6, pp. 2227–2236, 2012.
21. S-C. Zhuang, H-L. Yuan, and X-B. Wang, "Ultrabright Entanglement-Based Quantum Key Distribution over 404 km Fibre." *IEEE Journal of Quantum Electronics*, vol. 60, no. 1, pp. 1–9, 2023.
22. A. G. Fowler, C. Jones, and M. Martinis, "Surface Codes: Towards Practical Large-Scale Quantum Computation," *IEEE Transactions on Quantum Engineering*, vol. 3, pp. 1–15, 2020.

13 Next-Generation Quantum Algorithms
Trends, Techniques, and Applications

G. Deebanchakkarawarthi, N. Kavitha, Sivakumar Annamalai, and Mohamed Uvaze Ahamed Ayoobkhan

13.1 INTRODUCTION

Quantum computing (QC) redefines computational limitations by leveraging quantum mechanical principles such as superposition, entanglement, and quantum interference. Quantum computers operate with qubits, whereas conventional computers access the data using binary bits (0 or 1). The QC occurs in various states instantly, and the computational state space is increased exponentially. The data processing in this sort of approach is governed by the laws of quantum physics, which is the most prominent computing paradigm [1].

The recent developments in quantum hardware have further enhanced progress. "Willow," a Google superconducting quantum processor, exhibits an excellent architecture and error moderation strategies, resulting in the practicality of near-term quantum applications. Coherent times and gate reliabilities are enhanced by IBM's Quantum Eagle and IonQ's trapped-ion systems, evident that the quantum advancement era in the specific domain is fast approaching.

Investments from governments, academic circles, and industry people paved the way for quantum technologies, such as machine learning (ML), cybersecurity, ML, and materials science [2].

13.2 THE EMPHASIS ON ALGORITHMS

Algorithms define the utility, but hardware is the enabler. Quantum algorithms are the progresses that direct quantum systems to successfully explain issues.

- New developments in hybrid algorithms, such as VQE and QAOA.
- ML, graph theory, and quantum simulation algorithms.
- The new category of adaptive and feedback-based algorithms.

DOI: 10.1201/9781003587835-13

These advances aim to resolve problems that cannot be fixed by standard methods by capitalizing on the benefits of quantum parallelism and entanglement [3].

13.2.1 Essential Ideas

Awareness of the fundamental quantum concepts is essential to understand these algorithmic advancements: In distinction to traditional bits, qubits are accomplished of prevailing in a superposition of states 0 and 1.

Superposition: The capability of a quantum system to occur in several states at once permits parallel computing. Many quantum protocols depend on non-local correlations made possible by the phenomenon known as **entanglement**, in which the state of one qubit is dependent upon that of another [4].

Quantum gates are the unitary transformations, and they work with the qubits and are considered important components of quantum circuits.

These concepts permit quantum computers to more successfully explore enormous solution areas than conventional systems.

13.2.2 Speedup of Quantum

Quantum Speedup consists of a performance improvement that quantum algorithms have over the most well-known conventional algorithms [5].

For example,

Grover's algorithm improves the efficiency of solving unstructured search problems by accomplishing a quadratic improvement in speed.

Shor's algorithm, on the other hand, significantly fast-tracks the process of factoring large integers, offering an exponential computational benefit.

In the noisy intermediate-scale quantum (NISQ) era, attaining real-world speedup is a crucial objective, predominantly in fields such as ML, chemistry, and optimization. Significant events in the development of quantum algorithms are depicted in Table 13.1.

13.2.3 Quantum vs. Classical Search Complexity

In unstructured search, QC delivers a substantial edge over conventional computing. In conventional computing, the time complication upsurges linearly with the number of things, whereas incisive searching through an unsorted collection of items requires verifying each item individually. This suggests that the time essential to pinpoint a specific item grows consistently with the database's size. However, thanks to QC, Grover's search technique can search the same unsorted database in significantly fewer steps, providing a potent substitute. Grover's approach makes use of quantum

TABLE 13.1
Significant Events in the Development of Quantum Algorithms

Year	Algorithm	Contributor(s)	Problem Domain	Speedup Type
1994	Shor's algorithm	Peter Shor	Integer factorization	Exponential
2009	Harrow–Hassidim–Lloyd (HHL) algorithm	Harrow et al.	Linear systems	Exponential (under conditions)
2014	Quantum Approximate Optimization Algorithm (QAOA)	Farhi et al.	Combinatorial optimization	Heuristic
2019	Variational Quantum Eigensolver (VQE)	Peruzzo et al.	Quantum chemistry	Hybrid heuristic
2021	Quantum Singular Value Transformation (QSVT)	Gilyén et al.	Broad applications	Framework-level
2023	Quantum Natural Gradient Descent (QNGD)	Koczor et al.	Variational algorithms (VQE, QAOA)	Improved optimization efficiency
2023	Quantum Hamiltonian Learning with GFlowNets	Zhang et al.	Quantum machine learning (QML)	Sample-efficient learning
2024	Quantum Adversarial Learning Algorithm (QALA)	Li et al.	Quantum generative adversarial networks (GANs)/ML security	Hybrid heuristic
2024	Quantum Gradient Estimation with Reduced Shots	Broughton et al.	Variational algorithms	Precision-improved estimation

Applications

- QAOA with adjustable depth or parameters.
- Feedback-driven parameter changes for the VQE.
- Through trial, measurement, and feedback, the agent (quantum system) learns a policy in quantum reinforcement learning.

Advantages

- **Noise Adaptivity**: Particularly useful in surroundings that are noisy or fluctuate.
- **Real-Time Learning**: While a system is being executed, it learns from its results.
- **Hybrid Enhancement**: Combines quantum and classical processing to provide useful power.

Issues

- **Measurement Collapse**: Quantum measurement-induced collapse restricts feedback.
- **Timing and Latency**: For real-time feedback to be useful, it needs to happen quickly.
- **Resource Overhead**: Latency or decoherence may be introduced by frequent measurements and logic control.

13.3.2.2 Case Study: Feedback-Controlled Quantum State Preparation

With the constraints of hardware, the major challenge lies in preparing the desired quantum state (ψ).

Method: In the initial stage, a feedback controller iteratively advances and measures a unitary operation's fractional qubit state at each stage. If the anticipated result is varied from the measured reliability, then advanced gates (rotation angles or entangling gates) are modified by the controller.

Result: As established on a trapped-ion system, the performance of the static circuit solutions is outstripped by this adaptive approach in terms of reliability in noisy surroundings.

13.3.3 Quantum Gibbs Sampling

Simulating Systems at Non-Zero Temperatures, the thermal (Gibbs) states of quantum systems are prepared using a quantum computational technique called Quantum Gibbs Sampling. The thermal (or Gibbs) state of a quantum system with Hamiltonian H at temperature TT is defined by

$$\rho_{\text{Gibbs}} = e^{-\beta H} / Z, \text{where}\, \beta = 1/kT, Z = \mathrm{Tr}\left(e^{-\beta H}\right)$$

where

- ρ_{Gibbs} is the Gibbs density matrix,
- H is the Hamiltonian of the system,
- Z is the partition function, acting as a normalization constant, and
- k is the Boltzmann constant.

In QML, quantum thermodynamics, and simulations of quantum materials, generating such states is essential. Under certain circumstances, quantum algorithms promise more effective state preparation than classical techniques, such as Metropolis–Hastings Markov Chain Monte Carlo (MCMC), which scale poorly with system size. The Quantum Gibbs Sampling flow diagram is shown in Figure 13.3.

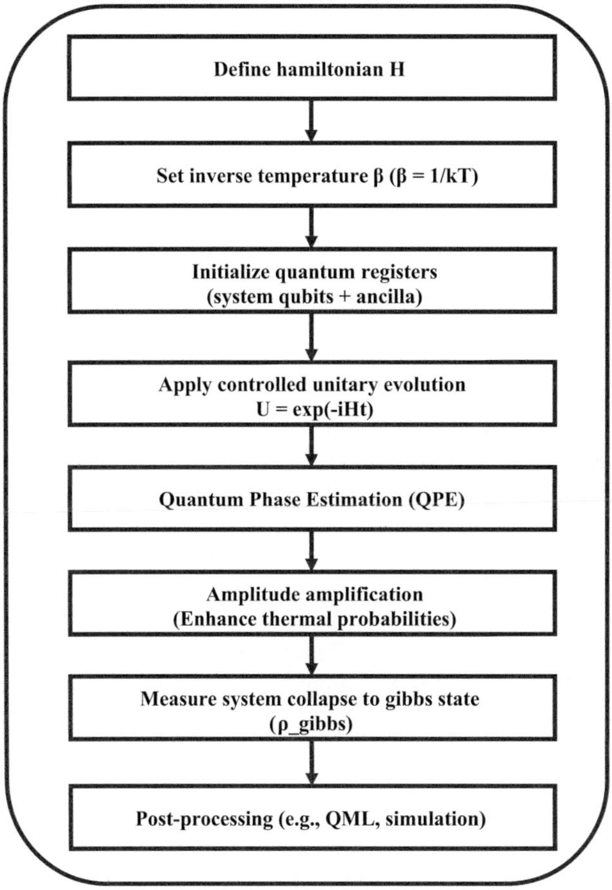

FIGURE 13.3 Quantum Gibbs sampling flow diagram.

13.3.3.1 High-Precision Sampling

Quantum Gibbs Sampling allows the preparation of quantum states proportional to the Boltzmann distribution of a given Hamiltonian. This is crucial for the following:

- Energy-Based Models (EBMs) in ML.
- Bayesian Inference for probabilistic modeling.
- Anomaly Detection in cybersecurity and sensor networks.

Recent algorithms utilize quantum rejection sampling and quantum Metropolis–Hastings methods to improve sampling accuracy, even from non-convex and high-dimensional distributions.

Applications:

- Quantum Chemistry: Simulating molecular behavior at non-zero temperature and reaction thermodynamics.
- Statistical Physics: Exploring canonical ensembles, phase transitions, and heat capacities.
- QML: Training Quantum Boltzmann Machines (QBMs) and other energy-based models.
- Material Science: Modeling thermal properties of strongly correlated systems.
- Optimization: Sampling-based optimization such as Simulated Quantum Annealing.
- Finance and Risk Modeling: Stochastic modeling using quantum-enhanced thermal distributions.

Advantages

1. Quantum Speedup: Under certain assumptions, Quantum Gibbs Sampling offers a polynomial (or better) speedup over classical MCMC.
2. State Efficiency: Efficient encoding of exponentially large probability distributions over quantum states.
3. Thermal Simulations: Enables accurate simulation of systems at thermal equilibrium—not just ground states.
4. Quantum ML Integration: Acts as a backend for generative models and quantum neural networks using Boltzmann distributions.
5. NISQ Relevance: Some variational thermalization techniques can be adapted to near-term devices.

Challenges and Open Issues

1. **Circuit Depth**: Many proposed algorithms require long coherence times and deep circuits.
2. **Scalability**: Resource requirements (qubits and gates) increase significantly with system size and precision.
3. **Noise Sensitivity**: Amplitude estimation and phase estimation are noise-sensitive, making them hard on NISQ devices.

4. **Partition Function Calculation**: Direct computation of $Z = Tr(e^{-\beta H})$ is not feasible on quantum computers—approximations are needed.
5. **Error Accumulation**: In iterative techniques, gate errors and decoherence accumulate, affecting the thermal state's fidelity.
6. **Implementation Complexity Algorithms** such as Quantum Metropolis or purification methods are non-trivial to implement in practice.

13.3.3.2 Case Study: QBM with Quantum Gibbs Sampling

Repetitive sampling from a heat distribution over a quantum Hamiltonian (H) is necessary for training a QBM. This is intractable in a classical sense because the Hilbert space is exponentially large.

Method: $\rho_{Gibbs} = e^{-\beta H} / Z$ is used to create samples using a Quantum Gibbs Sampling technique. The quantum processor uses controlled unitary evolution and phase estimation techniques to prepare thermal states.

As a result, we have the following:

- Gibbs samples with more fidelity than conventional approximations.
- Enhanced QBM training convergence on small-scale issues.
- Thermal sampling has been shown to be scalable for generative modeling tasks in QML.

Experimental Platforms:

- Superconducting qubits and trapped-ion systems for small-scale experiments.
- Thermal state simulations for **Ising Hamiltonians** with up to 6–8 qubits were shown.

13.4 OTHER PROMINENT DEVELOPMENTS

13.4.1 Boolean Formula Evaluation

Evaluation of Boolean formulas entails calculating the results of Boolean expressions made up of logical gates (AND, OR, NOT, etc.). Quantum walks are a more efficient way to analyze read-once Boolean formulas in the quantum domain, where each input variable appears exactly once.

13.4.1.1 Important Quantum Development: NAND Trees

1. A NAND tree is a binary tree where each internal node performs a NAND operation. The classical evaluation requires $O(N^{0.753})$ time, but a quantum algorithm by Farhi et al. uses continuous-time quantum walks to evaluate them in $O(\sqrt{N})$ time.
2. Ambainis et al. further optimized this using discrete-time quantum walks, providing an optimal solution for balanced trees.

Applications

1. Circuit Verification: Efficient checking of logic circuits for correctness.
2. Logic Programming: Faster rule evaluation in logic-based artificial intelligence (AI) systems.
3. AI and Robotics: Decision-making systems based on logical formulas can benefit from faster evaluation.

13.4.2 Quantum Linear Systems Algorithm (QLSA)

To solve linear systems of equations, a Hermitian matrix is used; the HHL algorithm was created in 2009. Instead of directly computing the conventional vector, a quantum state is produced by the algorithm to exhibit the resolution vector to normalization. A polylogarithmic time O (log N) system is solved by the HHL algorithm, which involves matrix sparsity, a number of low conditions, and an efficient simulation of the matrix exponential. A quadratic time is required based on the matrix properties and the size involved, which is considered a significant advance over the conventional methods. In prominent techniques such as quantum principal component analysis and quantum support vector machines, the learning in QML is shown by QLSA. Apart from that, the algorithm implies a major role in solving the differential equations in computational physics and simulation of large quantum systems, competent signal reconstruction and noise reduction tasks in the case of signal processing tasks.

The algorithm has various issues despite its potential. In the early stages, both the development of efficient quantum random access memory (RAM) and accurate Hamiltonian representation are the major concerns—the removal of the significant conventional process from the quantum states is considered difficult in an inherent manner.

Applications

- QML: To develop the data in an effective manner, Quantum support vector machines and quantum principal component analysis (PCA) are mostly formed on the HHL algorithm.
- Quantum methods are used in signal processing, which is explored for tasks such as signal reconstruction and filtering, and potential accelerations are offered for complex signal indulgence.
- Quantum algorithms are used in computational physics for solving partial differential equations and simulating physical systems, which provides more accurate and scalable modeling.

Challenges

- Extracting classical information from the solution vector is non-trivial.
- Needs further development in quantum RAM and Hamiltonian simulation.

13.4.3 Quantum Graph Algorithms

Compared to conventional approaches, quantum walks are influenced by quantum graph algorithms, enabling effective handling of intricate graph problems.

Computing minimum spanning trees (MSTs), triangle detection, and identifying shortest paths are important enhancements of these techniques. The graph traversal approaches are combined with Grover's algorithm, providing a quantum speedup for the shortest path problems, especially in sparsely connected graphs or unweighted graphs, and this overpowers the conventional Dijkstra's algorithm. As an advantage to the sparse graph, the least finding procedures are used for edge selection speedup in case of MST calculations. Triangle identification encompasses the cycle of three-length identification in the graph, which is the most investigated issue. The complication to lessen O ($n^{1.297}$) is carried out by the quantum algorithms proposed by Magniez et al., [16] which involves the quantum walk built techniques. The proposed technique is efficient than the conventional runtime around O ($n^{1.41}$). Central graph structures and speedy analysis are crucial in analyzing web graphs, secure cyber systems, and molecular structure modeling, where these innovations have real-world consequences.

13.4.4 Grover's Algorithm and Extensions

For effective design and a wide range of efficacy, Grover's algorithm is used in QC. It attains a quadratic speedup to handle issues such as resolving decision difficulties or unsorted database identification for a better verification of solutions. N elements listed in a target item are identified by O (N) through a central quantum amplitude amplification of Grover's method, which is less than O (N) investigations of conventional algorithms. For enhancing the likelihood of the subroutines of the quantum amplification of amplitude concepts are prolonged than the formulation of the original Gover's algorithm.

Complex NP-hard tasks such as Max-Cut, Boolean Satisfiability (SAT), and the Traveling Salesman Problem are optimized by the prolonged Grover's relevance interpretations. Intricate combinational issues are solved by combining the quantum state research with the QAOA. Several such advancements are investigated in various domains, such as ML, operational research, and cryptanalysis, signifying the Grover's algorithm influence in heuristic quantum methods.

13.4.5 Deutsch–Jozsa Algorithm

To speed up the classical deterministic algorithms exponentially for a definite problem the Deutsch–Jozsa algorithm plays a major role. It is used to define the Boolean function f:{0, 1} n → {0, 1} is constant (producing the same output for all inputs) or balanced (yielding an equal number of 0s and 1s). The Hadamard transformation and quantum interference algorithm leverage quantum parallelism used to acquire a precise response within a single quantum query, whereas a classical deterministic method needs up to $2^{n-1} + 1$ evaluations. Even though the Deutsch–Jozsa algorithm is used to solve larger theoretical problems and is hardly used in real-world scenarios, it acts as a base for developing Simon's and Shor's algorithms, which are mainly used in practical applications. Presently, this algorithm endures to resolve valued theoretical and educational models in quantum algorithm research, primarily focusing on quantum speedup principles and algorithmic benefits.

13.5 FUTURE DIRECTIONS AND CHALLENGES

13.5.1 Hardware Limitations

The current systems continue with certain notable constraints, as the QC technologies move toward significant progress. There exist major limitations, such as a restricted number of qubits, that directly impacts the ability to implement large-scale and complex quantum algorithms. The decoherence phenomena caused by unwanted interactions between qubits and their environment remain an unsolvable issue and challenge the accuracy. The limited connectivity and minimal reliability are the cause of delayed quantum gate performance. The difficulty in maintaining stability in deeper or border circuits, executing meaningful quantum programs at scale, is the obstacles that challenge the hardware-related issues. Quantum hardware limitations and their impact are shown in Table 13.3.

13.5.2 Algorithm Development

It is necessary to keep pace with the growing robust quantum algorithms due to the evolution in quantum hardware. There is a high demand for algorithms that produce reliable performance in the presence of noisy qubits. In recent times, researchers have concentrated on problem-specific quantum heuristics, leading to practical advantages even in the absence of fully fault-tolerant systems. For the new possibilities of intelligent computing, a promising direction involves designing a hybrid model that integrates quantum optimization, QML, and symbolic AI. By implementing these hybrid approaches, more prompt benefits will be acquired on both the classical and quantum paradigms.

13.5.3 Bridging Theory and Application

There always exists a contradiction between theoretical development in QC and its real-world implementations. In bridging the contradictions, ideas from physicists, computer scientists, engineers, and subject experts are considered. To achieve appropriateness, it is essential to create quantum benchmarks that mirror actual problem structures rather than fabricated test cases. The open-source software frameworks, such as Qiskit, Cirq, and Penny Lane, are widely used for the development and

TABLE 13.3
Quantum Hardware Limitations and Their Impact

Limitation	Impact
Decoherence	Loss of quantum information
Gate errors	Incorrect gate operations
Qubit count	Restricts algorithm complexity
Qubit connectivity	Limits circuit design flexibility
Error correction	High overhead and resource consumption

testing of algorithms. The researchers can rely on these quantum algorithms for building reproducible prototypes and models, and for implementing.

13.5.4 Error Correction

To achieve fault-tolerant, scalable, and robust quantum computers, effective Quantum error correction (QEC) techniques need to be developed. The QEC shields logical qubits from localized mistakes by using topological properties. For hardware-efficient encoding schemes, various unconventional approaches, such as cat codes and Bacon-Shor codes, are used by specific quantum platforms, which play an exceptional role. Due to the existence of noise, the evolution of fault-tolerant gate implementations becomes crucial to guarantee that the quantum operations remain reliable. The continual growth in QEC paves the way for long-duration, steady computations on large-scale quantum systems in the future.

13.6 CONCLUSION

13.6.1 An overview of the Developments

This chapter explores the development of quantum algorithms, key improvements highlighting the reformations in the traditional approaches for computation. Strategies such as VQAs and feedback-driven hybrid frameworks are used to handle optimization and simulation trials on quantum hardware, which contribute predictable optimization techniques with quantum state engineering.

Quantum Gibbs Sampling and QBMs are some of the Quantum sampling techniques that help in developing powerful tools in ML and probabilistic analysis. Additionally, quantum solutions to computationally challenging classical problems, including the HHL algorithm for solving linear equations, quantum walk-based methods for assessing Boolean expressions, and graph-focused algorithms for challenges such as triangle detection and shortest path computation, are also surveyed in this chapter. Practical and more domain-specific quantum algorithms are also reviewed rather than theoretical developments.

13.6.2 Prospects for the Future

The advanced computational and innovative abilities are well-defined by the quantum technologies algorithms explained in the chapter. The intricate challenges in multiple disciplines are solved by relating the investigations of the quantum algorithms to the real-world systems. For instance, the simulations of quantum in the area of material science, the QC is used to identify the materials and new compounds custom-made with the chemical and physical properties. A security framework development is prompted by regulating the hazards posed by Shor's quantum algorithms by adjusting the cryptographic landscape. The real-world applications spread wider as these technologies evolve.

Quantum heuristics renders a vast solution for the applications in logistics and managing the supply chain. Additionally, the ongoing refinement of quantum algorithms is aimed at transforming areas such as model training, clustering, and complex decision-making within data-intensive environments. As development continues in quantum hardware reliability and error correction techniques, these emerging applications are anticipated to become increasingly viable and impactful.

13.6.3 Demand for Action

To encourage and accelerate the advancements, it is important that professionals, students, and researchers dynamically contribute to the QC ecosystem. Over cloud-based platforms such as IBM Quantum, Google Cirq, Amazon Braket, and Xanadu's PennyLane, interested developers are encouraged to start inspecting quantum algorithms exploiting real quantum hardware and easily manageable simulants. These platforms provide collaborative settings for testing, deploying, and developing quantum algorithms at different levels of abstraction.

Furthermore, interdisciplinary cooperation will be essential for determining and articulating issues that are most appropriate for quantum solutions—filling in the gaps between computer science, mathematics, quantum physics, and application fields such as healthcare, finance, and chemistry. Last but not least, readers are encouraged to add to the expanding collection of open-source resources, scholarly works, and neighborhood projects that are working together to influence the direction of quantum-enhanced computing. Together, by taking part in this transition, we create the foundation for a new era of computation that goes beyond the capabilities of traditional machines.

REFERENCES

1. Harrow, A. W., Hassidim, A., & Lloyd, S. (2009). Quantum algorithm for linear systems of equations. *Physical Review Letters*, 103(15), 150502.
2. Farhi, E., Goldstone, J., & Gutmann, S. (2014). A quantum approximate optimization algorithm. *arXiv preprint* arXiv:1411.4028.
3. Peruzzo, A., McClean, J., Shadbolt, P., Yung, M. H., Zhou, X.-Q., Love, P. J., … & O'Brien, J. L. (2014). A variational eigenvalue solver on a photonic quantum processor. *Nature Communications*, 5, 4213.
4. Rebentrost, P., Mohseni, M., & Lloyd, S. (2014). Quantum support vector machine for big data classification. *Physical Review Letters*, 113(13), 130503.
5. Kimmel, S., Lin, C.-Y., Low, G. H., Ozols, M., & Yoder, T. J. (2017). Hamiltonian simulation with optimal sample complexity. *npj Quantum Information*, 3(1), 13.
6. Temme, K., Bravyi, S., & Gambetta, J. M. (2017). Error mitigation for short-depth quantum circuits. *Physical Review Letters*, 119(18), 180509.
7. Preskill, J. (2018). Quantum computing in the NISQ era and beyond. *Quantum*, 2, 79.
8. Mitarai, K., Negoro, M., Kitagawa, M., & Fujii, K. (2018). Quantum circuit learning. *Physical Review A*, 98(3), 032309.
9. Benedetti, M., Lloyd, E., Sack, S., & Fiorentini, M. (2019). Parameterized quantum circuits as machine learning models. *Quantum Science and Technology*, 4(4), 043001.
10. Havlek, V., Córcoles, A. D., Temme, K., Harrow, A. W., Kandala, A., Chow, J. M., & Gambetta, J. M. (2019). Supervised learning with quantum-enhanced feature spaces. *Nature*, 567(7747), 209–212.
11. McArdle, S., Endo, S., Aspuru-Guzik, A., Benjamin, S. C., & Yuan, X. (2020). Quantum computational chemistry. *Reviews of Modern Physics*, 92(1), 015003.

12. Cerezo, M., Arrasmith, A., Babbush, R., Benjamin, S. C., Endo, S., Fujii, K., … & Coles, P. J. (2021). Variational quantum algorithms. *Nature Reviews Physics*, 3(9), 625–644.
13. Blekos, K., Papageorgiou, A., & Angelakis, D. G. (2023). A review on quantum approximate optimization algorithm and its variants. *arXiv preprint* arXiv:2306.09198.
14. Gunlycke, D., Taylor, C. A., & Joiner, C. A. (2024). Cascaded Variational Quantum Eigensolver (CVQE). *arXiv preprint* arXiv:2303.15237.
15. Küngurtsev, I., Antonelli, A., & Tóth, G. (2024). Iteration complexity of variational quantum algorithms. *Quantum*, 8, 1042.
16. Jeffery, S., Kothari, R., & Magniez, F. (2013). "Nested quantum walks with quantum data structures." In *Proceedings of the Twenty-Fourth Annual ACM-SIAM Symposium on Discrete Algorithms*, pp. 1474–1485. Society for Industrial and Applied Mathematic.

14 Applications of Deep Learning Technology for Mobile and Quantum Computing

Fadi Al-Turjman and Ramiz Salama

14.1 INTRODUCTION

Our everyday lives now would be impossible without mobile phones and tablets. In one way or another, cellphones and tablets are used for tasks such as communicating with loved ones, handling money, or documenting life's greatest events. However, these devices' capabilities are always evolving. Deep learning is the driving force behind a new wave of innovation. A branch of artificial intelligence called "deep learning" enables robots to learn by processing vast volumes of data. Deep learning algorithms are able to achieve this in part because they are able to recognize complex correlations and structures in data, which largely mirror the fundamental architecture and operation of the human brain. Due to this characteristic, both mobile computing and quantum computing have undergone a revolution, opening up possibilities that were previously thought to be limited to science fiction. Consider a smartphone camera that can replicate the depth-of-field effect of professional cameras, produce amazing visual effects, and recognize things in the frame with ease. It can also be adjusted for low-light shooting. All in all, deep learning is transforming this. Beyond image processing, deep learning is significantly altering how we interact with our gadgets. These days, virtual assistants do more than simply respond to a strict set of basic directions. All of these developments in natural language processing have made it possible for them to understand complicated sentences to determine the meaning of the user and to reply with subtle dialogues, which makes hands-free interaction incredibly smooth. The same changes are evident in mobile keyboards, which have developed into intelligent assistants with features such as emoji predictions based on your emotions, automatic word predictions for the next word in your sentence, and even the ability to suggest GIFs to inject some humor into your conversations. Beyond ease of use, deep learning has already emerged as a crucial tool in the battle for mobile security. This entails using deep learning algorithms for mobile security, with the primary goal being the prevention of fraud. This is accomplished by identifying irregularities in user behavior and attempting to safeguard sensitive information, such as financial transactions, on a mobile device.

 DOI: 10.1201/9781003587835-14

The mobile device experience is now more customized than ever before because of deep learning. Recommendation engines that filter goods, services, and content based on your interests and preferences will be powered by this technology. Every time you browse social media, shop, or look for a movie on your mobile device, deep learning algorithms work in the background to provide you with an interesting and pertinent experience. The only thing is that deep learning's advantages should not be limited to connected environments. Some of the functionalities can function without an internet connection thanks to advancements in mobile deep learning. Users will benefit from continuity and functionality in a network-limited or network-unavailable environment by implementing smaller and more effective deep learning models. This research explores the fascinating field of mobile computing deep learning. We will demonstrate how this technology is bringing mobile devices up to speed with humans, enhancing user experience, and influencing how people engage with mobile devices in the future.

14.2 PREVIOUS WORK

In fact, deep learning for mobile and quantum computing has been a very popular study topic in recent years. This is attested to by the rise of research publications in the form of studies, articles, and industry reports on various uses and developments. However, this study will concentrate on some of the research studies released between 2021 and 2024 to offer a current and pointed appraisal. However, to obtain a balanced viewpoint, we must also take into account the foundational studies that were published prior to 2021 and established this fascinating subject.

14.2.1 Here Is a Breakdown of the Focus of Research

Core Technologies (before 2021 and 2021–2024): Our work on deep learning focuses on the following methods and fundamental structures that may be used in the creation of mobile applications. This involves efforts to compress huge models into mobile-friendly ones using knowledge distillation, lightweight model compression approaches, and effective convolutional neural networks (CNNs). Particular Uses (2021–2024): The research project is primarily focused on the current uses of deep learning in several fields of mobile computing throughout the period 2021–2024.

Image Recognition and Enhancement: To advance computational photography, research will be done on deep learning methods, real-time picture enhancement algorithms, and object detection and recognition in mobile device photos.

Natural Language Processing (NLP): This session will showcase the latest advancements in on-device NLP for mobile devices, emphasizing research in sentiment analysis, intelligent text prediction, and deep learning for virtual assistants.

Fraud Detection: We will investigate deep learning-based anomaly detection with an emphasis on user behavior analysis and real-time fraud prevention in financial and mobile banking applications.

Personalized Content and Suggestions: Investigations into Recommendation Systems for Mobile Applications Using Deep Learning-Based Content Personalization Algorithms, Collaborative Filtering Methods, and User Preference Modeling.

Offline Functionality: Recent efforts to make deep learning features operational offline on mobile devices will be examined. We will talk about computationally efficient deep learning inference on mobile devices, knowledge distillation, and model compression. This study contemplates it can describe the current state of the art in deep learning for mobile computing by looking at this wide variety of research and identifying potentially intriguing future destinations for such quickly developing research.

14.2.2 Quantum Systems

In this subsection, we discuss quantum systems that surpass classical computing units in some tasks as follows.

14.2.2.1 Quantum Bits (Qubits)

Quantum bits, or qubits, are the elementary units in quantum computers. Unlike bits in classical systems that can only be in the state of either 0 or 1, qubits share the property of superposition and thus can be in a number of states at the same time. This ability skyrockets the computational power of quantum systems. Various forms of qubits have been realized, including:

Superconducting Qubits: These are implemented in Quantum systems such as Google Sycamore and International Business Machines (IBM) Quantum processors that utilize superconducting circuits, which are operated in sub-zero temperature conditions.

Trapped-Ion Qubits: Ions encased by electromagnetic fields are used by ion traps, which are later controlled by lasers. Photonic Qubits: Systems such as Jianzhong have photonic qubits that integrate photons as quantum-based information processors.

14.2.2.2 Quantum Gates and Circuits

Gates are mathematically defined functionalities that efficiently explore the different quantum states for a quantum gate, working strictly on the quantum state of the qubits. For example, Hadamard Gate: Superposition. Controlled-NOT (CNOT) Gate: Relates to other qubits. Pauli Gates (X, Y, Z): Executes specific rotations on the qubits. These different gates are used in quantum circuits, which combine them to solve problems on certain algorithms, such as random circuit sampling or quantum optimization tasks.

14.3 UTILIZING DEEP LEARNING IN MOBILE COMPUTING APPLICATIONS

The research for this project will thoroughly examine the uses of deep learning for mobile computing using a literature review methodology. This analysis will be updated and more thorough in the following ways.

14.3.1 Search Strategy and Data Sources

Academic Databases: The Association for Computing Machinery (ACM) Digital Library, Institute of Electrical and Electronics Engineers (IEEE) Xplore, and ScienceDirect are the primary academic databases from which we will draw information for our study. High levels of dependability and scientific quality are guaranteed by the vast array of peer-reviewed research studies, conference proceedings, and journals they provide.

Method of Search: To return exactly the information found in the chosen databases, the search will be conducted using a combination of carefully chosen keywords. The keywords will be used to search databases for information about mobile computing (such as mobile devices and on-device learning), deep learning (such as CNNs and recurrent neural networks), and specific applications (such as fraud detection, image recognition, and natural language processing). To produce as many search combinations as possible that produce valuable findings for the study, all feasible Boolean operators—including AND, OR, and NOT—will be applied.

Inclusion and Exclusion Criteria: To ensure that the selection process is as beneficial as possible, there will be particular criteria for the articles that are included or excluded. Articles about recent advancements that are published between 2021 and 2024 will be given a higher priority. Additionally, preference will be given to articles that mainly address or explain the use of deep learning in mobile computing applications. Articles published before 2021 will be excluded, with the exception of key works, those that offer studies lacking in methodological depth or a clear assessment measure, or those that cover a wider range of deep learning applications that are not necessarily for mobile computing applications.

Snowballing Strategy: In addition to the original keyword search, we will look for pertinent research using the snowballing strategy. Since they might offer insightful information or present alternative viewpoints on the issue being studied, we will closely review the reference lists of a few important articles and investigate the cited works. Research that might be pertinent but missed by a first keyword search can be found using this method.

14.3.2 Data Collection and Analysis

Data Extraction: Following the sorting of the pertinent research studies, a methodical approach to extracting the necessary data must be taken. This could involve adding important information such as:

Details About the Publication: Title, authors, publication date, and journal/conference name.

Methodology: This lays out the precise deep learning architectures and techniques that were employed in the study.

Applications: The field of mobile computing applications that are being examined, such as fraud detection, picture recognition, and natural language processing.

Metrics for Evaluation: The authors' approach to assessing the effectiveness of their deep learning system.

Key Findings and Contributions: The study's main discoveries and breakthroughs.

Data Management: To guarantee proper citation management and to make the entire data analysis process simpler, the extracted data will be arranged using Mendeley or Zotero reference management software. Additionally, a spreadsheet or database for classification could be used to organize the information extraction according to the topic of the research field.

14.3.3 Critical Analysis and Synthesis

Critical Evaluation: The research methodology, the reliability of the findings, and the study's overall influence on deep learning for mobile computing are all included in the critical evaluation of the data. These consist of the generalizability of the results, the suitability of the assessment criteria, and the soundness of the experimental design. Thematic analysis is the process of identifying recurring themes and ideas in the chosen research. This is accomplished by coding the extracted data according to topics that may have been pre-specified or discovered, such as emergent applications, future research directions, and the difficulties of mobile deep learning. It is feasible to gain some understanding of the current state of the art as well as anticipated future advancements in the subject by examining the occurrences and relationships between these themes.

Conclusion and Integration: To provide a meaningful picture of the application of deep learning in mobile computing, this project will then synthesize the findings from the many research articles. The most significant of these will be covered in detail, along with discussions of the compelling uses, difficulties, and restrictions related to deep learning on mobile devices.

14.3.4 Ethical Considerations

Bias in Deep Learning Models: It is likely that deep learning models pick up on any bias in the data they were given. The bias in deep learning models that will be utilized in mobile computing applications is one of the likely ethical issues that this research project will bring up and examine. The significance of guaranteeing equity and inclusivity in the creation and implementation of such technologies is emphasized, and potential mitigation techniques are examined. Concerns around privacy and security in relation to the implementation of deep learning models on mobile devices will also be covered in this project. We will look at best practices for safeguarding user privacy and data security in mobile deep learning applications, as well as any concerns associated with data collection and storage. Using this thorough and methodical approach to the literature evaluation, this initiative aims to offer.

14.4 RESULTS AND DISCUSSION

We shall discover a multitude of innovative applications in the way we use our mobile devices in this overview of deep learning for mobile computing. This section attempts to consider some of the major fields where deep learning is having a significant influence, examining its advantages and disadvantages as well as the enormous promise it has for the future. Deep learning research for mobile computing applications has revealed a broad and creative environment that will transform our daily interactions with our gadgets and pave the way for new possibilities. In this section, we go into deeper detail about some of the most significant effects, advantages, and drawbacks of deep learning while also examining some fascinating potential future developments.

14.4.1 Image Identification and Improvement: Redefining Mobile Photography

Mobile photography has been essentially transformed by deep learning algorithms, mainly using CNNs. We may now access the following properties:

Identification of objects and scenes in a frame is now possible with mobile cameras, enabling functions such as automatic scene optimization during photo capture. Photos can be considerably more efficiently organized and searched thanks to object tagging.

Image Enhancement and Denoising: Low-light photos can be analyzed and improved using deep learning models to cut down on noise and improve overall image quality.

By catching details in both light and dark in a single frame, we may also develop methods for taking pictures on mobile devices that have a great dynamic range.

Filters and Creative Effects: Deep learning enables a variety of filters and creative effects. For instance, a style transfer algorithm can produce a look akin to that of a well-known artist. It can also be used in conjunction with backdrop segmentation techniques that enable sophisticated bokeh effects to blur the background and produce a professional portrait appearance.

Discussion: The mobile photo is significantly enhanced by the effectiveness of deep learning. The performance of older systems may be limited by model size and processing complexity, and research on accurate object detection in complex scenes or changing light conditions is still ongoing. These fields are rapidly evolving, primarily as a result of recent advances in on-device processing and effective model architectures.

14.4.2 NLP: Mobile Communication Transformed

Through a revolution in natural language processing, deep learning is significantly altering how people interact with mobile devices. The principal uses are as follows:

Better Understanding Virtual Assistants: Deep learning-powered virtual assistants can now comprehend challenging natural language queries. Through their responses, they provide contextually relevant information, allowing one to interact hands-free by utilizing voice commands to operate smart home devices, manage calendars, or even obtain real-time information.

augmented reality (AR) will no longer be limited to headgear thanks to deep learning; instead, they will be made available on mobile devices. The foundational components for creating genuinely realistic and engaging AR/VR applications will be real-time object detection, scene understanding, and mapping.

Edge Computing: When combined with edge computing, deep learning can enable real-time data processing at the network's edge, near mobile devices. For mobile applications, this can increase responsiveness and lower latency.

14.5 CONCLUSION

Its impact on mobile computing extends well beyond the recently reviewed capabilities. Deep learning has enormous potential to have a significant impact on everything from mobile device environmental monitoring to healthcare and education. Consider smartphone apps that can use image recognition to diagnose illnesses, or that can automatically analyze environmental data to track changes in the climate. These create enormous opportunities that lay the groundwork for creating a future in which mobile devices can be effectively used for good. But with all of that in mind, ethical considerations must be the top priority for further advancements in deep learning for mobile computing. This entails protecting user privacy, reducing algorithmic bias, and collecting data responsibly. Researchers, developers, legislators, and the general public must collaborate to realize that kind of agenda in the future and make sure that deep learning enables mobile technology in ways that benefit both humanity and the environment. To sum up, deep learning has the potential to revolutionize the field of mobile computing. We can build a future where mobile devices will not only improve our lives but also enable us to address some of the most important problems facing the globe as we proceed and explore the exciting potential it unlocks, balanced with responsible development, ethical considerations, and user privacy, while harnessing this force for good.

REFERENCES

1. Zhang, Y., Liu, B., Gong, Y., Huang, J., Xu, J., & Wan, W. (2024, April). Application of machine learning optimization in cloud computing resource scheduling and management. In *Proceedings of the 5th International Conference on Computer Information and Big Data Applications* (pp. 171–175).
2. Wang, Y., Bao, Q., Wang, J., Su, G., & Xu, X. (2024). Cloud computing for large-scale resource computation and storage in machine learning. *Journal of Theory and Practice of Engineering Science*, 4(03), 163–171.
3. Xu, Z., Gong, Y., Zhou, Y., Bao, Q., & Qian, W. (2024, October). Enhancing kubernetes automated scheduling with deep learning and reinforcement techniques for large-scale cloud computing optimization. In *Ninth International Symposium on Advances in Electrical, Electronics, and Computer Engineering (ISAEECE 2024)* (Vol. 13291, pp. 1595–1600). SPIE.
4. Wang, J., Lu, T., Li, L., & Huang, D. (2024). Enhancing personalized search with ai: a hybrid approach integrating deep learning and cloud computing. *Journal of Advanced Computing Systems*, 4(10), 1–13.
5. Wang, Y., & Yang, X. (2025). Machine learning-based cloud computing compliance process automation. arXiv preprint arXiv:2502.16344.

6. Ahmed, Q. O. (2024). Machine learning for intrusion detection in cloud environments: A comparative study. *Journal of Artificial Intelligence General Science*. ISSN: 3006-4023, 6(1), 550–563.
7. Akinbolaji, T. J. (2024). Advanced integration of artificial intelligence and machine learning for real-time threat detection in cloud computing environments. *Iconic Research and Engineering Journals*, 6(10), 980–991.
8. Shang, Y. (2024). Prevention and detection of DDOS attack in virtual cloud computing environment using Naive Bayes algorithm of machine learning. *Measurement: Sensors*, 31, 100991.
9. Polamarasetti, A. (2024, November). Role of artificial intelligence and machine learning to enhancing cloud security. In *2024 International Conference on Intelligent Computing and Emerging Communication Technologies (ICEC)* (pp. 1–6). IEEE.
10. Devi, T. A., & Jain, A. (2024, May). Enhancing cloud security with deep learning-based intrusion detection in cloud computing environments. In *2024 2nd International Conference on Advancement in Computation & Computer Technologies (InCACCT)* (pp. 541–546). IEEE.
11. Feng, Y., Qi, Y., Li, H., Wang, X., & Tian, J. (2024, July). Leveraging federated learning and edge computing for recommendation systems within cloud computing networks. In *Third International Symposium on Computer Applications and Information Systems (ISCAIS 2024)* (Vol. 13210, pp. 279–287). SPIE.
12. Reddy, P., Adetuwo, Y., & Jakkani, A. K. (2024). Implementation of machine learning techniques for cloud security in detection of ddos attacks. *International Journal of Computer Engineering and Technology*, 15(2): 1–15.
13. Sanagana, D. P. R., & Tummalachervu, C. K. (2024, May). Securing cloud computing environment via optimal deep learning-based intrusion detection systems. In *2024 Second International Conference on Data Science and Information System (ICDSIS)* (pp. 1–6). IEEE.
14. Polamarasetti, A. (2024, November). Machine learning techniques analysis to efficient resource provisioning for elastic cloud services. In *2024 International Conference on Intelligent Computing and Emerging Communication Technologies (ICEC)* (pp. 1–6). IEEE.
15. Rehan, H. (2024). Revolutionizing America's cloud computing the pivotal role of AI in driving innovation and security. *Journal of Artificial Intelligence General Science*. ISSN: 3006-4023, 2(1), 239–240.
16. Wang, Y., Yang, C., Lan, S., Zhu, L., & Zhang, Y. (2024). End-edge-cloud collaborative computing for deep learning: A comprehensive survey. *IEEE Communications Surveys & Tutorials*, 4, 2647–2683.
17. Rao, S. M., & Jain, A. (2024). Advances in malware analysis and detection in cloud computing environments: A review. *International Journal of Safety & Security Engineering*, 14(1), 1–14.
18. Li, H., Wang, S. X., Shang, F., Niu, K., & Song, R. (2024). Applications of large language models in cloud computing: An empirical study using real-world data. *Spectrum of Research*, 4(1), 1–9.
19. Zheng, H., Xu, K., Zhang, M., Tan, H., & Li, H. (2024). Efficient resource allocation in cloud computing environments using AI-driven predictive analytics. *Applied and Computational Engineering*, 82, 17–23.
20. Wiryasaputra, R., Huang, C. Y., Lin, Y. J., & Yang, C. T. (2024). An IoT real-time potable water quality monitoring and prediction model based on cloud computing architecture. *Sensors*, 24(4), 1180.
21. Mistry, H. K., Mavani, C., Goswami, A., & Patel, R. (2024). The impact of cloud computing and AI on industry dynamics and competition. *Educational Administration: Theory and Practice*, 30(7), 797–804.

22. Padmanaban, H. (2024). Quantum computing and AI in the cloud. *Journal of Computational Intelligence and Robotics*, 4(1), 14–32.
23. Wang, Y., & Yang, X. (2025). Research on enhancing cloud computing network security using artificial intelligence algorithms. arXiv preprint arXiv:2502.17801.
24. Wali, G., & Bulla, C. (2024, July). Suspicious activity detection model in bank transactions using deep learning with fog computing infrastructure. In *International Conference on Computational Innovations and Emerging Trends (ICCIET-2024)* (pp. 292–302). Atlantis Press.
25. Simuni, G., & Atla, A. (2024). The role of AI and machine learning in optimising cloud migration processes. *International Journal of Business Analytics & Intelligence*, 12(2): 1–7.
26. Singh, J. A. J., Gnanasoundharam, J., Birunda, M., Sudha, G., Maniraj, S. P., & Srinivasan, C. (2024, March). Wearable sepsis early warning using cloud computing and logistic regression predictive analytics. In *2024 11th International Conference on Reliability, Infocom Technologies and Optimization (Trends and Future Directions) (ICRITO)* (pp. 1–6). IEEE.
27. Zhang, M., Yuan, B., Li, H., & Xu, K. (2024). LLM-cloud complete: Leveraging cloud computing for efficient large language model-based code completion. *Journal of Artificial Intelligence General Science*. ISSN: 3006-4023, 5(1), 295–326.
28. Abd Elaziz, M., Al-qaness, M. A., Dahou, A., Alsamhi, S. H., Abualigah, L., Ibrahim, R. A., & Ewees, A. A. (2024). Evolution toward intelligent communications: Impact of deep learning applications on the future of 6G technology. *Wiley Interdisciplinary Reviews: Data Mining and Knowledge Discovery*, 14(1), e1521.
29. Xu, K., Zheng, H., Zhan, X., Zhou, S., & Niu, K. (2024). Evaluation and optimization of intelligent recommendation system performance with cloud resource automation compatibility.
30. Zhang, X. (2024). Machine learning insights into digital payment behaviors and fraud prediction. *Applied and Computational Engineering*, 77, 203–209.

15 Effective Quantum, Artificial Intelligence (AI), and Cloud Implementation

Fadi Al-Turjman and Ramiz Salama

15.1 INTRODUCTION

Today's business environment is marked by fierce rivalry and a constant need for efficiency, productivity, and agility. To obtain a competitive advantage in this ever-changing environment, associations are continuously looking for novel outcomes. Artificial Intelligence (AI) and Pall computing are two technologies that are rapidly changing the way organizations function [1]. This design explores the mutually beneficial interaction between AI and Pall, examining how their combined strength is bringing about revolutionary transformation in the field of diligence. To reduce timeouts and ensure seamless output, consider a production facility where AI-powered prophetic conservation may analyze detector data to discover implicit outfit problems before they occur. By making product recommendations based on past purchases and browsing behavior, AI can perfectly capture customer gestures in the retail industry, resulting in greater client loyalty and satisfaction. The healthcare industry can use AI to speed up research and development and solve patient problems by doing jobs such as medical picture analysis and medication discovery. This design goes beyond the hypothetical possibilities of Pall and AI. Through a rigorous analysis of real-world case studies, it seeks to provide a useful road map for successful execution [2]. The aforementioned case studies will highlight organizations from many industries that have used AI and Pall to produce tangible outcomes. We will look at the particular difficulties these associations encountered, the AI and Pall outcomes they imposed, and the measurable advantages they attained. Similarly, the investigation will focus on the crucial elements that lead to effective integration. Strategies for changing operations and leadership will receive a lot of attention. In what ways did these associations get their pool ready to give up AI and Pall? Did they implement training initiatives and encourage a creative culture to guarantee stoner support and a seamless surrender? We will also look at the importance of data integration and medicine. We will learn about the fashionable data cleaning, governance, and security strategies used by prosperous associations by looking at the case studies. To replicate their success, it is essential to comprehend how businesses made sure their

DOI: 10.1201/9781003587835-15

AI models were powered by reliable data sources [3]. Nowadays, in the digital world, security issues are paramount. The case studies will analyze the fashionable security measures that successful AI and Pall adopters enforce. Investigating features used to protect sensitive data within the Pall landscape, such as data encryption, access controls, and trouble discovery procedures, may be part of this. To reduce time-outs and ensure seamless output, consider a production facility where AI-powered prophetic conservation may analyze detector data to discover implicit outfit problems before they occur. By making product recommendations based on past purchases and browsing behavior, AI can perfectly capture customer gestures in the retail industry. resulting in greater client loyalty and pleasure. The healthcare industry can use AI to speed up research and development and solve patient problems by doing jobs such as medical picture analysis and medication discovery [4]. This design goes beyond the hypothetical possibilities of Pall and AI. Through a rigorous analysis of real-world case studies, it seeks to provide a useful road map for successful execution. The aforementioned case studies will highlight organizations from many industries that have used AI and Pall to produce tangible outcomes. We will look at the particular difficulties these associations encountered, the AI and Pall outcomes they imposed, and the measurable advantages they attained. Similarly, the investigation will focus on the crucial elements that lead to effective integration. Strategies for changing operations and leadership will receive a lot of attention. In what ways did these associations get their pool ready to give up AI and Pall? Did they implement training initiatives and encourage a creative culture to guarantee stoner support and a seamless surrender? We will also look at the importance of data integration and medicine. We will learn about the fashionable data cleaning, governance, and security strategies used by prosperous associations by looking at the case studies. To reduce time-outs and ensure seamless output, consider a production facility where AI-powered prophetic conservation may analyze detector data to discover implicit outfit problems before they occur [5]. AI can improve customer satisfaction and loyalty in the retail industry by making product recommendations based on past purchases and browsing behavior. The healthcare industry can use AI to speed up research and development and solve patient problems by doing jobs such as medical picture analysis and medication discovery. This design goes beyond the hypothetical possibilities of Pall and AI. Through a rigorous analysis of real-world case studies, it seeks to provide a useful road map for successful execution. The aforementioned case studies will highlight organizations from many industries that have used AI and Pall to produce tangible outcomes [6]. We will look at the particular difficulties these associations encountered, the AI and Pall outcomes they imposed, and the measurable advantages they attained. Similarly, the investigation will focus on the crucial elements that lead to effective integration. Strategies for changing operations and leadership will receive a lot of attention [7]. In what ways did these associations get their pool ready to give up AI and Pall? Did they implement training initiatives and encourage a creative culture to guarantee stoner support and a seamless surrender? We will also look at the importance of data integration and medicine. We will learn about the fashionable data cleaning, governance, and security strategies used by prosperous associations by looking at the case studies. To replicate their success, it is essential to comprehend how businesses made sure their AI models were powered by reliable data sources. Nowadays, in the digital world, security issues are paramount. The case studies will analyze the fashionable security measures that successful AI and Pall adopters enforce. Investigating features used to protect sensitive data within the Pall landscape, such as data encryption, access controls, and trouble discovery procedures, may be part of this. For associations looking to create strong perpetuation plans and unleash the revolutionary potential of this crucial technical tool, the case study assignments will be an invaluable resource.

15.2 QUANTITY OF PRIOR PUBLICATIONS

Quantum computing is often considered a field that has the ability to change a lot of things, including how we address certain problems and how we perceive processes. At the same time, it was once said that it would not take long before quantum supremacy is achieved. This is a confrontational point, as several researchers are already stating that some computer problems will never be achievable by quantum computers. Quantum computing operates on physically different principles than classical computing [8]. While the classical computer operates with binary codes (0 and 1), the quantum computer uses quantum bits—qubits—which may be in several states at a time, due to the effect of superposition. Also, thanks to quantum entanglement, qubits can interact with each other in a way that practically increases computing efficiency by several orders of magnitude. Thanks to these properties, quantum computers are able to perform tasks in the areas of cryptography, optimization, AI, and others that are resource-intensive for classical systems.

Moreover, the subject of AI and Pall applications is rapidly changing, with new research emerging all the time to shed light on fashionable methods, tackle emerging issues, and investigate the ever-expanding potential of these technologies [9]. This plan will draw on a wealth of research that has been published in the last 2 years (2022–2024) to provide a thorough grasp of the existing geography. Next, we get into some of the most important elements of this most recent investigation.

15.2.1 Operations Specific to Industry

The adapted operation of AI and Pall across various diligences is the subject of a large amount of recent research. Research looks at how particular diligence affects AI and Pall to solve their particular problems and support expansion opportunities. Here are other examples after that. AI-powered predictive conservation in manufacturing optimizes product timelines, decreases time-outs, and lowers costs, according to Manufacturing Research by Mistry et al., 2024 [10]. The application of Pall-grounded robotics for reduced product inflexibility and scalability in production installations is the subject of another study by Paroha et al., 2024 [11]. Money The use of AI for fraud detection and threat operation in the financial sector is the subject of recent research by Kommisetty et al., 2024 [12]. The study examines how Pall computing makes it easier to store and analyze the enormous amounts of financial data needed to develop and implement efficient AI models. Healthcare Research by Thota et al., 2024 [13] explores how AI works for medical picture processing, emphasizing how it could improve patient care and individual delicacy. To improve accessibility and convenience for patients in remote locations, a different study by Gooda et al., 2025 [14] investigates the usage of Pall-grounded telemedicine platforms to provide remote healthcare services.

15.2.2 Management of Change and Leadership

Effective leadership and change operation techniques are essential for the successful integration of AI and Pall. Recent research focuses on this crucial element, providing invaluable insight for associations undergoing transformation. Leadership strategies that encourage a culture of innovation and hand buy-in during AI and Pall relinquishment are examined in studies such as Mamidi et al., 2024 [15]. Additionally, research looks at fashionable methods for training and development initiatives to provide employees with the skills they need to succeed in an AI-powered plant.

15.2.3 Security and Data Management

The availability and quality of data are critical to the performance of AI models. Data operation techniques for AI and Pall executions are the subject of recent research. Research such as Olabanji et al., 2024 [16] investigates data governance, security, and cleansing strategies in the Pall landscape. Additionally, research by Thummala et al., 2024 [17] explores fashionable methods for data integration between AI models and enterprise systems, ensuring a perfect information flow for peak performance.

15.2.4 Moral Aspects

Important ethical questions are brought up by the additional abandonment of AI. These businesses are examined in recent research, which focuses on the appropriate development and application of AI technologies. Research conducted in 2024 by Seenivasan et al., 2024[18] explores implicit impulses in AI algorithms and suggests ways to mitigate them. Additionally, research by Zangana et al., 2024 [19] examines the ethical defenses of AI-driven decision-making systems as well as the necessity of accountability and transparency. This design will provide a thorough knowledge of the current status of AI and Pall executions by looking at this collection of recent research. The insight gleaned from this research will guide case study analysis, resulting in a comprehensive discussion of effective tactics and fashionable practices. By presenting real-world examples that highlight the transformative potential of this significant technical advance, this design seeks to add to the current conversation.

15.3 MATERIALS AND PROCEDURE

This section describes the rigorous process used to choose and analyze case examples that demonstrate effective AI and Pall executions. This method guarantees a thorough and impartial discussion of the important elements influencing their success.

15.3.1 Selection Criteria for Case Studies

The following standards will be applied to the selection process to guarantee a unique and insightful set of case studies.

Depiction of Industry: The case studies will cover a range of topics, demonstrating how AI and Pall are related in several industries. Manufacturing, banking, healthcare, retail, and other industries will fall under this category [20].

Stack of Technologies: To address particular difficulties, the case studies will delve into several technological stacks and examine the application of various AI models (such as machine literacy and natural language processing) and Pall platforms (such as Amazon Web Services, Microsoft Azure, and Google Cloud Platform).

Measurable Achievement: The selected case stories will show measurable progress made with AI and minimize perpetration. Criteria such as improved client satisfaction, cost savings, increased effectiveness, or improved product development procedures may fall under this category.

Reliability of the Sources: Each case study's information will come from credible and trustworthy sources. These sources might be approved corporate reports, periodicals that are admired for their diligence, or scholarly journals that concentrate on technology-related crimes.

15.3.2 Information Gathering and Evaluation

A systematic procedure for gathering and analyzing data will be approved after the case studies are named.

Birth of data: Relevant data will be rigorously extracted from the selected sources for every case study. Information on the association, the particular AI and Pall technologies used, the difficulties faced, and the outcomes attained will all be covered.

Analysis of Themes: To find recurring themes and patterns in the case studies, a thematic analysis will be carried out. The focus of this investigation will be on identifying the critical elements that lead to effective AI and Pall executions. The specialized functions of AI models in various contexts, data operation procedures, security issues, and leadership and change operation techniques are examples of implicit themes.

Comparison of Cases: To find similarities and contrasts in perpetration approaches and issues, the case studies will be rigorously compared and varied. This will provide valuable insight into the inflexibility of effective techniques in various organizational contexts.

15.3.3 Triangulation of Data

Data triangulation will be used to ensure the reliability and validity of the exploration findings. This entails using information from a variety of sources to support the claims made in each case study against support the stated successes, for example, firm reports can be compared against industry news articles or critical reports.

15.3.4 Moral Aspects

The exploration process will be conducted with ethical considerations in mind. To acknowledge the sources utilized, appropriate citation guidelines will be adhered to. Additionally, measures will be made to anonymize or redact any sensitive information, such as particular fiscal data in case studies, to ensure confidentiality. This design seeks to provide a comprehensive and insightful examination of successful AI and Pall executions by adhering to this exacting criterion. Together with the theme analysis, the selected case studies will provide associations starting their own AI and Pall peregrinations with valuable assignments and fashionable practices [21–23].

15.4 RESULTS AND DISCUSSION ARE AS FOLLOWS

This section explores the fundamentals of the design by showcasing the selected case studies and promoting an in-depth conversation about the crucial elements that made them successful.

Figure 15.1 depicts case studies from 2021 to 2030.

15.4.1 Using AI to Revolutionize Logistics Acme Corporation's Chain Optimization

The intricate force chain network of Acme Corporation, a well-known worldwide logistics provider, was inefficient. Their operations were hindered by detentions, erroneous demand forecasting, and growing transportation expenses. Acme implemented a Pall-grounded AI solution to overcome these issues. Real-time data on force conditions, dispatch routes, and request trends were analyzed by machine

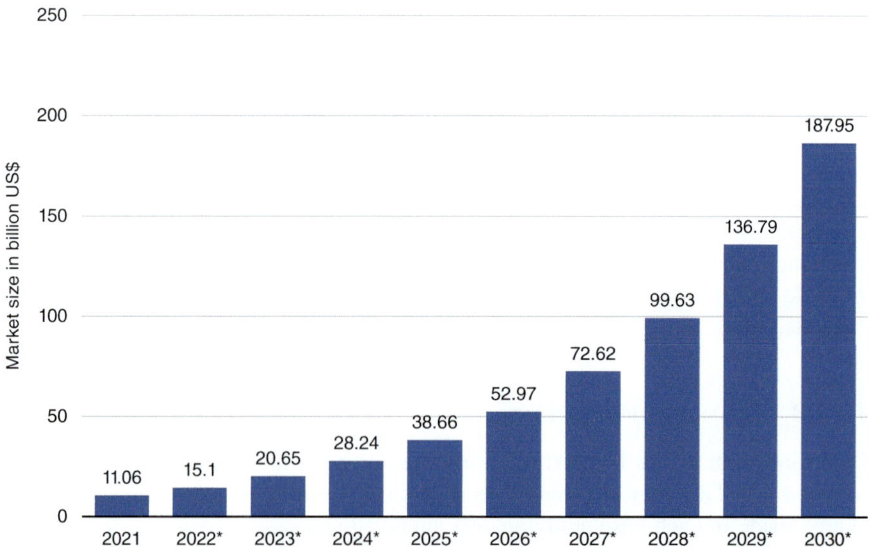

FIGURE 15.1 Case studies 2021 to 2030.

learning algorithms. They were able to anticipate demand fluctuations, optimize delivery routes, and assist with stockouts as a result. Talk about the effectiveness of AI in force chain operations is highlighted in this case study. For Acme, real-time data analysis and AI-enabled intelligent decision-making resulted in considerable cost savings, improved delivery times, and increased customer happiness.

15.4.2 Bodying the Customer Journey with AI-Powered Suggestions at RetailCo

Due to the huge amount of data and varying customer preferences, RetailCo, a significant online retailer, struggled to define client segments. A Pall-grounded AI recommendation system was enforced. Analyzed customer evaluations, past purchases, and browsing gestures using natural language processing techniques. RetailCo was able to recommend relevant products as a result, which raised customer engagement and enhanced conversion rates. Talk about the role of AI in client relationship management is highlighted in this case study. RetailCo created a more personalized buying experience by utilizing AI for tailored suggestions and Pall computing to manage large databases, increasing customer loyalty and sales.

15.4.3 Using AI to Speed Up Drug Discovery at Pharmalab

The goal of pharmaceutical exploration firm Pharmalab was to speed up the typically laborious and expensive drug development procedure. They promoted a Palliative AI platform that analyzed vast amounts of natural data and molecular structural databases. As a result, they were able to find promising drug campaigners more quickly and efficiently. Talking about this case study demonstrates how AI has the potential to revolutionize scientific research. While AI techniques facilitated quick analysis and the identification of implicit medical campaigners, grid computing provided the scalability required to handle large datasets. It is implied that this will speed up the development of life-saving details and update the pharmaceutical industry.

15.4.4 Inter-Case Conversation

Upon analyzing these many case stories, a number of important patterns emerge as critical elements for effective AI and Pall executions.

Management of Change and Leadership: A culture of innovation and "hand buy-in" is fostered by a strong leadership vision. Programs for training and development are necessary to give employees the skills they need to adopt AI-driven processes.

Security and Data Management: The availability, confidentiality, and quality of data that powers AI models are guaranteed by strong data governance procedures.

Strong Security Elements on Exercise: Pall platforms safeguard private data and promote confidence in AI-powered procedures.

Pay Attention to Business Needs: Successful implementations make it simple to identify the business issues that AI and Pall End are meant to solve. Associations can monitor their effectiveness and make sure the technology provides tangible benefit by focusing on particular pretenses and tracking advancement using measurable standards. Flexibility and agility, the Pall platform's gauging capacity enables future growth and enables associations to adjust their AI models in response to changing request conditions and commercial requirements. These case studies demonstrate how AI and Pall may transform enterprises across disciplines when properly implemented. For organizations thinking of starting their own AI and Pall peregrinations, they provide invaluable insight and fashionable practices.

15.5 CONCLUSION

The bleak quest for innovation and expansion forces companies to adopt cutting-edge technologies. To unlock a new era of opportunity, this design has dug into the mutually beneficial link between AI and Pall computing. Through rigorous analysis of real-world case studies from several disciplines, it has shed light on the transformative potential of this technology tool and the critical elements that lead to successful implementations. The case studies demonstrated how AI can solve important business problems by analyzing enormous amounts of data, forming wise judgments, and automating processes. AI offers a wide range of applications with observable returns on investment, from bodying client gestures to optimizing force chains to speeding up scientific research. However, AI's actual potential depends on its ability to acquire reliable and secure data. Pall computing can help with this by providing a scalable and affordable platform for data storage, processing, and analysis. Businesses may use data-driven perception to make well-informed decisions and gain notable performance improvements thanks to the combination of AI and pall. To reduce time-outs and ensure seamless output, consider a production facility where AI-powered prophetic conservation may analyze detector data to discover implicit outfit problems before they occur. AI can improve customer satisfaction and loyalty in the retail industry by making product recommendations based on past purchases and browsing behavior. The healthcare industry can use AI to speed up research and development and solve patient problems by doing jobs such as medical picture analysis and medication discovery. This design goes beyond the hypothetical possibilities of Pall and AI. Through a rigorous analysis of real-world case studies, it seeks to provide a useful road map for successful execution. The aforementioned case studies will highlight organizations from many industries that have used AI and Pall to produce tangible outcomes. We will look at the particular difficulties these associations encountered, the AI and Pall outcomes they imposed, and the measurable advantages they attained. Similarly, the investigation will focus on the crucial elements that lead to effective integration. Strategies for changing operations and leadership will receive a lot of attention. In what ways did these associations get their pool ready to give up AI and Pall? Did they implement training initiatives and encourage a creative culture to guarantee stoner support and a seamless surrender? We will also look at the importance of data integration and medicine. We will learn about the fashionable data cleaning, governance, and security strategies used by prosperous associations by looking at the case studies. To replicate their success, it is essential to comprehend how businesses made sure their AI models were powered by reliable data sources. Nowadays, in the digital world, security issues are paramount. The case studies will analyze the fashionable security measures that successful AI and Pall adopters enforce. Investigating features used to protect sensitive data within the Pall landscape, such as data encryption, access controls, and trouble discovery procedures, may be part of this. In summary, the case studies demonstrated how AI can solve important business problems by analyzing enormous amounts of data, forming wise judgments, and automating processes. AI offers a wide range of applications with observable returns on investment, from bodying client gestures to optimizing force chains to speeding up scientific research. However, AI's actual potential depends on its ability to acquire reliable and secure data. Pall computing can help with this by providing a scalable and affordable platform for data storage, processing, and analysis. Businesses may use data-driven perception to make well-informed decisions and gain notable performance improvements thanks to the combination of AI and Pall.

REFERENCES

1. Parisa, S. K., & Banerjee, S. (2024). AI-Enabled Cloud Security Solutions: A Comparative Review of Traditional vs. Next-Generation Approaches. *International Journal of Statistical Computation and Simulation*, 16(1), 1–152.
2. Banerjee, S. (2024). Intelligent Cloud Systems: AI-Driven Enhancements in Scalability and Predictive Resource Management. *International Journal of Advanced Research in Science, Communication and Technology*, 2, 266–276.
3. Ugbebor, F. O. (2024). Intelligent Cloud Solutions Bridging Technology Gaps for Small and Medium-Sized Enterprises. *Journal of Artificial Intelligence General Science*. ISSN: 3006-4023, 7(01), 161–186.
4. Devaraj, S. M. (2024). Cloud, Ai, And Digital Transformation: A Winning Combination. *International Journal of Computer Engineering and Technology*, 15(5), 1020–1032.
5. Salako, A. O., Fabuyi, J. A., Aideyan, N. T., Selesi-Aina, O., Dapo-Oyewole, D. L., & Olaniyi, O. O. (2024). Advancing Information Governance in AI-driven Cloud Ecosystem: Strategies for Enhancing Data Security and Meeting Regulatory Compliance. *Asian Journal of Research in Computer Science*, 17(12), 66–88.
6. Farzaan, M. A. M., Ghanem, M. C., El-Hajjar, A., & Ratnayake, D. N. (2024). Ai-enabled system for efficient and effective cyber incident detection and response in cloud environments. arXiv preprint arXiv:2404.05602.
7. Muppalaneni, R., Inaganti, A. C., & Ravichandran, N. (2024). AI-enhanced data loss prevention (DLP) strategies for multi-cloud environments. *Journal of Computing Innovations and Applications*, 2(2), 1–13.
8. Akinbolaji, T. J. (2024). Advanced integration of artificial intelligence and machine learning for real-time threat detection in cloud computing environments. *Iconic Research and Engineering Journals*, 6(10), 980–991.
9. Rehan, H. (2024). Revolutionizing America's Cloud Computing the Pivotal Role of AI in Driving Innovation and Security. *Journal of Artificial Intelligence General Science*. ISSN: 3006-4023, 2(1), 239–240.
10. Mistry, H. K., Mavani, C., Goswami, A., & Patel, R. (2024). The Impact of Cloud Computing and AI on Industry Dynamics and Competition. *Educational Administration: Theory and Practice*, 30(7), 797–804.
11. Paroha, A. D. (2024, April). Integrating IoT, AI, and Cloud Technologies for Sustainable Oilfield Operations. In *2024 9th International Conference on Cloud Computing and Big Data Analytics (ICCCBDA)* (pp. 120–126). IEEE.
12. Thota, R. C. (2024). Optimizing Edge Computing and AI for Low-latency Cloud Workloads. *International Journal of Science and Research Archive*, 13(1), 3484–3500.

13. Kommisetty, P. D. N. K., & Nishanth, A. (2024). AI-Driven Enhancements in Cloud Computing: Exploring the Synergies of Machine Learning and Generative AI. *Iarjset*, 10, 1–9.
14. Gooda, S. K., Mohanraj, P., Veni, J., Ashish, A., Kannadhasan, S., & Thamizhkani, B. (2025). Cloud-Based Solutions for Scalable Enterprise Resource Planning Systems Benefits and Implementation Strategies. In *ITM Web of Conferences* (Vol. 76, p. 05002). EDP Sciences.
15. Mamidi, S. R. (2024). The Role of AI and Machine Learning in Enhancing Cloud Security. *Journal of Artificial Intelligence General Science*. ISSN: 3006-4023, 3(1), 403–417.
16. Olabanji, S. O., Marquis, Y., Adigwe, C. S., Ajayi, S. A., Oladoyinbo, T. O., & Olaniyi, O. O. (2024). AI-Driven Cloud Security: Examining the Impact of User Behavior Analysis on Threat Detection. *Asian Journal of Research in Computer Science*, 17(3), 57–74.
17. Thummala, V. R., & Singh, P. (2024). Developing Cloud Migration Strategies for Cost-Efficiency and Compliance. *International Journal of Multidisciplinary Innovation and Research Methodology*, 3, 1–14. ISSN, 2960-2068.
18. Seenivasan, D. (2024). AI Driven Enhancement of ETL Workflows for Scalable and Efficient Cloud Data Engineering. *International Journal of Engineering and Computer Science*, 13(06), 10–18535.
19. Zangana, H. M., & Zeebaree, S. R. (2024). Distributed Systems for Artificial Intelligence in Cloud Computing: A Review of AI-Powered Applications and Services. *International Journal of Informatics, Information System and Computer Engineering*, 5(1), 11–30.
20. Ali, S. I., Abdulqader, D. M., Ahmed, O. M., Ismael, H. R., Hasan, S., & Ahmed, L. H. (2024). Consideration of Web Technology and Cloud Computing Inspiration for AI and IoT Role in Sustainable Decision-making for Enterprise Systems. *Journal of Information Technology and Informatics*, 3(2), 4.
21. Thota, R. C. (2024). AI-augmented Predictive Analytics for Proactive Cloud Infrastructure Management. *Journal of Science & Technology*, 5(4), 246.
22. Prakash, S., Malaiyappan, J. N. A., Thirunavukkarasu, K., & Devan, M. (2024). Achieving Regulatory Compliance in Cloud Computing through ML. *AIJMR-Advanced International Journal of Multidisciplinary Research*, 2(2), 1–12.
23. Akinade, A. O., Adepoju, P. A., Ige, A. B., & Afolabi, A. I. (2025). Cloud Security Challenges and Solutions: A Review of Current Best Practices. *International Journal of Multidisciplinary Research and Growth Evaluation*, 6(1), 26–35.

16 Quantum Supremacy and Its Applications

Ramiz Salama and Fadi Al-Turjman

16.1 INTRODUCTION

Quantum supremacy is an important idea in the history of quantum computing (QC): it refers to the point in time when quantum computers lead over classical ones for some specific designated problems. Earlier thought to be merely a theoretical possibility, quantum supremacy has become the focus of zealous efforts in both science and technology. It highlights not only the brute force of quantum mechanics but also the ability to tackle problems that are considered too hard for classical machines to resolve [1]. QC operates on physically different principles than classical computing. While the classical computer operates with binary codes (0 and 1), the quantum computer uses quantum bits—qubits—which may be in several states at a time, due to the effect of superposition. Also, thanks to quantum entanglement, qubits can interact with each other in a way that practically increases computing efficiency by several orders of magnitude. Thanks to these properties, quantum computers are able to perform tasks in the areas of cryptography, optimization, artificial intelligence (AI), and others that are resource-intensive for classical systems. The pursuit of quantum dominance has been motivated by many years of theoretical as well as practical work [2]. Google made a significant announcement in this respect in 2019, arguing that its quantum processor Sycamore managed to perform a task within just 200 s, which would otherwise take the fastest classical supercomputer thousands of years to complete. This achievement worked as an impetus for further developments with organizations such as International Business Machines (IBM) and Ion, making remarkable contributions as well. This chapter sets a target to map the entire history of quantum supremacy's development, its diversification, and contemporary achievements, as well as the challenges facing the future. By combining a number of studies published from 2021 to 2023, this research demonstrates the speed and the revolutionary nature of change that quantum technology is able to bring. The subsequent parts will focus on the principles, techniques, and societal aspects of the novel technology in question. The real-world issues concerning computations are now going to be approached in a new dimension due to the extent of quantum supremacy, which cuts across all areas, including quantum physics [3]. There are issues that grow tremendously in their scope that can be addressed by classical computers that can perform linear operations or work within deterministic medians that are finite. For example, classical computing is inadequate for interesting tasks such as factoring large numbers (important in secure communications) or simulating molecules (molecule-targeted

DOI: 10.1201/9781003587835-16

After Google made a claim about quantum dominance in 2019, research activity was directed toward attempts to confirm and test its results with different modalities and computational frameworks. For example, according to IBM representatives, Google's experiment was weak because the sampling problem resolved by Sycamore, in their opinion, could be synthetically resolved by a classical system with a higher level of algorithms. As a consequence, there was a more serious focus on how to create robustness tests of benchmark definitions on quantum supremacy. From 2021 to 2023, scientists proposed an alternative based on photonic QC, which has advanced rapidly to supplement the superconducting qubits [14]. Scientists from China working at USTC have shown quantum superiority in practice using photonic systems that can handle classes of problems that classical computers cannot handle. Through advanced techniques, they reached advanced photon sources and optimized optical systems, exhibiting a different pathway to supremacy achievement. Simultaneously, achievements have been recorded in error correction and noise suppression, two major bottlenecks to scaling up QC. IBM's most ambitious work to date in fault-tolerant quantum architecture, characterized by an ambitious roadmap for quantum processors containing multiple thousands of qubits, exhibits the power of computation with errors correction. The implementation of approaches such as quantum error correction (QEC) codes and enhanced qubit connectivity increased the confidence level on logical quantum operations, thereby bringing practical QC into focus. Aside from the aforementioned improvements in hardware and methodology, improvements in software and algorithms have also been achieved. Scientists have targeted specific areas, such as the design of new quantum algorithms suitable for NISQ devices [15]. Research has also included application areas such as variation quantum eigensolver (VQE) and quantum approximate optimization algorithms (QAOA). These efforts are aimed at demonstrating quantum advantage in tasks that are relevant to various industries, including finance, logistics, and materials science. The impressive developments in QC research are attributed to its collaborative and multidisciplinary nature, particularly because various scholars, private enterprises, and governments continue to channel significant resources into the technology. As quantum supremacy demonstrations become more numerous and diverse, so too will their scope [16]. The increasing focus of the community on quantum supremacy has not only accelerated the quest for relevant technologies but also leaped the boundaries of theory. The researchers have set a goal to make the term quantum supremacy more precise by specifying the computational problems for which quantum advantage can be claimed beyond all doubt. Of these, random circuit sampling persists as a pioneering test because of its use in Google's Sycamore experiment. Recent studies (2021–2023) have also brought improvement to the quality and understanding of Random Circuit Sampling (RCS) techniques. Assiduously pursued is the inquiry on "quantum volume," which is a quantitative term coined by IBM to encapsulate the general performance and capacity of a quantum system. Quantum volume tackles such aspects of performance as qubit, gate, and fidelity and noise level, so it is a more integrative metric of a quantum computer's ability to realize supremacy. IBM's quest to enhance the quantum volume parameter of their processors, the 127-qubit Eagle and 433-qubit Osprey, among others, has raised the performance levels of the hardware and has opened prospects for scalable quantum systems [17]. In addition to the progress made in metrics and benchmarks, some researchers have set out to examine the potential classical computing possesses when it comes to the simulation of quantum systems. In a number of studies, classical algorithms have been enhanced to enable better solving of quantum problems, which pushes the boundaries of the definition of supremacy further. For instance, tensor-network simulations have been able to efficiently substitute quantum computations, effectively reducing the gap in performance efficiency between classical and quantum systems. Such studies not only support the claims of quantum supremacy but also contain information on the limits and capabilities of classical computation.

The scope of efforts has also enlarged to cover the dominance of quantum systems other than superconducting qubit systems. There has been a wide variety of quantum supremacy demonstrations in photonic systems, ion-trap processors, and hybrid architectures. Ion, for example, has progressed significantly in trapped-ion QC, emphasizing its superior coherence times and connectivity. In the same way, the photonic quantum computer of the University of Science and Technology of China (USTC), Jiu hang, won over competition in a boson sampling task, bringing more evidence to this case [18]. In the timeframe between 2021 and 2023, quantum supremacy research has not only changed, but its prospects look bright. This is because there is a consensus on the need for collaboration and increased levels of investment, as witnessed on the global stage. Countries across the world, especially the USA, China, and the European Union, have made quantum technology one of their key enablers in their strategic plans. Major funding for quantum research has, for instance, resulted from the US National Quantum Initiative Act and China's Quantum Information Science project, thereby creating an environment that is both competitive and collaborative for quantum supremacy to be further advanced. There is also academic research that has been perceived to be quite instrumental in enhancing the theories of quantum supremacy, as well as its development. Some scholars have published articles that were airbrushed in prominent publications, including Nature, Science, and Physical Review Letters, regarding the novel quantum algorithms, among other works related to the limits of classical simulation [19]. Some forms of collaboration, such as those between Google and Caltech or IBM and universities, contributed to the speed when it came to the integration of basic science and its marketable outcomes. A common aspect that has been recurrent in the recent literature is the focus on the scalability of quantum systems. While early instances of quantum supremacy concerned unique efforts, development now seeks to go toward quantum computers that can be reprogrammed to tackle multiple tasks. Research has suggested new designs, including error-corrected logical qubits and modular quantum systems, as some of the ways to address the problem of noise and coherence of qubits [20].

An additional defining focus area has been the practical implications of quantum supremacy. Certain researchers have begun to tackle such crucial real-world issues as supply chain optimization, financial modeling, and speeding up drug development processes. These attempts seek to prove not only theoretical benefits but practical usefulness as well, and so go beyond the stage of experimental supremacy and market competitiveness. To conclude, the enormous number of articles published from 2021 up until the present has contributed to a better understanding and practical application of quantum supremacy. These changes are representative of how fast the

16.4.1 Random Circuit Sampling

RCS has been instrumental in proving quantum supremacy. This entails performing a preset order of quantum gates chosen at random on a quantum circuit and measuring the output. The challenge of performing this task stems from the fact that, as quantum systems get larger, the probability distribution that depicts quantum circuits becomes overwhelming to replicate on normal computers.

16.4.2 Shor's Algorithm

Even if it is never used directly in the demonstrations of supremacy, its worth is in its general idea since it shows that quantum computers would be able to factor large integers much faster than their classical counterparts, where a large growth in efficiency is expected. There are important implications for cryptography that should be relevant to quantum supremacy.

16.4.3 Variation Quantum Algorithms (VQA)

These NISQ architectures include algorithms such as the QAOA and VQE. They are hybrids by nature, encompassing classical optimizers and allowing quantum computations to be harnessed in multiple domains, such as energy minimization and optimization.

16.5 HARNESSING QUANTUM SUPREMACY: HARDWARE ARCHITECTURE

Building quantum machines that exhibit superiority over classical computing systems in terms of performance requires emerging quantum hardware designed for speed, precision, and scalability. A few features related to hardware implementation are discussed in the following.

16.5.1 Superconducting Qubits

For instance, Google Sycamore and IBM's processors are produced using Josephson junctions and have to be maintained at very low temperatures to reduce noise and DE coherence.

16.5.2 Photonic Systems

Jiu hang, and several others operate with photons and components of various optical systems, which help to provide these systems with regard to scalability and tolerance to faults.

16.5.3 Trapped-Ion Systems

In such systems, qubits are encoded in ions confined in electromagnetic fields. Their coherence times are quite long, and they can be efficiently manipulated, making them useful for some specific quantum applications.

16.6 EXPERIMENTAL SETUP

Experimental validation of quantum supremacy in QC requires the establishment of particular models that guarantee the accuracy of results. Important factors are discussed in the following.

16.6.1 Qubit Initialization and Control

Qubits should be initialized to some particular state and used in quantum gates with high fidelity. There are control mechanisms used depending on the type of qubits; these include microwave pulses, lasers, etc.

16.6.2 Circuit Depth and Qubit Connectivity

The depth of quantum circuits (number of sequential gates) and the connectivity between qubits are also the factors that limit how resources are used efficiently and the accuracy of calculations. A high connectivity means that additional gates are not required to perform an interaction simulation between qubits that are placed in remote areas.

16.7 SCALABILITY CHALLENGES

While the existing QC systems are capable of outperforming classical computers in a number of pre-defined issues, the principle of scalability is the first challenge. The scalability of the architecture requires higher systems of qubits.

16.7.1 Error Correction

Error-correcting codes such as the Surface Code are vital requirements in building a fault-tolerant quantum topology.

16.7.2 Improved Fabrication Techniques

Enhanced densities of qubits and the uniformity of the qubit's performance are very critical for the purpose of scaling quantum processors.

16.8 QUANTUM SUPREMACY DEMONSTRATION PROTOCOLS

The protocols for demonstrating quantum supremacy must be constructed in a precise manner with an underlying emphasis on experimental fidelity as well as the result validation. These protocols include the ones discussed in the following.

16.8.1 Task Selection

To perform research, scientists choose challenges that cannot be solved using classical computers, but can be handled swiftly when implemented on quantum systems. Random Circuit Sampling and Boson Sampling are popular since they are nontrivial and have utility that is unique to the quantum domain.

16.8.2 Execution and Data Collection

Several sets of quantum circuits are run to obtain output distributions. This is important because quantum computations are probabilistic, and some form of statistical analysis needs to be done on the inevitable noise that will be present on the complex circuits.

16.8.3 Classical Verification

An output of QC processes is subjected to a comparison with a simulation of classical technologies for some models of relatively small-sized circuits. In the case of larger systems, however, quantum efficiency is corroborated with the help of statistical relations.

16.9 STATISTICAL ANALYSIS OF RESULTS

Because of the probabilistic character of quantum mechanics, the procedures used for demonstrating quantum supremacy include a great deal of statistical effort. Quantitative metrics include.

16.9.1 Fidelity

Promotes interaction while also reporting on the integrity margins of output from a quantum system and its theoretical average. The higher the fidelity, the correct the computation.

16.9.2 Cross-Entropy Benchmarking

This approaches the evaluation of quantum circuits' performance as an integration of the sampled output probabilities to those corresponding to the theoretical framework and has been utilized in great depth in Google's Sycamore experiment.

16.9.3 Scalability Testing

Performance characterization at the propounded scale involves researchers studying the fractions of the performance as the scale (at the number of qubits) or the scale (at the number of circuit depth) varies for the cases of the given system capabilities.

16.10 ERROR-MITIGATION TECHNIQUES

As of the time of writing, the NISQ era is characterized by noise and errors. Due to the presence of errors, researchers adopt a number of error-mitigation strategies in the following manner.

16.10.1 Post-Processing

Basically, after computation, the raw results are subjected to a number of corrective processes to improve their performance. Zero-noise extrapolation is one such technique that is often applied.

16.10.2 Gate Calibration

The quantum gates' performance is highly eroded if not constantly calibrated, as this reduces the errors made during computation processes.

16.10.3 Physical Factors

Also, many quantum systems are housed within a normal physically isolated system, such as a cryogenic chamber, to generally reduce further sources of splash, such as noise, particularly due to disturbances, variations in the atomic structure, or even electromagnetic radiation.

16.11 TOOLS AND SOFTWARE

The current efforts toward obtaining quantum supremacy are done through the combination of respective hardware and software tools.

16.11.1 Quantum Programming Frameworks

Different libraries, such as Qiskit (IBM), Cirq (Google), and Pennylane, enable the design and simulation of quantum circuits by researchers.

16.11.2 Classical Simulators

To demonstrate the effectiveness of small-scale quantum circuits, they are used to benchmark against algorithms on classical systems. Supercomputing clusters aid tensor network simulators, which are excellent for the task as well. Summary of key quantum algorithms and their associated advantages for supremacy tasks shown in Table 16.1.

TABLE 16.1
Summary of Key Quantum Algorithms and Their Associated Advantages for Supremacy Tasks

Quantum Algorithm	Primary Application	Key Advantage
Shor's algorithm	Factoring large integers for breaking cryptographic keys	Exponential speedup over classical algorithms
Grover's algorithm	Unstructured database search	Quadratic speedup for search problems
RCS	Benchmarking quantum supremacy	Demonstrates quantum computational advantage
Boson Sampling	Simulating bosonic systems for benchmarking	Efficient simulation beyond classical capabilities
QAOA	Optimization problems in logistics and finance	Solves practical optimization tasks on NISQ devices
VQE	Finding ground-state energies in molecular systems	Useful for chemical and material simulations

16.11.3 Custom Hardware Controllers

The intricacies of quantum processors' operations necessitate the development of specialized controllers that manipulate qubits with the necessary precision. These controllers issue microwave pulses, laser signals, or other control inputs that correspond to the qubit's specifics.

16.12 BENCHMARKS FOR QUANTUM SUPREMACY

To demonstrate quantum supremacy, benchmarks are critically important as they provide a test completion that classical systems cannot feasibly accomplish. The most prominent standards include.

16.12.1 A Subsection Sample RCS

There is no doubt that RCS sets the upper bounds for quantum supremacy demonstration. One needs to execute a quantum circuit that has random gates added to it to create output distributions that classical computations struggle to simulate. Naima settings adjust the depth and width of the circuit to challenge the classically achievable computational limits.

16.12.2 Boson Sampling

Also called "Tuinau" in light-based quantum systems, this benchmark has been designed to perform measurements of the universe contained within an interferometer with waves of photons passing through the device. Systems such as Jiuzhang have used this benchmark to proclaim quantum advantage.

16.12.3 Quantum Volume

IBM introduced quantum volume, a singular measure of a quantum computer system in terms of the quality and interconnectedness of qubits and the fidelity of quantum gates. Quantum volume is then a necessary step in the journey of achieving quantum supremacy toward practical levels.

16.13 VALIDATION CRITERIA

The questions surrounding claims of quantum supremacy should be settled by theoreticians and experimenters along the lines of satisfactory verification and reproducibility, the two most important being.

16.13.1 Reproducibility

Wherever quantum systems are reported to demonstrate quantum supremacy, they should maintain their supremacy status if the same is tried out under similar apparent conditions again. Any deviation in the dividend is evaluated for possible factors causing the aberration or the turbulence.

16.13.2 Computational Complexity

The task chosen for the purposes of demonstrating quantum supremacy must be demonstrably impossible to solve using classical systems. This is done by the usual approach of employing classical algorithms for target scaling.

16.13.3 Independent Verification

The quantum supremacy claims are given a wider validation by way of other scientists conducting peer-reviewed articles and replicating results that were previously generated.

16.14 PRACTICAL CONSIDERATIONS

The demonstration of quantum supremacy is very important scientifically. Nevertheless, it is not sufficient for most needs owing to.

16.14.1 Energy Efficiency

Most quantum systems, especially those that heavily rely on cryogenic setups, are power hungry. Efforts are being made to enhance the energy efficiency of the system to ensure sustainability.

16.14.2 Integration with Classical Systems

There are studies about building quantum-classical hybrid systems to utilize both systems. These persistent hybrid architectures make it possible for quantum operations to execute well-defined steps while classical systems perform the rest of the instructions.

16.14.3 Scalability to Real-World Applications

Moving from experimental proofs to realistic cases requires quite a number of things, among them fault-tolerant quantum systems, which can deal with multiple problems on an extensive scale.

16.15 ETHICAL AND SECURITY IMPLICATIONS

Quantum supremacy is also rapidly raising a lot of ethical issues apart from technical ones. This includes the potential of creating circumstances that would undermine existing cryptographic systems which guard global data security. To alleviate the situation, scientists are working toward formulating post-quantum cryptography algorithms that can protect sensitive information. Figure 16.2 describes a comparative chart of quantum and classical performance on benchmark tasks

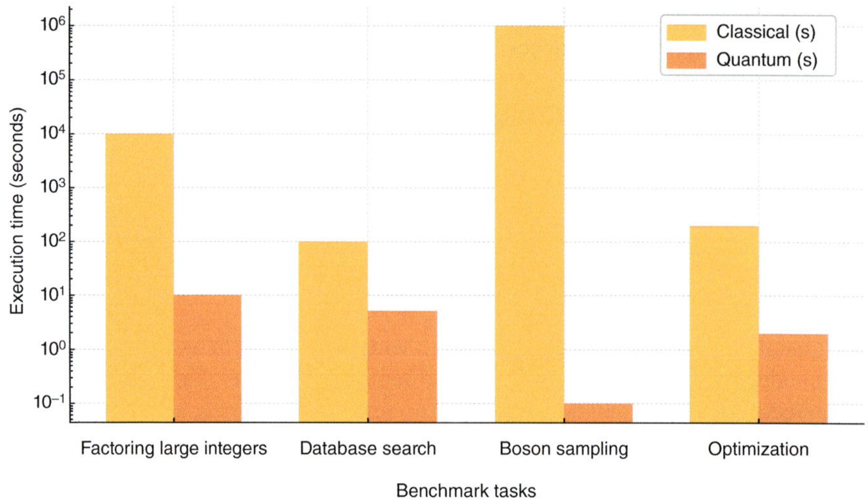

FIGURE 16.2 Comparative chart of quantum and classical performance on benchmark tasks.

16.16 RESULTS AND DISCUSSION

16.16.1 The Progress That Has Been Made with Quantum Supremacy

There have been some instances that have approached the area of quantum supremacy, where quantum devices managed to tackle some problems faster than even the strongest classical supercomputers. One of the most notable achievements still is Google's Sycamore processor, which executed 256 random circuits in 2 min within 200 s—that is a task that supercomputers are estimated to do in around 10,000 years. This outcome not only supported the theoretical claims of quantum supremacy, as it had been predicted long before, but also demonstrated the performance of current quantum computers.

16.16.2 Performance Analysis Relative to Baseline Performance Measures

Another important notion that arises from quantum supremacy demonstrations is that different tasks work more efficiently and effectively either on quantum or classical systems. In Table 16.2, the lead quantum processors are measured against the current best classical supercomputers in RCS and boson sampling tasks.

TABLE 16.2
Comparative Performance of Quantum vs. Classical Systems in Random Circuit Sampling (RCS) Tasks

System	Task	Estimated Classical Time	Quantum Time	Key Metric Achieved
Google Sycamore	Random circuit sampling	10,000 years	200 s	1.5×10^3 speedup
Jiuzhang (USTC)	Boson sampling	600 million years	min	Photonic quantum advantage
IBM Osprey	Circuit complexity	Infeasible	s	Increased quantum volume

16.17 APPLICATION-SPECIFIC RESULTS

While tasks such as Resource Constrained Scheduling may be considered artificial in most quantum supremacy demonstrations, they are important in terms of their application to real-life scenarios, such as the ones discussed in the following.

16.17.1 Optimization Problems

There are quantum algorithms such as QAOA that appear to be quite useful for solving combinatorial optimization problems in logistics and finance, or scheduling problems.

16.17.2 Machine Learning

Models of machine learning enhanced by quantum systems have proven to cut down on the time and energy utilized in training on complicated datasets, which are Tensor Processing (TP)-intensive functions.

16.17.3 Cryptography and Security

Shor's algorithm is a potential risk to classical encryption by all means but has yet to be realized at the scale level. These outcomes have increased the rush toward post-quantum cryptography constructions

16.18 KEY OBSERVATIONS

From the previous demonstration of quantum supremacy, several important observations were made: Noise and Error Impact: Noise continues to be one of the main limitations, especially for deeper circuits. Although the efficiency of error correction techniques has been more effective, they remain a cost in terms of the required computational resources and energy.

16.18.1 Quantum Supremacy and Its Research Potential

Quantum supremacy is synonymous with accomplishments that surpass the capabilities of classical computation. Such accomplishments, when exhibited, have an overwhelming impact in numerous domains, including but not limited to science, technology, as well as industry. These accomplishments are not purely theoretical but also have a practical application, which allows a new paradigm in computation for the potential of existence.

16.18.2 Cryptography and Data Security

Research efforts for the implausibly plausible post-quantum time are on the rise. Suffice it to say, these post-quantum cryptography protocols utilize mathematically grounded principles to deliver optimal data security originally devised for systems that have existed for decades. There is a good reason to begin constructing the future of data secured through or for dimensions beyond quantum encryption systems, because the current state of encryption systems is open to attack when quantum supremacy is achieved. Shor's algorithms, among others, have the plausibility of factorizing huge numbers at an astonishingly faster rate than traditional systems can, one advanced in a significant manner away from common RSA encryption. This greatly motivated centuries of global research toward the development of post-quantum encryption systems to ensure the standards of data security do not outdate with time.

16.18.3 Drug Discovery, Materials Science

Under quantum supremacy, new possibilities were made available in the simulation of molecular correlation file interactions and chemical processes. Where such possibility is available, undertaking tasks such as determining the ground-state energy of molecules, which handle classic systems' high computational resource usage, stand to gain immensely from quantum processors. This could spark a paradigm shift in the scope to which drug articles, material structures, and energy storage solutions will be brought to the market and the efficiency levels at which they will operate.

16.18.4 AI and Machine Learning

The previous quantum-enhanced machine learning models showed potential over the classical models in handling large datasets. Automation of certain processes, such as matrix inversion, highly requires quantum processors to speed up the operations that involve encoding of AI models. Potential advancement in autonomous systems, predictive analytics, and natural language processing is expected.

16.19 CHALLENGES IDENTIFIED IN RESULTS

Despite the success that has been witnessed in the quest for quantum supremacy, it also brings with it plenty of challenges that futurists still need to overcome for global adoption.

16.19.1 Quantum Systems Scalability

These qubits are, however, still too operationally short and saturated with errors, hence even quantum systems with supremacy can only be used for specific tasks. Furthermore, for these systems to be saleable to do general computation, further development in qubit coherence, interconnectivity, and error suppression is still paramount.

16.19.2 Energy and Infrastructure Requirements

Superconducting qubits qualify as being part of quantum computers, which also need the most exotic cryogenic systems to function. This, therefore, has a high energy cost and requires so much infrastructure, again meaning that users are limited.

16.19.3 Validation of Results: Evaluation of Results

Validation of the results for the demonstrations of supremacy has become increasingly rigorous with the shift of such activities closer to solving real-world issues. Cross-checks, verification through simulations, are unable, as far as quantum systems are concerned, the bigger the system, the thicker the barriers, and complexity comes into play.

16.20 COMPARATIVE ANALYSIS WITH CLASSICAL SYSTEMS

Even though there is growth in quantum supremacy, classical systems are still in normal computing usage. Comparative analysis indicates that quantum systems are highly proficient in circuits of random sampling, for example, or factoring large numbers in tasks requiring a great deal of time and resources. Classical systems are not very useful in regard to economy, energy costs, and sometimes flexibility, and are limited in their area of usage. There are also new directions which combine different methods—quantum and classical ones to benefit from the advantages of both paradigms.

16.20.1 Industry Impact

The industries that are likely to be affected in the short run by quantum supremacy are likely to include:

Finance: Enhancing a portfolio in general understanding toward securing against risks, including false transactions, predictions, or decisions, and evaluation of potential threats.

Logistics: Improvement of the processes of commodities distribution through enhancement of appropriate routes or resolving strategies aimed at easing congestion.

Energy: There is bound to be an enhancement of power systems, accompanied by drafting advanced materials aimed at batteries that are expected to be eco-friendly.

16.20.2 Current Challenges and Their Solutions

With the advancement of quantum computers, various researchers and even industries are working around some of the major challenges that hinder the widespread use of quantum supremacy. Some of such solutions are mentioned in the following:

16.20.3 Error Correction and Fault-Tolerance

Reliable quantum computation depends on the reliable correction of the erasure of logical information. Codes such as the Surface Code and Quantum Low-Density Parity-Check (LDPC) codes have provided possibilities for error correcting. Although current systems reserve a large fraction of the number of physical qubits for error correction, efforts are being made to make further developments on fault-tolerant architectures to reduce this overhead.

16.20.4 Higher Qubit Coherence Times

For executing larger and more intricate circuits, it is essential to have qubits with long coherence times. Higher stability is being achieved through advances in materials science, qubit architectures, and isolating techniques. For example, covering qubits in traps has resulted in longer coherence times for trapped ion qubits in comparison with the superconducting qubits.

16.20.5 Hybrid Quantum-classical Systems

As a practical measure toward addressing real-world problems, the use of both quantum and classical models is necessary. In this approach, more complicated quantum processes are flown to Quantum processors while simpler operations and general control are left to classical systems. Algorithms, as the VQE, have already begun to demonstrate results in areas such as optimization and chemistry, where the algorithm can be accessed and relied on as a hybrid.

16.21 MORE PRACTICAL USES

The latest achievements regarding quantum supremacy seem to be translating into more usable real-world applications. There are some noticeable parallels.

16.21.1 Logistic and Supply Chains Optimization

The performance of quantum algorithms is being evaluated in the context of route planning, inventory, and forecasting. Organizations such as Volkswagen and DHL are testing out quantum applications to optimize international supply chain components.

16.21.2 Enhancement of Cryptography Using Quantum Technology

Various nations and organizations are seeking to have quantum encryption standards that can withstand future attacks. Techniques that do cover this domain include post-quantum lattice encryption protocols.

16.21.3 Simulations of Quantum Systems by Using Quantum Computers

Quantum computers can now be used to simulate actual quantum systems, such as the structures of molecules and reactions. Such simulations can fast-track processes such as drug development and the designing of materials with desirable features, including superconductivity.

16.22 SCALABILITY POSSIBILITIES

Although expansiveness is far-fetched at the moment, the field's ultimate objective is scalability and universality. Current attempts being made to scale quantum systems include the ones presented in the following.

16.22.1 Qubit Count Scale Up

Organizations such as IBM and Google have developed visions of constructing quantum processors with thousands of qubits. With regard to this, IBM's Osprey (433 qubits) and plans of having a system with 1,000+ qubits by 2025 are commendable.

16.22.2 Minimizing Error Rates

Advances in qubit construction and its fabrication, gate fidelity, and quantum noise suppression are fundamental to the scaling of quantum computers. To a great extent, low error rates enable the construction of more intricate circuitry and its practicality.

16.22.3 The Concept of Quantum Computer Networks

Quantum computers will communicate among themselves with ease over the internet in a quantum network composed of several smaller quantum systems. Such collaborative quantum networks distribute processors, garnering the strengths of small and quantum systems.

16.23 THE QUEST FOR AN ENDURING QUANTUM SUPREMACY

In laying out the course of action toward achieving quantum supremacy, there are several steps that warrant focus in this regard:

Designing building blocks for quantum systems that are module-based and can withstand faults. Formulating universal quantum algorithms that are customized for differing fields. Establishing standardized international norms for the measurement of quantum's performance.

16.24 CONCLUSION OF RESULTS DISCUSSION

The phrase quantum supremacy has become a key marker, showing the actual possibilities of quantum computers and their usage. However, there are shortcomings, but the outcomes of the above-mentioned experiments offer a firm base for constructive

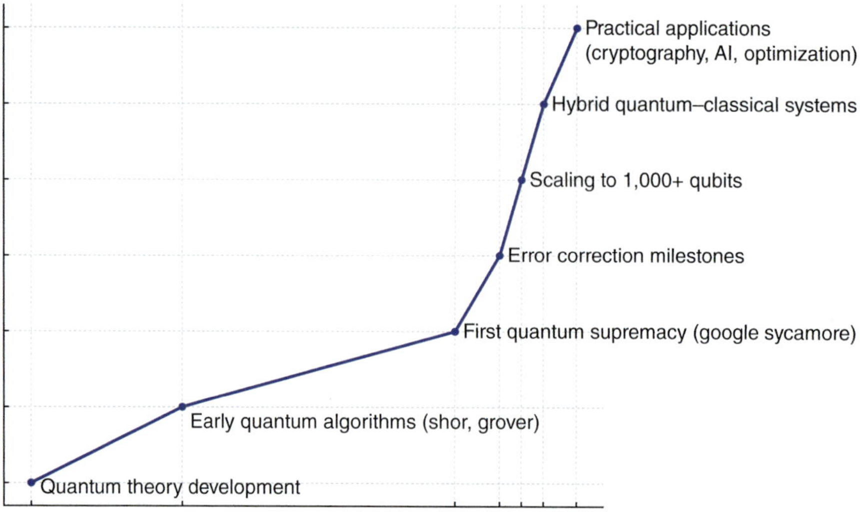

FIGURE 16.3 Roadmap of quantum computing (QC) advancements from supremacy to practical applications.

progress. These insights will help to create scalable quantum systems that will address practical needs and advance many areas of the economy in an unprecedented way. Figure 16.3 describes a roadmap of QC advancements from supremacy to practical applications

16.25 CONCLUSION

16.25.1 Summary of Key Findings

Quantum supremacy is a key event in computational history, having showcased the ability of QC hardware in executing specific tasks a great deal faster than classical systems. With the success of Google's Sycamore system as well as Jiu hang, the quest for quantum supremacy has gained traction, and quantum advantage has now been proven. The key points are:

Validation of Supremacy: A number of experiments have provided empirical evidence that quantum systems can perform better than classical systems in quantum tasks such as Random Circuit Sampling and Boson Sampling.

Broader Applications: Other than benchmarks, quantum supremacy extends the horizon for progress in other fields, including cryptography, optimization, AI, as well as materials science.

Challenges to Overcome: In spite of these achievements, issues such as noise, error correction, scalability, and integration with classical systems need to be solved for widespread usage.

16.25.2 Broader Implications

The relevance of quantum supremacy's significance is certainly not about how many calculations can be done within a second. The fateful occurrences follow to industry or society, for that matter, worldwide, including:

Industry Transformation: A few industries, such as finance, logistics, and even healthcare, will be on QC's waiting list because its features of solving optimization problems, running simulations, and improving data processing have yet to reach them.

Cryptographic Revolution: At the same time, the threats involve the critics of these systems, quantum supremacy seems to be a catalyst for the introduction of post-quantum cryptography, so data will be secured in a quantum world.

Global Technological Race: The purpose of the race among countries and companies to reach and exploit quantum supremacy has geopolitical and economic importance.

16.25.3 Ethical and Social Considerations

Quantum supremacy is a powerful force, but within its force are ethical and social issues as follows:

Equitable Access: As QC resource accessibility for everyone is an issue that should be dealt with to avoid a technological divide between developed and undeveloped countries.

Regulatory Frameworks: Setting and enforcing standards and regulations on quantum technologies will be imperative to avoid misuse and abuse in the realms of warfare and spying.

16.25.4 Existing Barriers

However, tasks that go above and beyond may show some quantum supremacy, but until that point, make throughout designs for particular problems that are seemingly feasible. This practical utility, however, depends on overcoming factors that are listed in the following:

Error Rates: Actual quantum-based applications will be mathematically impossible if there is no tolerance for noise governance.

Scalability: At the qubit and number of systems, the boundaries of previous technology are reached. Therefore, the targets for qubits need to exceed thousands, with the constraints being high thresholds in noise.

Energy and Cost Efficiency: Adequate resources do not exist in quantum informational apparatuses, including cryogenic systems, preventing a wide-scale adoption from occurring.

16.25.5 What's Plan Ahead

Quantum supremacy and its broader applications' future will depend on overcoming the existing obstacles and capitalizing on the recent victories. Addressing which are some forcing initiatives going forward are therefore, extensive plans in this direction are as follows:

Scaling Quantum Systems: To avoid noise, increasing the number of qubits, provided the system does not outsmart the coherence time, is critical. Achieving this scalability, it is clear that developing modular and distributive models' architectures of quantum compute systems is needed.

Advancing Error Correction Techniques: Achieving practical measurement and performance figures for quantum systems capable of tolerating the scrutiny associated with practical applications would require amazing leaps in the error correction codes and noise-mitigating mechanisms that will guarantee the fault-tolerant approaches for QC center models and setups.

Developing Simple Algorithms: This small development will allow closing the emerging gap in order of experimental supremacy and its industrial relevance toward the expanding circle of quantum algorithms aimed at solving specific practical tasks.

Encouraging Global Cooperation Partnerships: A unified approach is required involving shared quantum research efforts within academia, industry, and governments. Open access and global standards will speed up the pace of progress and ensure fair benefits.

16.25.6 Long-Term Associated Risks Potential

The long-term promise of quantum supremacy is in its power to transform computation and computation systems across virtually all industries and areas of science:

Health Care and Drug Discovery: Drug target identification in quantum simulations can be accelerated, enabling drugs to be developed relatively quickly and efficiently.

Climate and Landscape Ecology: QC can help in the optimization of energy systems, the enhancement of climate models, and the invention of new sustainable materials.

Artificial Intelligence: AI models based on quantum technologies may allow solving such multidisciplinary tasks as natural language processing, construction of autonomous systems, and many other tasks within the predictive intelligence area.

16.25.7 Closing Reflections

It has been contended that quantum supremacy is not an end in itself; rather, it is the beginning. In other words, it marked the first time that quantum mechanics may be used to tackle certain computational problems. While the current systems are in the

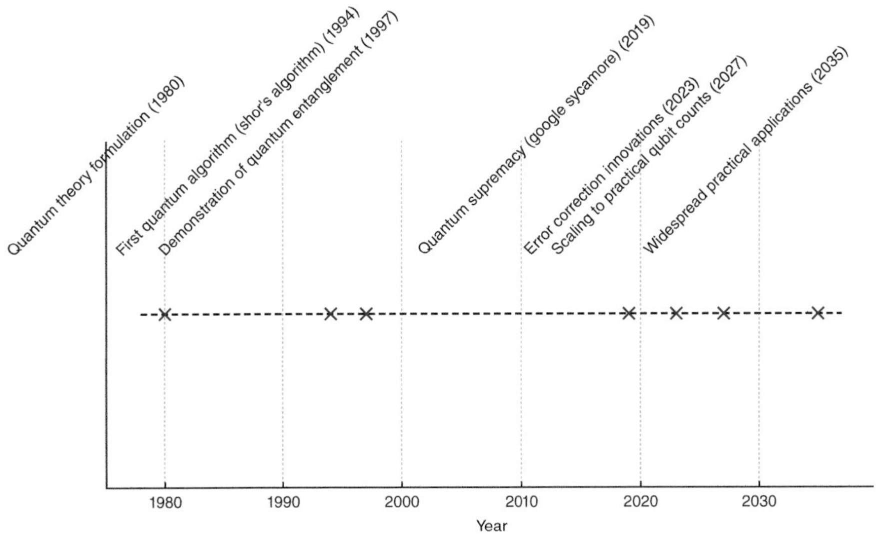

FIGURE 16.4 Timeline of quantum computing (QC) milestones and future projections.

NISQ era, the advancements already made can be demonstrated as a teaser of what is yet to come in the times when quantum computers are omnipresent. Implementing a practical application of the existing concepts, which have already been developed, will certainly demand more resources. This brings forth new opportunities for research and collaboration. In fact, QC has the potential to change the game in several realms, including industrial, scientific, and social. Figure 16.4 describes the timeline of QC milestones and future projections.

REFERENCES

1. Karamchand, G. (2024). The Road to Quantum Supremacy: Challenges and Opportunities in Computing. *Aitoz Multidisciplinary Review*, 3(1), 19–26.
2. Singh, H. (2025). Future Directions and Challenges, Quantum Supremacy, and Beyond. In *Quantum Technology Applications, Impact, and Future Challenges*, pp. 141–162. CRC Press.
3. Akash, M. S., & Jamema, S. A. (2025). Quantum Supremacy and Its Implications for Classical Computing. *World Journal of Advanced Engineering Technology and Sciences*, 42(1–6), pp. 1–6.
4. Saiyed, A. I. (2025). Hybrid Quantum-Classical Cryptographic Protocols: Enhancing Security in the Era of Quantum Supremacy. *Spectrum of Research*, 5(1), 1–7.
5. Puthussery, E. S., & Poonia, R. C. (2024, February). Quantum Computing's Path to Supremacy: Progress in the NISQ Epoch. In *International Conference On Innovative Computing and Communication* (pp. 315–325). Singapore: Springer Nature Singapore.
6. Kenarangui, N., Powalka, A., & Kish, L. B. (2025). "Quantum Supremacy" Challenged. Instantaneous Noise-based Logic with Benchmark Demonstrations. arXiv preprint arXiv:2506.00063.

7. Zhang, H. (2024). Quantum Entanglement and Qubit Interactions: The Key to Quantum Supremacy. *Theoretical and Natural Science*, 41, 112–118.
8. Lee, H., & Jun, K. (2025). Quantum Supremacy in Tomographic Imaging: Advances in Quantum Tomography Algorithms. arXiv preprint arXiv:2502.04830.
9. Jaramillo, J., Mathieu Beau, and Adolfo del Campo (2024). Quantum supremacy of many-particle thermal machines. *New Journal of Physics* 18, no. 7 (2016): 075019.
10. Amin, M. H., Raymond, J., Kinn, D., Hamze, F., Hamer, K., Pasvolsky, J., … & Kortas, S. (2025). Blockchain with Proof of Quantum Work. arXiv preprint arXiv:2503.14462.
11. Steane, Andrew. (1998). Quantum computing. *Reports on Progress in Physics*, 61, (2), 117.
12. Pawan, Y. N., & Kolla, B. P. (2025). Quantum Simulations and Classical Hybrid Machine Learning. In *Quantum Computing* (pp. 43–68). Morgan Kaufmann.
13. Bae, J., Yoo, G., Nakamura, S., Ohnishi, S., & Kim, D. S. (2024). Hardware Efficient Decomposition of the Laplace Operator and Its Application to the Helmholtz and the Poisson Equation on Quantum Computer. *Quantum Information Processing*, 23(7), 270.
14. Zidan, M., Eisa, A. M., Qasymeh, M., & Shoman, M. A. I. (2024). A Quantum Algorithm for System Specifications Verification. *IEEE Internet of Things Journal*, 11, 24775–24794.
15. Priya, S. M., Prasath, S. R., Anitha, S., Jesintha, D. K., & Julie, E. G. (2024). Quantum Computing: Current Advancements and Future Prospects. In *Emerging Trends in IoT and Computing Technologies* (pp. 132–137). CRC Press.
16. Misra, S., & Rani, P. (2024, June). Quantum Machine Learning: A Comprehensive Overview and Analysis. In *2024 15th International Conference on Computing Communication and Networking Technologies (ICCCNT)* (pp. 1–5). IEEE.
17. Jung, E. (2024). *The Impact of Quantum Information Science and Technology on National Security* (Doctoral dissertation, Purdue University).
18. Raheman, F. (2024). Defining Quantum Advantage for Building a Sustainable MVP to Deliver Quantum Computing Services. *Open Journal of Applied Sciences*, 14(6), 1530–1549.
19. AbuGhanem, M., & Eleuch, H. (2024). Full Quantum Tomography Study of Google's Sycamore Gate on IBM's Quantum Computers. *EPJ Quantum Technology*, 11(1), 36.
20. Raskar, D., Iyer, R., & Maralapalle, V. C. (2025). Quantum Data Processing and Analysis: Revolutionizing Data Science. In *Quantum Computing for Healthcare Data* (pp. 189–214). Academic Press.
21. Yuan, Suzhen, Mao, X., Chen, L., & Xue, Y.. (2013). Quantum digital image processing algorithms based on quantum measurement. *Optik*, 124(23), 6386–6390.
22. Preskill, J. (1998). Quantum computing: pro and con. *Proceedings of the Royal Society of London. Series A: Mathematical, Physical and Engineering Sciences*, 454(1969), 469–486.
23. Singh, A., Kumar, Y., Yadav, P., Tripathi, N., Bhargava, A., & Rana, A. (2024, May). Overcoming Quantum Hardware Challenges: Navigating the Landscape of Quantum Computing. In *2024 International Conference on Communication, Computer Sciences and Engineering (IC3SE)* (pp. 1904–1911). IEEE.
24. Thamilarasi, V., Naik, P. K., Sharma, I., Porkodi, V., Sivaram, M., & Lawanyashri, M. (2024, March). Quantum Computing-Navigating the Frontier with Shor's Algorithm and Quantum Cryptography. In *2024 International Conference on Trends in Quantum Computing and Emerging Business Technologies* (pp. 1–5). IEEE.

Index

Pages in *italics* refer to figures and pages in **bold** refer to tables.

E

F

G

H